LEARNING FROM TEACHING IN LITERACY EDUCATION

NEW PERSPECTIVES ON PROFESSIONAL DEVELOPMENT

EDITED BY
EMILY M. RODGERS
AND
GAY SU PINNELL

HEINEMANN • PORTSMOUTH, NH

Heinemann
A division of Reed Elsevier Inc.
361 Hanover Street
Portsmouth, NH 03801–3912
www.heinemann.com

Offices and agents throughout the world

The editors and publisher wish to thank those who have generously given permission to reprint borrowed material:

Figure 5–7 is reprinted from *Systems for Change in Literacy Education: A Guide to Professional Development* by Carol A. Lyons and Gay Su Pinnell. Copyright © 2001 by Carol A. Lyons and Gay Su Pinnell. Reprinted by permission.

Figure 7–2 is adapted from a Spiral of Learning (Figure 2.1) in *Systems for Change in Literacy Education: A Guide to Professional Development* by Carol A. Lyons and Gay Su Pinnell. Copyright © 2001 by Carol A. Lyons and Gay Su Pinnell. Reprinted by permission.

Library of Congress Cataloging-in-Publication Data
    Learning from teaching in literacy education : new perspectives on professional development /
    edited by Emily M. Rodgers and Gay Su Pinnell.
       p. cm.
    Includes bibliographical references.
    ISBN 0-325-00483-8
    1. Reading teachers—In-service training. 2. Primary school teachers—In-service training.
    I. Rodgers, Emily M. II. Pinnell, Gay Su.
    LB2844.1.R4 L42 2002
    428.4'071'5—dc21   2002006124

Editor: Leigh Peake
Production: Elizabeth Valway
Cover design: Linda Knowles
Typesetter: Argosy
Manufacturing: Steve Bernier

Printed in the United States of America on acid-free paper
06 05 04 03 02 RRD   2 3 4 5

CONTENTS

ACKNOWLEDGMENTS

This volume describes what we have learned about the effective professional development of literacy educators. We are deeply grateful to the contributors for their insights about the complexity of bringing about sustainable changes to instructional practices. We hope that readers enjoy and learn from their research-based reports as much as we have.

We thank Rebecca Kitchen and Pauline Taylor who keep our offices running so smoothly and efficiently. They are really the lynchpins of our projects! Becky played a large part in the production of this book and we are very grateful to her. We are also grateful to Jeff Spieles for his help—especially for his careful checking of citations and references. We also recognize the contributions of Lori Pugh, Bonnie Lake, and Linda Ruffin at our literacy project office.

Special thanks go to Francisco Gomez-Bellange who keeps us centered on student-outcomes with his impeccable analysis and reporting of the results of our work in Reading Recovery and thanks as well to Jane Williams who leads the evaluation of children's achievement in classrooms.

In our work at Ohio State we daily enjoy the friendship and collegiality of Susan Fullerton and Mary Fried; both demonstrate to us daily the importance of continued learning. We also wish to acknowledge Carol Lyons' contribution to our thinking as well as Pat Scharer's good ideas and constant encouragement. We thank these superb staff developers for teaching us about coaching and teachers' learning: Laurie Desai, Justina Henry, Kecia Hicks, Andrea McCarrier, Lynda Mudre, and Joan Wiley.

We would also like to thank the staff at Heinemann, in particular Leigh Peake and Elizabeth Valway, who kept us on course from start to finish.

We dedicate this volume to the staff developers who provide ongoing professional development to literacy teachers. They demonstrate on a daily basis the power of learning from teaching.

1 | PROFESSIONAL DEVELOPMENT SCENARIOS
What Is and Might Be

EMILY M. RODGERS
GAY SU PINNELL

In every school district across the country, every year, literacy teachers receive some form of professional development; however, change in classrooms is not always the result. The difficulties in bringing about reform in education have been well documented. We probably all agree that things do need to change. We might agree, for example, that an achievement gap is growing between higher and lower performing students, as a recent NAEP report identified (U.S. Department of Education 2001). We might also agree that the recently announced Federal Department of Education's goal to improve student achievement by raising teacher and principal quality is well reasoned and necessary (Department of Education's Strategic Plan 2002).

Yet we still know very little about "what works" in professional development. The popular method to communicate new techniques and knowledge is to simply tell teachers what to do, perhaps showing videotapes as demonstration, and depending on reading materials to do the rest (See Hughes et al., this volume). Teachers sometimes refer to this professional development experience as a "one-shot workshop" or "sit-and-get." We are skeptical about this didactic style of professional development and feel it is just a small step forward from the days when teachers were considered "trained" when they entered the profession and from that time needed only cursory looks at specific materials in order to know how to use them.

First, individuals, including teachers, do learn by being told, and demonstrations help, but learners need a wide variety of demonstrations to internalize action. Learners learn best by doing; and they learn faster if they have expert support as they try out new ideas.

Second, for an innovation to "work," teachers must embrace it, be committed to it, and do all of the little extra things that make it effective as they are working with children. For example, good teachers typically embroider every kind of approach with minute adjustments to the individual children in their classes. They encourage just at the right time; they make the activity fun; they bring in children's own interests and backgrounds; they praise and celebrate children's learning. The crucial role of teacher motivation and engagement in a teaching approach's success is acknowledged in The National Reading Panel Report, in this case, to teach phonics:

> Few if any studies have investigated the contribution of motivation to the effectiveness of phonics programs, not only the learner's motivation to learn but also the teacher's motivation to teach. The lack of attention to motivational factors by researchers in the design of phonics programs is potentially very serious . . . [Future research should] determine which approaches teachers prefer to use and are most likely to use effectively in their classroom instruction. (Report of the National Reading Panel 2000, 97)

Professional development has to be more than "sit-and-get"; teachers' current practices, knowledge, and motivation must be taken into account in any reform of instructional practices.

WHAT IS AND WHAT COULD BE IN PROFESSIONAL DEVELOPMENT

To frame this section, we'd like to look at three scenarios. The first scenario describes typical professional development for teachers while the two scenarios that follow describe what could be a model for professional development.

Scenario #1: District-Based Staff Development

Carol has an important role in her school district. Her task is daunting and complex. She is charged with providing the support systems that teachers need to assure that the district's elementary school students meet standards for literacy. And that means performance on the state proficiency test as well as meeting district-designated benchmarks. She is assigned to ten elementary schools as a staff developer and coach.

Understandably, Carol is very busy. She organizes district-level committees on standards and the adoption of materials; she is in charge of managing the professional development for teachers around preparation for proficiency tests. She attends a great many meetings and also works with grant writers to generate funds for the district. When there is a district-wide in-service, she performs a major organizational role and also documents the attendance of participants.

Carol has a high level of expertise. She has taken courses and reads a great deal. She has attended many national conferences and workshops and has a sound understanding of the underlying theory of how people learn to read. She has also acquired an understanding of staff development and school change. An issue for her is that, with her district-level duties, she has had little time to try out new procedures with children even in a rudimentary way. When she makes presentations or facilitates workshops with teachers, she is talking from the written materials she has perused rather than from her own experience. She is an excellent presenter but tends to rely on forms and directions to teachers, rather than helping them deeply engage in processes.

Carol represents a very traditional model of professional development in which a staff developer at the district office provides a series of experiences, usually in the form of presentations. It is difficult to imagine how the district's professional development can be improved because Carol is obviously stretched to the limit. Small districts such as hers may have one or two staff developers in her role; large districts may have a director and a staff of individuals, each assigned to particular schools or working across the total number of schools. This traditional model of professional development seems to reach many teachers, but the quality of the sessions is questionable regardless the expertise of personnel. District staff developers typically do not know if teachers incorporate the new ideas in their teaching or whether or not the professional development can be linked to student achievement (See Hughes et al., this volume).

Now let's consider another scenario.

Scenario #2: School-Based Teacher Education

Eric is a teacher-educator and a teacher of children. Based at an elementary school, he spends about half of his time teaching language and literacy in a classroom; he also coaches teachers. Eric prepared for his role by taking part in a year-long course in which he had time to refine his classroom application of the new approaches he was learning. In fact, Eric is always developing expertise at the classroom level as new research informs his work, and he engages in continuous professional development to help him in his role.

In Eric's school, teachers complete sixty hours of an initial course designed to help them use a combination of research-based instructional approaches that are integrated in a language and literacy framework. The teachers enjoy reading, discussing, viewing videotapes of teaching, and hearing about new approaches in onsite, after-school sessions over the course of the year; however, the real learning occurs when Eric works with the teachers in their classrooms. On a regular basis, he observes, demonstrates, and coaches so that teachers are highly supported when taking on new learning.

The teachers have begun to reflect on their teaching, to analyze it, and to help each other. Even after the initial course, teachers continue in staff development sessions and coaching. Even more important, some say, is the informal access they have to Eric. They can drop into his classroom or small office to share what is happening in their classrooms. They can get a quick piece of advice or a recommendation for books and materials. They have colleagues who are interested in how their work is going. The conversations in the teachers' room have taken an entirely new turn, because teachers are sharing their successes.

Eric works mainly with teachers in grades 3 through 6; he has a counterpart staff developer who works with K–2 teachers and also teaches for half a day in a classroom. The two half-time staff developers work closely with the principal and a school leadership team who guide the implementation of change. A particular concern of theirs is measuring achievement using "hard data," so they regularly examine benchmark assessment as well as yearly performance on standardized tests. The teachers in this school have taken accountability into their own hands. They know that the achievement of each student entering the school is the entire staff's responsibility.

The professional development for the teachers in Eric's building does not end there. Another layer provides instructional support for teachers who are working with the lowest achieving students and that is the next scenario.

Scenario #3: School-Based Professional Development for Early Interventions

Eric's school provides an intensive early intervention program called Reading Recovery for the lowest achieving first graders. The staff recognizes that as classroom instruction improves, the gap between average students and those who are experiencing great difficulties learning to read may also grow unless they not only receive good classroom but also extra help.

In this building, first graders who are struggling receive one-to-one tutoring by a teacher who has been specially trained to teach effective early reading strategies. These teachers have taken part in year-long graduate course work taught by Raquel, the district's "teacher-leader." As a teacher-educator, Raquel, who has also taken part in a year-long graduate course of study to prepare her for her role, trains and then continues to provide ongoing support to the Reading Recovery teachers. What makes the professional development for these teachers different from the kind that Carol, presented in the first scenario, provides?

Like Carol, Raquel works district-wide, but the kind of professional development Raquel offers is grounded in real examples of teaching and learning. Teachers meet weekly for an academic year when they are learning how to teach Reading Recovery and, following the initial training, approximately every six weeks. In these sessions, teachers take turns teaching children behind a one-way glass. Freed from teaching, others in the class can sharpen their observational powers, reflect on teaching actions, specify in language what the child's behavior is and what it indicates in terms of learning, and formulate hypotheses as to the most effective way to teach. Teachers use a structured format; knowing each child in detail, they can plan a systematic sequence of activities designed to take advantage of exactly what the child knows and needs to know next. Throughout their professional development, teachers learn to be effective decision makers.

Raquel teaches children in one-to-one lessons every day herself; the rest of the time, she visits and coaches teachers in their work. Children's progress is monitored daily with precision, so that Raquel knows exactly at what level each child in the system is working. She also works closely with the principal and leadership team in each school she serves; she reports on the progress of children regularly, and they all work together to assure efficiency and effectiveness.

The professional development that Eric and Raquel provide is complex. The teachers receive a high level of support initially while they are taking on the new instructional practices, but this support is scaled back once the teachers become more proficient. Even then, the professional development isn't withdrawn, but continues as long as the teacher remains in the role. This sustained contact is rarely seen in traditional teacher professional development.

Another distinguishing feature of this model is that the staff developers themselves continue to teach children, keeping themselves grounded in practice. In addition to the teaching of children and teachers, attention is paid to student outcomes. The staff developer oversees the systematic collection of data on students' achievement, which are then analyzed and shared with stakeholders. In other words, everyone pays attention to the fidelity and results of the treatment.

Even complex plans for professional development such as the ones provided by Raquel and Eric may come to be regarded as passing fads. In Raquel's district for example, even though many elementary schools in the district remain strongly supportive of an early intervention such as Reading Recovery, a new Associate Superintendent is convinced that one-to-one interventions are too costly and that systematic phonics instruction delivered to the whole class will take care of all reading problems. It seems likely that the early intervention model for professional development will be dropped.

Complex designs for professional development, such as the ones described previously, are still relatively rare and suggest what *might* be. In today's educational climate it is more likely that teachers will receive scanty and haphazard professional development. It is not uncommon for teachers to attend several different professional development sessions within a short span of time and hear competing messages and directions for "what works." No wonder it is sometimes difficult to get teachers to fully participate in new initiatives. We expect them to embrace whatever "new" vision comes along, but we do not offer them a multifaceted design for professional development that provides varying levels of support, over an extended period of time, along with the materials needed to be successful.

WHAT MIGHT BE

What if we had the power to buy whatever we need to improve literacy education? What would we want? Our answer would be that we would "buy" effective, ongoing professional development. But, despite what federal, state, and local politicians tend to promise, no amount of dollars can achieve the vision overnight. It will take more than a massive infusion of funds to make a sustained change in literacy education.

It is also risky to suggest that by simply waving a punishing set of standards over educators' heads, schools will magically develop the capacity they need to assure that every child meets rigorous criteria for reading and writing. As Walmsley and Allington (1995) have so succinctly said, "There is no quick fix."

In addition to dollars and a system of accountability (which arguably standards might provide) we believe that school systems themselves have to change. This can happen if educators work together to build a system that has the capacity to

- analyze problems and find solutions;
- evaluate itself; and
- teach itself.

A system that has learned how to do these things will not be trying the professional development flavor of the month, but will have developed educators who can themselves target problem areas and decide together what support is needed to remedy the situation. Anders, Hoffman, and Duffy (2000) make this point well when they say:

> Reading educators should be trying to develop teachers who analyze reading instructional situations and then in a thoughtful way, construct appropriate responses. (733)

How to accomplish this? Professional development is the key, but we need a broad and systemic district-wide approach that works within each building to do what needs to be done. We also know that professional development is not an isolated event and does not exist within a vacuum. It's not a matter of calling a good consultant to spend one—or even ten—days with a school staff. The two aspects that must work together to assure this march toward systemic change are

- integration of research with practice, and
- long-term professional development with clear parameters.

Integration of Research with Practice

We begin with research because the rigorous collection and analysis of data are at the heart of school reform. In any change effort, we must be able to measure whether and to what extent we are succeeding in terms of children's learning. Teachers' opinions certainly count in the mix of evidence, but they also must look systematically at their students' progress. Research provides an invaluable feedback loop that allows us to continually refine what we do. For example, a group of teachers looking at students' writing scores found that good ideas were coming through in the samples they evaluated, but that spelling was well below expectations. That motivated the teachers to enter a year-long study group to support each other in implementing a phonics and spelling program across the grades.

Another group of teachers found that children's test scores showed they were reading accurately and decoding quite well, but had trouble answering questions and writing about texts. The teachers decided to look at a variety of ways to demonstrate and teach for comprehension.

In both of these examples, research and teaching are closely aligned. The need for new approaches emerged from the teachers' attention to data, and was not imposed from the outside. Further, the teachers' exploration of the issues, in whatever professional development format they use, will continue to be grounded in the teaching of children and not simply by listening to didactic-style presentations. It is also notable that these teachers are working very independently. Not only have they identified an instructional issue that needs to be resolved, but they have also designed their own professional development experiences. Research and practice can be aligned in these ways when staff developers, like Eric and Raquel, are school based and continue to work with students themselves.

Long-term Professional Development with Clear Parameters

Much of the criticism leveled at typical professional development practices is that they don't provide for systemic change. Usually a few teachers attend a professional development session featuring an invited speaker. It is up to these few teachers to then bring back to their colleagues what they have learned at the session. As well, there is often no coherence to the professional development experiences and teachers may see them as a series of unconnected topics.

There should be a clear design for professional development experiences that is related to the needs in the district. Staff developers may want to ask themselves the following questions:

- How are students presently progressing in literacy?
- What literacy-related goals do we want to achieve as a school district in one year, two years, and beyond? (In other words, what changes do we want?)
- How much professional support do we need to bring about the instructional changes required for change? Choices may range from closely guided professional development provided by a specially trained staff developer working side by side with the teacher in the classroom to teachers deciding for themselves how to structure their professional development.
- What structures need to be put in place in the system to support the change? For example, perhaps an arrangement with a local university is needed to provide graduate credit for the extra time the teachers will be working with the staff developers. Teachers may need to be reassigned to work with small groups or individuals, meaning changes in teacher

allocation and scheduling, or they may need new instruments or materials to carry out the new instructional practices.

• How will we know when we get there? A plan is needed to collect achievement on students and teachers. In other words, how will we determine the fidelity of the treatment and its results?

These are just some of the questions to be addressed in the design of a plan for professional development, which will, in turn, build capacity within systems. This complex design is far different from the haphazard and scanty approaches typically available to teachers.

In this volume we present an array of chapters, each describing a complex model of professional development for literacy teachers and suggesting what might be possible. The research and experience represented in these chapters encompass many varied settings. Across them all we have learned that true expertise means developing internal systems for *learning while teaching* and *teaching while learning*.

2 | A NATIONAL OVERVIEW OF PROFESSIONAL DEVELOPMENT PROGRAMS IN READING

MARIE TEJERO HUGHES
MICHELE MITS CASH
SUZETTE AHWEE
JANETTE KLINGNER

Highly qualified teachers are crucial to students' success in learning to read, yet many teachers begin their teaching careers without having the skills and knowledge to help all students become proficient readers. A meta-analysis conducted by the National Reading Panel identified research-based practices and strategies considered effective in teaching students to read (National Reading Panel 2000). The researchers concluded that it is essential for teachers to possess knowledge in each of these pedagogical domains: (a) a sophisticated understanding of how students learn to read, (b) knowledge of the difficulties experienced by some students and how to provide necessary support, and (c) the ability to effectively implement a variety of multi-level instructional practices.

Along with this essential base of knowledge, teachers must also possess skills in specific instructional areas (e.g., phonological awareness, word identification, fluency, reading comprehension, vocabulary, study skills, and motivation). Many researchers agree that teachers do not acquire this knowledge or these skills during the course of their teacher preparation programs, which typically varies between one-to-three reading methods courses, depending on the institution. It would, therefore, be unrealistic to expect novice teachers of classrooms full of diverse students to be able to teach all their students to read proficiently. To become accomplished, teachers must be lifelong learners, always honing their teaching skills through participation in high-quality professional development opportunities.

PROFESSIONAL DEVELOPMENT CAN MAKE A DIFFERENCE

When educators receive high-quality professional development directly focused on their classroom curriculum and instructional techniques, they

9

tend to use research-based instructional practices associated with higher reading achievement (Darling-Hammond 2000; Joyce and Showers 1995). In addition, teachers who integrate effective reading interventions into their curriculum lead effective school-based programs that are designed to meet the needs of struggling readers (Broaddus and Bloodgood 1999). By participation in high-quality continuing professional development, teachers are able to stay abreast of best reading practices (American Federation of Teachers 1999).

Research suggests that appropriate professional development for teachers can and does produce higher reading achievement in students (Anders, Hoffman, and Duffy 2000; National Reading Panel 2000). Every dollar spent on preparing teachers to become qualified practitioners can result in increased student achievement outcomes (Ferguson 1991). Yet, outcomes associated with professional development vary widely because of differences in program content, structure and format of the experience, as well as the context within which new practices are implemented (Guskey 2000; National Staff Development Council 1995). Determining causal relationships regarding professional development programs and improvements in student learning is difficult because of the complexities associated with the intervening variables (Guskey 1997; Guskey and Sparks 1996).

There is evidence that professional development programs that offer intense levels of support and opportunities for reflection are more likely to have positive effects (Anders, Hoffman, and Duffy 2000). Due to the difficulties in determining causal relationships when designing professional development programs, directors who initiate these programs should keep teachers as a central focus in determining the content and structure, as well as how they will integrate the new information into their instructional repertoires.

Regrettably, the majority of professional development programs fail to result in changes in reading instruction. Few teachers have opportunities to participate in long-term quality professional development programs that have the potential to promote significant and lasting change (Porter et al. 2000). One-shot or sit-and-get sessions continue to be typical of professional development programs offered to teachers. These programs lack sub-

FIGURE 2–1
Why Do Most Professional Development Programs Fail to Change Reading Instruction?

Why Do Most Professional Development Programs Fail to Change Reading Instruction?

- "One-shot" or "sit-and-get" sessions continue to be typical.
- Programs lack a research base.
- Programs lack follow-up and observation.
- Programs tend to be "top-down." Information is mandated from the upper level.
- There is little consideration for teachers' background or experience.

stantive, research-based content and systematic follow-up, which is required for sustainability (Snow et al. 1998). These professional development activities tend to be linear or top-down in approach, where teachers simply listen to the latest ideas regarding teaching and learning from experts. In professional development opportunities of this type, little consideration is given to what teachers have experienced or their past knowledge and background. Further, teachers are seldom observed following the practices taught in professional development, which would assist them in perfecting their implementation of the practices presented (Hoffman 1996).

EFFECTIVE PROFESSIONAL DEVELOPMENT

Over the past twenty years we have learned much about what constitutes effective professional development for teachers.

Research has revealed salient characteristics of effective models that should be considered in the design of programs. First, research provides evidence that intensive and extensive levels of support monitoring and coaching help in increasing skills (Anders and Evens 1994; Moore 1991). Research also supports teacher reflection (Bos and Anders 1994); as well as ongoing conversations and dialogue among colleagues (Combs 1994). Participation in professional development should be voluntary (El-Dinary and Schuder 1993) and ideally should encompass entire school faculties (Joyce and Showers 1995). Collaboration among different role groups is essential (Short and Kauffman 1992); and teachers will need ongoing assistance in assimilating new information into existing belief structures (Malouf and Schiller 1995).

The role of professional development is not just to train teachers on specific reading practices, but also to help teachers personally develop into strategic and reflective practitioners. Teachers who are able to directly relate new practices to everyday realities tend to be more effective. Ongoing support is needed for this complex integration of new information, and ownership is the key. Teachers taking ownership of their learning and feeling pride

What Research Says: Requirements of Effective Professional Meetings	
Support:	Monitoring
	Coaching
	Teacher reflection
	Conversation
	Voluntary participation
	Full-school participation
	Collaboration among role groups
	Assisting

FIGURE 2–2
What Research Says:
Requirements of Effective
Professional Meetings

in their practice should be the goal of every professional development program (Finch 1999).

Recently, professional development programs in the area of reading have been responding to the need for better-prepared teachers by offering opportunities that are more in-depth and provide ongoing follow-up and support. It is still common, however, to see a list of one-shot type professional development opportunities posted on faculty bulletin boards across the nation. Contributing to the problem of underprepared teachers are the high costs associated with providing a continuum of support and feedback to practicing teachers. In any structural format, professional development for teachers is an expensive endeavor.

PROFESSIONAL DEVELOPMENT OFFERED BY SCHOOL DISTRICTS

Most states and districts estimate that three percent to five percent of their school district budgets are spent on professional development programs (Corcoran 1995). While expenditures vary from district to district, they typically include such costs as personnel salaries associated with planning and delivering the workshop, supervising and evaluating personnel, providing for substitute coverage, adding extra school days designated for professional development, and paying teacher stipends for participation in professional development. Additionally, money is often spent on professional development without questioning whether teachers and students are significantly benefiting from these efforts (Robb 2000).

It therefore becomes critical to measure the long-term impact of these programs in terms of the extent of teacher implementation and subsequent sustainability of practices, as well as to support teachers' endeavors to meet the challenges they face in their classrooms (Duffy, Roehler, and Putnam 1987). We still know very little about the procedures that school districts should follow when designing professional development activities. We know even less about methods for determining implementation success and teacher accountability. To begin answering these questions, we needed to first determine what professional development programs school districts were offering elementary teachers in the area of reading. In this chapter, we describe a study we undertook to determine the content, structure, and context of the programs, as well as the school districts' methods of assessing implementation and sustainability.

SURVEY RESPONDENTS

We selected school districts using the information available from the National Center for Educational Statistics, randomly selecting two school districts that represented each metropolitan status (rural, suburban, urban) from each state. When a state had fewer than two school districts in any metropolitan status, an alternative school district was randomly selected until six school districts were identified for the state. In states that had fewer than six school districts in total, all districts were included in the survey mailing. Taken together, a total of 294 school districts were identified nationwide. In addition, we included the twenty largest school districts in the United States. A total of 314 school districts participated in the investigation.

One survey was sent to the program director of reading/language arts and one to the program director of special education at each of the identified school districts, making a total of 628 surveys mailed. Directors were asked to complete the survey or forward it to a colleague who was better able to provide the information. After six weeks, a total of 292 surveys were returned (forty-six percent), 149 from reading/language arts directors and 143 from special education directors. The directors represented 216 of the 314 school districts sampled.

In addition to the survey, we conducted a follow-up telephone interview with fifty-six directors (twenty-six reading/language arts, thirty special education) who indicated interest. This group of directors have been in the field of education an average of 22.58 years and have held their current positions for an average of 5.12 years.

HOW RESPONSES WERE COLLECTED AND ANALYZED

Survey

The research literature relating to professional development in reading served as a guide in determining what concepts, formats, and programs to address in the survey developed for this investigation (e.g., Hoffman and Pearson 2000; Snow, Burns, and Griffin 1998). The National Survey of Professional

School Districts	
Metropolitan Status	
Rural	87
Suburban	109
Urban	94
Unknown	2
Regions	
Northwest	43
Midwest	68
South	119
West	60
Unknown	2

FIGURE 2–3
School Districts

Development Practices in Reading for Elementary School Educators was developed for this investigation and contained nineteen items centered around three themes related to professional development programs: program content, program structure, and post-program accountability.

The first question we asked the directors was to identify their professional role in organizing professional development programs for their district. Four questions covered the content of what was offered by their school district. Specifically, what types of programs and or concepts were presented in workshops; what factors were important to decision makers when choosing content for workshops; and whether or not they felt that the professional development programs in reading were providing the teachers with the tools needed to be successful in meeting the needs of their students. Seven questions elicited information regarding program structure and included types of incentives offered to teachers for attending professional development programs; who generally conducts programs; and what was the format of the programs.

Another six questions focused on teacher accountability following participation in a professional development program. They addressed issues such as what percentage of teachers in the district attended at least one professional development program in reading; to what extent did teachers implement and sustain learning, and how implementation is monitored. The final question on the survey asked if the respondent would be willing to participate in a follow-up telephone interview.

Telephone Interview

The telephone interview consisted of a semi-structured interview format following the same three central themes as the survey: program content, program structure, and post-program accountability. During the interview, we asked directors to describe what was presented to teachers during workshops and what they believed was the main reason for choosing the topics. We also asked if they felt the professional development programs in reading were providing teachers with the tools and knowledge they needed to meet

FIGURE 2–4
Questions We Asked About Professional Development in Reading

Questions We Asked About Professional Development in Reading

What types of programs and concepts are presented in workshops?

What factors are important to decision makers when choosing content for workshops?

Do professional development programs provide teachers with the tools needed to be successful?

What are the key characteristics of effective professional development programs?

What obstacles may be encountered in implementing professional development?

How is accountability assessed?

the needs of all of their students and why they felt that way. Furthermore, we asked them to describe key characteristics of effective professional development programs, possible obstacles that may be encountered during implementation, and how districts assessed accountability of teachers in the implementation and sustained use of practices learned through professional development. To wrap up the interview, interviewers documented demographic information on the director.

Procedures

We mailed the survey with a pencil (for ease of completion) and a postage-paid return envelope, and requested that they complete and return the survey within two weeks of receipt. As an incentive, we offered directors an opportunity to win a gift certificate upon return of the completed survey. After the first mailing, we sent a second mailing to those school districts that had yet to respond.

Once all of the survey data had been entered into the database, directors who had indicated they would participate in the telephone interview were identified. We made at least five attempts to contact them. Sixty-two directors indicated they would participate in the interview, fifty-six (ninety percent) of whom completed the interview process. Trained researchers conducted interviews at times convenient to the directors. The length of the interviews ranged from thirty to forty minutes and were tape-recorded to ensure that relevant themes and concepts were accurately recorded.

The survey data were analyzed using the SPSS™ statistical software package to generate frequencies and descriptive information. Nonparametric analysis was used to determine statistical significance between comparative participant groups on appropriate survey questions.

Qualitative data from the interviews were themed by two of the researchers and constantly compared to attain one hundred percent agreement on the themes following guidelines established by Glaser and Strauss (1967). Themed data were organized around three central ideas: structure and content of the professional development reading programs, and post-program accountability for teachers. A systematic multiple-step procedure was implemented: (a) each researcher read the interviews and individually coded them; (b) the coded interviews were compared to identify characteristics shared by the interviewees; (c) after key characteristics were determined, the researchers reviewed all of the interviews and recoded them to reflect the noted themes and concepts.

WHAT DIRECTORS SAID ABOUT PROFESSIONAL DEVELOPMENT

The findings of this study can be grouped into three themes: Content of professional development, structure of professional development, and accountability. After examining the responses of both groups of directors, we found no significant difference between groups on any survey item or interview question. To further explore this issue, we analyzed for differences a data set containing only districts in which both the reading/language arts and special education directors (*n* = 74) responded to the survey. We found no significant differences between these two groups of directors. Therefore, we merged responses for both groups of directors (reading/language arts; special education) and percentages indicate the total number of respondents who provided information.

Most directors felt satisfied that their professional development programs provided teachers with the knowledge and skills needed to prepare students to meet established reading standards. A small number of directors (eight percent) felt that the professional development did not prepare the teachers in their districts to teach reading well.

CONTENT OF PROFESSIONAL DEVELOPMENT

On the survey, we asked directors to identify the professional development topics offered in their school district during the past year. These workshop topics were grouped into eight general categories (see Figure 2–5). The most frequently mentioned workshop topics focused on providing instruction on implementing specific packaged reading programs. Sixty-five percent of the directors indicated that reading programs such as Reading Recovery or Success for All were frequently topics of professional development. Specific reading practices like Making Words (Cunningham and Cunningham 1992) or Collaborative Strategic Reading (Klingner and Vaughn 1996) constituted the second most common category, with sixty-four percent of the directors indicating their district offered workshops in this area. Districts also provide in-services on teaching teachers a variety of general reading strategies. Besides focusing on programs, practices, and strategies for reading, districts also provided teachers with workshops geared toward developing the teachers' reading instructional skills. This type of professional development covered a wide range of topics including computer-based instruction, using multicultural literature, and collaborative learning.

Directors also rated how important certain factors were in influencing their selection of professional development topics.

We rated three factors as very important or important by at least eighty percent of the directors. The district's reading philosophy played a major role in determining what topics were presented at workshops. As one director commented to us, "It [the reading workshop] matched the district philosophy and the need that we had for a variety of students." As districts changed their reading philosophy, directors wanted to ensure teachers were knowledgeable of the new focus, as this director states, "We wanted teachers to have a better understanding of how phonics fits into the total balanced picture of reading."

In addition to reading philosophy, directors indicated that they considered the impact the reading in-service potentially has in increasing students' reading test scores. Specifically, directors talked extensively about the importance of ensuring students were prepared for high-stakes assessments much like these directors did, "We have new state testing. So we definitely needed to take a look at how we were instructing kids and really prepare them for the state tests, which we believe is a much more authentic testing. . . . The main reason for most of the staff development that's going on in the state is the new assessment." Directors also strongly felt that information presented to teachers should be research-based. As this director responded when asked what she looks for when selecting a topic, "It [reading practice] has been documented and researched that it's really one of the most important things for students who are learning to read."

STRUCTURE OF PROFESSIONAL DEVELOPMENT

Format and Presenter

Directors provided insight into the formats most commonly used by districts to disseminate information and prepare teachers, as shown in Figure 2–6. Most professional development opportunities presented to teachers across the country were conducted using either one-day workshops (seventy percent) or half-day workshops (sixty-four percent).

Most Common Professional Development Categories and Selection Factors	
Categories	**Percentage**
Specific reading programs	65
Specific reading practices	64
General reading strategies	58
Instructional techniques and methods	57
Phonological awareness	46
Reading comprehension	40
Emergent reading	31
Remedial reading	29
Factors	
Fits school district's philosophy	82
Expected to increase test scores	81
Research-based	81
Teacher's request	75
Professional experience	56

FIGURE 2–5
Most Common Professional Development Categories and Selection Factors

However, more extensive professional development was also used in many districts for some of the professional development, including multi-day workshops (fifty-five percent) and workshops with follow-up support (forty-five percent). More individualized professional development programs (e.g., coaching, modeling in class) were not as common; however, it is interesting to note that about a quarter of the directors indicated that the district offered them.

We also asked directors to identify who typically conducts the professional development programs in reading in their district. In most cases, the districts hired outside consultants (eighty-four percent) or used school district personnel (eighty percent). School-level administrators and lead teachers (fifty-nine percent) also regularly led professional development workshops. Directors indicated that publishers and developers of the program or practice presented at in-services forty-five percent of the time.

Incentives and Resources

Teacher participation in professional development programs organized by the school district was split between voluntary (fifty-three percent) and required (forty-seven percent) participation. Although in most cases, districts did provide some kind of incentive for teachers attending the in-services. Directors reported that frequently used incentives included providing the teachers with credit for attending professional development that could be used toward state recertification, providing teachers with release time to attend workshops during the workday, and/or giving teachers a stipend upon completion of the workshop. Several of the districts provided other incentives such as mileage reimbursement, classroom resources, and salary increases.

We also asked directors to describe the kind of resources and support most frequently provided by the school districts to teachers during and after the professional development program. The most common resources provided to teachers during the workshops were handouts about the presentation, supplemental materials such as charts and activities related to the topic, and books and videos related to the workshop. After attending the in-

FIGURE 2–6
*Format of Professional
Development for Reading*

Format of Professional Development for Reading	
Format	**Percentage**
One-day workshops	70
Half-day workshops	64
Multi-day workshops	55
Workshops with follow-up support	45
Individualized professional development	25

Percentages indicate proportion of directors indicating format. Respondents could mark more than one (i.e., coaching, modeling in classrooms).

service, teachers were given very minimal support or resources. The most common follow-up support available to teachers was the contact information of a person who could answer their questions. Several school districts, however, provided more extensive support such as in-class observations to provide feedback, support groups, additional training, and mentors.

Characteristics of Effective Programs

After directors gave an overview of how professional development programs in reading are conducted in the school districts, we asked them to describe in ideal terms the key characteristics of an effective program. Directors provided a plethora of ideas on how professional development opportunities could be structured more effectively. These are summarized in Figure 2–7.

The need to *provide teachers with follow-up support* was the most frequently mentioned element. As this director explained, "I would say getting teachers the basic information they need, but allow them time to process it in whatever ways they need to. A lot of times that means having conversations in small groups back at their schools, their study groups." Another director stated this need by saying, "The key is following up with a coaching model for support." Directors also talked about the importance of workshops being *interactive and hands-on with opportunities to model* the new practices. "I really like to offer staff development where the participants get to demonstrate their knowledge in the field. Either working in small groups to problem-solve or producing some type of action plan. I like for them not to just sit and listen and read. I want them to demonstrate in some manner that they have an understanding of what's been presented," stated one director. Another director also expressed this need, "Learning the basic components, having an opportunity to discuss and analyze those components with your peers, an opportunity to practice, an opportunity to implement, and an opportunity to evaluate afterwards whether you were successful or not."

Directors also discussed the importance of ensuring that teachers attending in-services *understood the need* for the practice or program and felt that the material presented would benefit them and their students. One director expressed the issue in this way: "Participants of the staff development have to

---

Suggestions from Directors:
Ideal Characteristics of an Effective Professional
Development Program

- Provide teachers with follow-up support
- Provide interactive and hands-on opportunities to model new practices
- Ensure that teachers understand the need for the practice or program
- Present practical strategies

FIGURE 2–7
Suggestions from Directors: Ideal Characteristics of an Effective Professional Development Program

feel a need to be there. If they don't think that there is something wrong with the way they are teaching now or there is anything better out there, then they won't come and won't play when they do come. There has to be a sense that I can do what I am doing better than I am doing it now." Other directors said, "That it [the workshop] meets the needs of the individuals who are attending. That there's a good match, that there are people who want this information." While discussing characteristics of effective professional development programs, some directors talked about the value of presenting *practical strategies*, so that teachers are able to implement easily the strategies in their class. Several directors made remarks similar to the following, "First, I think that they [the workshops] need to be very practical. I think that they need to be able to provide someone with immediate feedback. In other words, I think workshops need to give you stuff that you can come back and immediately implement parts of it or try out immediately."

Barriers to Implementing Programs

When we asked directors what barriers they faced in developing and organizing effective professional development programs, the barrier identified by most directors was *insufficient funds and resources*. One director stated, "Cost, in our state, because we are so frugal the teachers are rated at the bottom of the scale. We try to do a lot of creative things with a lot of good people, but it doesn't always bring in the outside resources or the new ideas and information that we should have."

Lack of funding concerned another director as well, "There's not money to pay for subs for teachers to do it [attend workshops] and there's really not money to pay teachers to come after school and, by contract they don't typically work after school." Another common barrier shared by directors was the *difficulty of scheduling* professional development programs. This director explained, "Time. It's such a double-edged sword. You want to offer staff development when you think that you can get the most captive audiences. Oftentimes that is during the workday, but then finding enough substitutes to cover those classes is very difficult. You're left with offering them after school or on the weekends. People who have families and have responsibilities cannot come very frequently to after-school workshops." Another director concurred by saying her barrier was "finding the time for staff to learn the material and practice it, and then assess whether the training is applicable to their situation."

FIGURE 2–8
Barriers to Implementing Professional Development Programs

Barriers to Implementing Professional Development Programs

- Insufficient funds and resources
- Difficulty of scheduling
- Teachers' fears of implementing new ideas

The next most common barrier expressed by directors was related to the teachers themselves. Directors talked about teachers' being *fearful of implementing new ideas*. "We have to overcome the teachers' fear of failure or to take a risk. Change is difficult and chaotic. I think it's important that in-services do give them confidence and they do reaffirm confidence in themselves and their abilities. Without that, they can't go out there and take the risks they need to make the effective changes in their classroom," remarked one director.

ACCOUNTABILITY

We further asked directors if there was a mechanism in place for collecting data on implementation and sustainability of practices presented at professional development programs. Only about fifty percent replied that their district had a means to determine, although sometimes limited, implementation and/or sustainability of practices presented at professional development workshops. When we asked directors why no accountability procedures were in place, thirty-four percent indicated that the main reason was *insufficient time*. The following two directors addressed this issue by saying, "The main barrier is time for the administrators to do that. You need a clone if you're going to do it. There has to be a will and support to do it, too. I don't think it's there yet" and "The barrier is time. There is not enough time to go to every school to evaluate the teachers." Another reason expressed by the directors was that there was a *lack of resources and personnel* to carry out any accountability procedures. "I think we could do much more, but we don't have the people and money to do much more," remarked a director. Other reasons cited by directors for not monitoring implementation of practices included *lack of support from administrators, not seeing a need for it,* and *not knowing what to measure*.

Even directors who stated the district gathered some data acknowledged that it was not systematic. Many concurred as this director did, "It's just informal with administrators doing a walk-through and just observing and asking at faculty meetings." Because many respondents indicated they did not collect systematic information, survey findings regarding how implementation is measured and the extent to which teachers integrated practices is based on the 145 directors whose districts collected this type of data.

Accountability Mechanism

Directors indicated that teacher implementation of the strategies and practices acquired through professional development programs was primarily assessed and determined by teachers' self-reports, such as "doing surveys every year and asking people" or "by talking with the principal" or through observations. One director said, "I visit each of our teachers on a regular basis. I can access whether or not they're using certain reading strategies. I can see whether they're implementing certain strategies." About a quarter of the districts surveyed monitored students' daily progress or their performance on achievement tests to evaluate whether or not teachers were implementing the practices covered in professional development sessions.

Practice Implementation

The majority of school district directors reported that in their opinion, teachers who attend professional development programs in reading only partially integrated the information presented during the workshops into their classroom teaching. Only about eight percent of the directors believed that teachers completely incorporated the material into their daily instruction. The remaining directors reported that they were unable to answer the question. For those teachers who did integrate all or part of the practices learned at workshops, information regarding their sustainability of the practice or program was not available in sixty-one percent of the cases. Of the remaining responses, seven percent of directors felt that practices learned were not sustained beyond twelve weeks, seventeen percent felt that three months to a year was the total extent of sustainability, and another fourteen percent felt that practices were sustained for more than one year.

When we asked what contributed to some teachers implementing all or most of the information presented during the professional development, overwhelmingly directors felt that practices and strategies were implemented when teachers were provided with *follow-up support* from the professionals as well as having a strong *faculty network* for communication and support. Directors expressed this with such comments as "Just this year we have been doing one where the program was introduced one day in August and then has been followed-up with at least a day or half-day after that, and that has really made the difference in implementation" and "we are meeting on a monthly basis, and teachers are going back to the classroom and practicing the strategies; and then we get back together as a group and it's like a renewal thing. You keep it fresh, you keep it going."

We also asked directors how the district helps teachers generalize the practices learned through professional development. Having *supports within the schools* themselves, *providing follow-up* as an integral part of professional development, and inviting only *motivated and enthusiastic teachers* who are committed to learning at the workshops were the primary methods mentioned, with most of the directors supporting at least one of them. Over half the directors indicated that incorporating a support system within their schools is the preferred method. More specifically, having teachers help each other would facilitate the generalization of these practices. One director stated, "some institutionalized form of peer coaching has to be present so that it is acceptable practice to have peers come in, watch you, coach you, and demonstrate things for you." Another director agreed, "what we're looking at is a mentoring program." Many of the directors also discussed the importance of including follow-up support to teachers. A special education director explained that teachers would generalize the practices "if there is an opportunity that some follow-up can be provided on an individual basis, in [the teachers' classrooms], to monitor how they may be using the knowledge they've gained through staff development activity."

According to many of these directors, an important factor in determining the generalization of practices included motivating teachers.

> Many times teachers will not try anything because they don't think it's going to work. You have to really work at trying to get them to see that it is practical [and] that it'll work. You ought to try it, to keep that open mind.

Other methods mentioned by a smaller number of directors included providing more time for teachers to learn and implement the practices, additional resources that would facilitate their implementation, and providing a wide variety of strategies and materials from which teachers could choose to implement. Four directors stipulated that the only way that teachers would generalize practices learned through professional development would be to mandate their implementation and sustainability.

Barriers to Practice Implementation

We asked directors for their opinions as to why many of the teachers did not implement or stopped implementing the practices and strategies shared with them during professional development opportunities. Many directors felt that teachers did not implement practices and strategies because teachers were *not committed to the practice*. As one director put it, "somebody tries something and it's moderately successful and they feel like well that wasn't great, I like it the way I always did it before, because they are comfortable with it." Another director suggested that "no matter how much we do—and we do a lot of training and staff development—oftentimes, we don't see that in the long run, students are benefiting because we don't see a lot of changes in instructional strategies in the classroom." In addition, the directors suggested another factor that might affect a teacher's commitment to implementing practices was *lack of administrative supports*. As one director put it, "if there's no support, and there's no time, then there's no special reason to continue it, unless it creates such miraculous results that it's self motivating, why should it continue?" Another factor was the length and depth of the *professional development program is inadequate* for teachers to learn and practice new skills. One director noted, "professional development in a classroom situation, based on theory, doesn't have any problems. You go back to the classroom and try to implement it and you run into people and then you have a lot of different variables that weren't part of the presentation. So you're constantly having to problem-solve to make it work." A final factor that directors shared was that it is *difficult to share workshop information with other teachers*, especially, as one director put it, "if only one could go and you need the whole elementary school to be involved in it; it's hard for her to come back and sell this to five or six other teachers or twenty when she's the only one who heard it and heard the professionals talk about it, so that's what's hard sometimes."

We asked directors to specify what needed to be in place for the generalization of practices to occur. Many of them said that the *support of both in-school and outside key stakeholders,* as well as *increasing the funding and resources,* were necessary for teachers to apply what they learned in their classrooms. One director specified that more money and time for training would facilitate more opportunities for practice and feedback. A director succinctly summarized his response with, "money has to be there." Directors also provided other responses relating to support from in-school and outside key stakeholders. Directors tended to focus on administrative support as portrayed in one director's statement, "You need administrators who promote this [and] who see value in it." Another director corroborated that "administration has to be supportive of that and work toward that." Other supports mentioned were (a) establishing a reading curriculum, (b) recognizing that teachers need time management training, (c) including teachers who are committed to using the strategy in program development, and (d) building in an evaluation component for teacher implementation.

PROFESSIONAL DEVELOPMENT NEEDS TO BE IMPROVED

Professional development programs offered by school districts are often ineffective in preparing teachers to meet the challenges of teaching reading to all students. A large number of teachers today report that they have not had adequate professional development to provide the reading instruction necessary to ensure that all students are able to meet established reading standards (Olson 2001). In an effort to provide the most effective professional development, districts try to offer a wide variety of opportunities that match their reading philosophy. However, this survey of school district directors confirms that there is still room to improve how teachers are prepared. School districts often lack the infrastructure and knowledge of what is needed to implement and monitor effective professional development in reading.

Across the country, one-shot professional development experiences continue to be the most common form of delivering information to teachers. About half the school districts that responded to our survey indicated they did provide some multi-day workshops and follow-up, although this usually took the form of "Call if you have questions." Within traditional sit-and-get professional development workshops, the contact time between the presenter and the teacher is minimal, and teachers are generally only given handouts and contact information to help them put it all together in their classrooms. To translate needed reforms into practice, school districts need information and guidance on the characteristics and conditions that can help them provide high-quality professional development. If teachers are to gain the most from professional development, districts and other providers of professional development need to re-examine the structure of their professional development delivery methods.

A National Overview | **25**
of Professional
Development
Programs in Reading

NEXT STEPS IN PROVIDING EFFECTIVE PROFESSIONAL DEVELOPMENT

Staff development programs that are effective incorporate relevant theory, demonstration, opportunities for practice, and feedback that is not only provided during the program, but post-program as well, and helps the teacher hone newly acquired skills. This continuum of services for professional development can be successful in preparing individuals to incorporate and implement new approaches, techniques, and curriculums in their classrooms. Within this framework, high-quality professional development programs should be structured to include three components: support, reflection, and collaboration. Recently, researchers have shown that these alternate methods to the sit-and-get process have been successful in changing and informing teachers' classroom practices.

In-service professional development opportunities need to provide for transfer of training, practice, feedback, and reflection, as well as support and reinforcement for the use of skills in natural settings. Our investigation confirms that professional development efforts across the nation are offering more in the way of the nontraditional workshop formats, which as the directors indicated, have a positive impact (see Figure 2–9).

Such examples include ongoing intensive supports (Anders and Evans 1994); coaching and mentoring support that links to actual practices (Moore 1991); time for teachers to reflect on their own practices as they are moved to change (Bos and Anders 1994); support for the process of change as an ongoing dialogue between stakeholders in the change process (Combs 1994; Hollingsworth 1994); and collaboration among university-based researchers, school-based teacher-educators and teachers (Jennings et al. 1994). Further, the use of teacher-led or action research (Gray-Schlegel and Matanzo 1993), portfolio development for students and teachers (Kieffer

---

Nontraditional Formats for Professional Development

- Coaching and mentoring
- Time for reflection
- Ongoing dialogue among all stakeholders
- "Choice of involvement"
- Collaboration among university and school personnel
- Teacher-led action research
- Portfolio development
- Book clubs

FIGURE 2–9
Nontraditional Formats for Professional Development

and Faust 1994), reflective journals (Botel, Ripley, and Barnes 1993), and book clubs (Flood et al. 1995) have all been shown to assist teachers in gaining new knowledge and practices. Effective methods such as those mentioned here provide for transfer of training through practice, feedback, and reflection, as well as provide full support and reinforcement for the use of skills in classroom settings. While the directors in our study felt that these methods are important and would like to offer more, time and money limit them.

As current practice stands, teachers tend to not implement instructional strategies and cannot sustain the use of research-based instructional practices within their classrooms because they do not know how to put into practice what they have learned. Clearly, the systematic follow-up of professional development programs is also necessary to assist teachers in the endeavor to sustain what they have learned. Follow-up as a means of supporting the classroom teacher also falls on a continuum and can take the specific form of ongoing conversations and dialogue as it currently does with principals or colleague teachers, or it may consist of more intensive and extensive levels of support, such as providing consultants in the classroom.

Although most administrators state it is important to supervise teachers to see if they are implementing the ideas and concepts conveyed during professional development, about half the school districts surveyed did not have a means of determining implementation. Directors who did monitor teacher implementation relied for the most part on teacher self-report and/or principal observations. Directors reported that they perceived that the majority of the teachers implemented some aspect of the information with which they were presented, but they were unable to provide solid evidence beyond self-report. Our finding confirms that most professional development programs focus on measuring teachers' satisfaction with the professional development or changes in teachers' attitudes, but that few measure the change in teachers' practice and degree of implementation (Killion 1998). Furthermore, most professional development efforts do not demonstrate evidence of their impact on student performance.

Our investigation suggests that district directors generally feel that teachers have access to sufficient programs to be prepared to teach reading. Yet, more than half of the respondents had no mechanism in place for evaluating effectiveness of programs. Guskey (2000) suggests when evaluating whether or not professional development programs have been effective, evaluators should be asking specific questions, such as who benefited and under what conditions. Further, even though a relationship between professional development and student achievement has been found to exist (Gusky 2000; Lieberman 1995b; Sparks 1997), most professional development programs do not utilize student performance measurements as part of the evaluation process when assessing the effectiveness of their programs. Although it is difficult to create and carry out an evaluation that links staff development and student achievement, the monitoring of teacher progress following professional development insures that activities are beneficial in terms of improving teacher skills and student achievement.

Time and money are the culprits for the lack of accountability in professional development programs; however, to be effective, professional development should be "results driven" (Sparks 1997); and therefore teachers should be evaluated after implementation (Anderson 1991). In spite of the difficulties for establishing accountability, every effort should be made to incorporate an evaluative component in professional development to allay the fear many have that money is spent with questionable benefits (Guskey 2000; Robb 2000). Researchers have suggested that teacher factors that contribute to the high costs of providing quality in-service education include an aversion to attending workshops at the end of the teaching day and very little time available for in-service training during the school year. Additionally, the provision of in-service training during the school day requires the high cost of substitute teachers, which can sometimes be prohibitive.

The purpose of professional development programs should be to provide teachers with the cognitive tools as well as instructional strategies that will help them develop their instructional strategies and improve reflective practices (see Figure 2–10).

Teachers who receive professional development that provides models and demonstrations, time for guided practice with feedback, and time for advance practice in the classroom with feedback and ongoing support, will be more successful in integrating new practices into their instructional repertoire; teachers who are able to directly relate new practices to everyday realities tend to be more effective.

In this national survey, comments made by directors support our assumption that these structural aspects needed to be in place for the generalization of practices to occur. Many of the directors suggested that support of key stakeholders (both in-school and in the community), as well as an increase in funding and resources, is necessary for generalization. One director specified, "more money and time for training would facilitate more opportunities for practice and feedback." For example, in-school stakeholders can form informal networks of peer coaches or provide a support system for teachers as a nonthreatening way to encourage them to acquire new skills. Additionally, practice and feedback facilitates teacher reflection, which is critical to effective professional development models. In order for teachers to sustain the use of the practices learned, educational leaders must

---

A Sequence of Action for Integrating New Practices

- Models and demonstration
- Guided practice with feedback
- Advance practice with feedback
- Ongoing support

FIGURE 2–10
A Sequence of Action for Integrating New Practices

provide "the resources for implementation to occur." Specifically, a large amount of training time as well as qualified trainers is important for teachers to acquire new skills. The more developed the structure of the professional development program, the better the sustainability of teaching practices by teachers and, in turn, higher student academic success.

3 | CONSTRUCTING A MODEL OF PROFESSIONAL DEVELOPMENT TO SUPPORT EARLY LITERACY CLASSROOMS

BILLIE J. ASKEW
TEDDI FULENWIDER
ROBYN KORDICK
SARAH SCHEUERMANN
PAT VOLLENWEIDER
NANCY ANDERSON
YVONNE RODRÍGUEZ

This is the first time in history that the success, perhaps even the survival, of nations and people has been so tightly tied to their ability to learn. Because of this, our future depends now, as never before, on our ability to teach.
(Darling-Hammond 1996a, 7)

This chilling challenge is echoed today in a variety of ways and in a variety of contexts. We know that educational change depends on what teachers do and yet the conditions of teaching appear to have deteriorated over the past twenty years (Fullan 2001). Demands on teachers have intensified, leading to reduced time for relaxation during the workday, lack of time to retool and stay current with the field, chronic and persistent overload, and reductions in the quality of service because corners are cut to save time (Hargreaves 1994). Teacher shortages are increasing across the country. Fullan (2001) proposes a new professionalism that is collaborative, open, and outward looking. This new professionalism makes huge demands on teachers' learning. While teachers are carrying out their everyday duties, they are also required to take

The authors wish to thank Verizon, their corporate partner, for their commitment to literacy and for their support of this project.

on significant new learning "on the job" where they can try out, refine, and get feedback with access to colleagues in a culture of learning.

These challenges prompted the collaborative teacher development project presented here. Three forces led to the initiation of this exploration: area Texas school districts, Texas Woman's University faculty, and a corporate partner, Verizon. With varying motives, all three forces were seeking a model for professional development in the area of early literacy.

Local school districts were requesting long-term, in-house professional development for teachers to address demands for higher levels of literacy performance in the early grades. They knew that the range of literacy performance within early grade classrooms calls for increased teacher knowledge and expertise. School district personnel also knew that traditional one-shot in-service sessions did not work (Darling-Hammond 1996b; Fullan 2001; Hughes et al., this volume).

University faculty were searching for ways to support ongoing teacher development in collaboration with local schools and districts. They also wanted to see if the three-tiered training model used in Reading Recovery (university-based trainers, district-based teacher-leaders, and school-based teachers) would be useful in professional development related to classroom literacy. Because Reading Recovery is an individual intervention for children with special needs (Askew et al. 1998), *only the training model was adapted from Reading Recovery*. Procedures, practices, and theoretical frameworks came from research and theory on classrooms. Faculty were interested in developing district-level literacy leaders who could work with classroom teachers while district-level Reading Recovery teacher-leaders focused on teachers working with low progress readers and writers in grade 1.

Finally, a corporate partner was interested in a literacy project that would influence teaching and learning in the early grades. Of several possibilities, they chose to support this professional development proposal because of its potential influence on teachers, and ultimately on the many children they teach.

Essentially, the question all three groups were asking was "What will it take to make a difference in the professional development of early grade teachers in

FIGURE 3–1
Training Models

	Training Models	
	Reading Recovery Training Model	*Adapted Training Model for Classrooms*
University	Faculty	Faculty
District	Reading Recovery teacher-leader	Classroom Literacy Facilitator
School	Reading Recovery teachers working one-to-one	Classroom teachers

the area of literacy?" The question called for development that included unique combinations of exploration, construction, and collaboration.

BUILDING ON WHAT WE KNOW ABOUT PROFESSIONAL DEVELOPMENT

In recent years, attention has been focused on the teaching profession. The National Commission on Teaching and America's Future (Darling-Hammond 1996b) concluded that the teaching profession must be restructured in two directions: toward increasing teachers' knowledge to meet the demands of their roles and toward redesigning schools to support quality teaching and learning. The commission's plan was aimed at ensuring that all schools have teachers with the knowledge and skills needed to enable all children to learn. "If a caring, qualified teacher for every child is the most important ingredient in educational reform, then it should no longer be the factor most frequently overlooked" (Darling-Hammond 1996b, 194).

The National Board for Professional Teaching Standards (NBPTS 1993) outlined what teachers should know and be able to do according to five domains as shown in Figure 3–2.

With an emphasis on the importance of the *teacher*, professional development has become a crucial aspect of education. Educators have attempted to move from the "hit and run" in-service sessions, which often contribute to one of the biggest problems facing schools today: fragmentation and overload (Fullan 2001). We seem to be able to identify the problems and we know what does not work. We even have many suggested solutions in the literature. But few solutions have been subjected to trial and error. Although there are examples of university-school collaborative efforts, few have provided models for replication and redesign. A notable exception is the Literacy Collaborative (Lyons and Pinnell 2001; also see Chapter 5, this volume). The collaborative project reported here attempts to provide another example of ongoing professional development for examination.

The authors of this chapter endorsed and operated on six characteristics of professional development proposed by Darling-Hammond and McLaughlin (1995) (see Figure 3–3).

Five Domains of Teacher Knowledge and Skills (NBPTS 1993)

1. Teachers are committed to students and their learning.
2. Teachers know the subjects they teach and how to teach those subjects to students.
3. Teachers are responsible for managing and monitoring student learning.
4. Teachers think systematically about their practice and learn from experience.
5. Teachers are members of learning communities.

FIGURE 3–2
Five Domains of Teacher Knowledge and Skills (NBPTS 1993)

These six characteristics closely match those attributed to successful Reading Recovery teacher development suggested by Pinnell (1997). See Figure 3–4.

The Reading Recovery professional development model has been cited as exemplary (Herman and Stringfield 1997) and was central to decision making within our exploratory venture. Reading Recovery is an example of a successful redesign process in that it

- equips specialists with a common body of proven knowledge and skills
- offers ongoing training and support to teachers and schools that adopt it
- shapes its methods according to the results of research (Wilson and Daviss 1994)

Bussell's (2001) study provided evidence that Reading Recovery teacher-leaders play an important leadership role that can serve as an example for others interested in reform. Teacher-leaders provide ongoing training and support to teachers, monitor aspects of implementation in schools, and supervise data collection.

AN OVERVIEW OF THE CLASSROOM FACILITATOR (CLF) PROJECT

The overall goal of the project was to develop a replicable professional development model for early literacy with a major emphasis on the training of *leaders* to provide professional development for teachers in local school districts. University faculty and district administrators initiated the Classroom Literacy Facilitator (CLF) Project. Figure 3–5 outlines actions taken to achieve this goal.

Who Were the Participants?

University faculty invited district administrators in the geographic area of the university to a meeting to consider participating in the development of a

FIGURE 3–3
Characteristics of Professional Development (Darling-Hammond and McLaughlin 1995)

Characteristics of Professional Development (Darling-Hammond and McLaughlin 1995)

1. Experiential—engaging teachers in tasks of teaching, assessment, and observation that illuminate the processes of learning and development;
2. Grounded in participants' questions, inquiry, and experimentation, as well as profession-wide research;
3. Collaborative—involving a sharing of knowledge among participants;
4. Connected to and derived from teachers' work with children, as well as to examinations of content and practices;
5. Sustained and intensive; and
6. Connected to other aspects of school change.

training model for Classroom Literacy Facilitators (CLFs). A district's participation would involve sponsoring an experienced and successful classroom teacher(s) to work with university faculty for an academic year while concurrently working in a designated classroom for at least two hours daily. These CLFs would first become district literacy facilitators and in subsequent years would then teach cohorts of classroom teachers across a full academic year through course work and on-site support.

Four districts participated in the development year, with two of the larger districts sponsoring two CLFs. Figure 3–6 describes participation in the initial training year. One university faculty member directed the project and taught two of the courses. Two other faculty members contributed in a variety of ways, including the teaching of the theory course.

YEAR 1: STRUCTURES ESTABLISHED AT THE ONSET OF THE PROJECT

Because the project was exploratory, faculty imposed few "givens" at the onset of participation. Faculty also decided not to impose a formulaic framework or advocate for any given reading program in the CLF training. Two general principles guided our work: (a) it is essential to understand how young children learn and what literacy opportunities are needed to ensure their success, and (b) classroom facilitators must be empowered with the knowledge and resources for making decisions and solving problems related to literacy learning in *their* schools. Faculty outlined the following general areas of emphasis: determining literacy program needs within schools and systems; working within existing programs to make modifications, additions, and changes; setting up and organizing classrooms; working with teachers; working with diverse learners; working toward accountability for student outcomes, etc.

Some requirements were specified (as summarized in Figure 3–7).

Even with good classroom instruction in early literacy, some children will need extra help of an intensive nature. Therefore, districts were required

---

Reading Recovery Teacher Development (Pinnell 1997)

Factors contributing to Reading Recovery teacher development include:

1. A structure that builds strong content knowledge
2. Observation of phenomena that are important to participants and that they encounter in their daily work
3. Guidance from an expert
4. Daily work of an investigative nature
5. Use of careful records to guide those investigations
6. Case examples for the group to consider together
7. A group of professional colleagues who work together across time
8. Recognition of the central role of language in learning

FIGURE 3–4
Reading Recovery Teacher Development (Pinnell 1997)

to provide Reading Recovery as a safety net for struggling children. They were also required to commit to data collection and research, to provide appropriate resources and materials for participating classrooms, and to establish demonstration classrooms for use in training.

YEAR 2: TRAINING FOR CLASSROOM LITERACY FACILITATORS (CLFS)

The training for CLFs included a range of interrelated components. We briefly describe each below.

Classroom Teaching

Each CLF-in-training worked in a classroom every morning. Two shared a first-grade classroom with another teacher and had total responsibility for the class each morning. The others worked alongside a selected classroom teacher each morning; these classrooms were to become demonstration classrooms. The daily work in classrooms grounded participants in practice and allowed for ongoing trials of literacy experiences discussed in university classes.

University Course Work

Classroom Literacy Facilitators were at the university at least two afternoons a week for eighteen semester hours of course work across two semesters.

Classroom Literacy Facilitator Project Overview		
Year 1	**Year 2**	**Year 3**
PLANNING	*INITIAL TRAINING FACILITATOR*	*INITIAL TRAINING TEACHER*
Selection of literacy facilitator	Teach in classrooms for part of day	Teach 15–30 teachers in a created course
Decisions about schedules and resources	Assess/monitor progress of children in classrooms	Provide class support and coaching for teachers
Evaluation design	Participate in university courses 2 times per week	Gather assessment data on children in classrooms
	Make field visits to classrooms	Participate in 4–6 professional development days at the university
	Work with early literacy scholars (recognized experts)	Work with early literacy scholars (recognized experts)
		Provide professional development opportunities for other teachers
		Give feedback to university for future direction

FIGURE 3–5   *Classroom Literacy Facilitator Project Overview*

The three courses each semester focused on (a) theoretical foundations of early literacy (literacy processes as well as literacy difficulties); (b) the teaching of children; and (c) the teaching of teachers, leadership roles and responsibilities, and implementation issues within systems.

The CLFs joined the Reading Recovery teacher-leaders-in-training for theory courses, which proved to be invaluable for both groups. As theoretical issues were explored, case studies of a variety of children across the combined class offered rich examples of diversity in literacy learning. Other courses were specifically designated for the classroom facilitators.

Because the project was exploratory, university syllabi for courses evolved and were co-constructed by faculty and CLFs. Major activities that emerged within course work are listed:

- wide reading and in-depth discussion of literature related to reading/writing processes and reading/writing difficulties (theory and practice)
- development of tentative and evolving literacy frameworks
- exploration of each component of the frameworks relative to theoretical support, procedural possibilities, assessment, resources, diversity, etc.
- critical analysis of classroom teaching via use of videotaped lessons
- classroom investigations; seeking answers to individual questions
- case studies of three children (high progress, average progress, and low progress)
- the use of data to make instructional decisions and to evaluate student outcomes
- exploration of implementation issues and change processes

The content also evolved as needs and questions emerged, using *principles* of good first teaching as a guide (Fountas and Pinnell 1999b). General topics of exploration are listed in Figure 3–8 on page 37. For each area of investigation, there were three levels of exploration: the child, the teacher, and the context. Within each area, attention was also given to theoretical underpinnings as well as practical applications, as shown in Figure 3–8.

Participants in Initial Year of CLF Project			
Districts	Number of CLFs	Teaching Experience	Training Year Assignment
A	2	Grade 1	Half-time grade 1 teacher
		Grade 1	Half-time grade 1 teacher
B	1	Kindergarten	Supporting a kindergarten class
C	1	Grade 1	Supporting a grade 1 class
D	2	Kindergarten	Supporting a kindergarten class
		Kindergarten	Supporting 2 kindergarten classes (one bilingual Spanish)

FIGURE 3–6
Participants in Initial Year of CLF Project

Eminent Scholar Series

To expand participants' access to the best thinkers in early literacy education and to expose them to multiple perspectives, we brought a variety of early literacy scholars to the campus. These scholars, sponsored by our corporate partner in an "Eminent Scholar" series, worked directly with the CLFs and the faculty. They also presented seminars for the greater professional community.

The CLFs met for at least a half-day with scholars. In an informal setting, the scholar shared information and responded to questions and comments. Having previously read the work of each scholar, CLFs were able to ask for clarification and further discussion. In some instances the scholars worked with CLFs in schools, demonstrating teaching practices with groups of children.

Reading faculty members also met with the scholars. They had two goals: (a) further discussion about the scholar's work and current research, and (b) conversations about faculty members' current academic research and publication potential.

Field Experiences

Because the project was new, we had no established "demonstration" classrooms for fieldwork. Faculty arranged for some visits in local districts for observation of exemplary teachers. CLFs cited the need for more opportunities to observe other teachers.

YEAR 3: TRAINING OF CLASSROOM TEACHERS

Following their training year, CLFs in three districts taught teacher classes across an academic year. Descriptions of the classes are shown in Figure 3–9.

YEAR 2: WHAT WE LEARNED FROM TRAINING CLASSROOM LITERACY FACILITATORS

Faculty and CLFs found that we were all on a steep learning curve! In this section we share the nature of learning from the perspective of the CLFs.

FIGURE 3–7
Requirements for Participation in the CLF Project

Requirements for Participation in the CLF Project
- offer Reading Recovery to provide a safety net for children with literacy difficulties even within good classroom programs,
- commit to data collection and research related to the project,
- commit to providing appropriate resources for participating classrooms, and
- commit to establishing demonstration classrooms for training purposes

Their journals kept throughout the year and their verbal and written course evaluations yielded the voices that emerge in this section. Ten central concepts were frequently discussed. Using these concepts, in the following section we summarize what we learned from CLFs.

Co-Construction Is Challenging

For professional development to be effective, it must offer serious intellectual content, take explicit account of the various contexts of teaching and experiences of teachers, offer support for informed dissent, be ongoing and embedded in the purposes and practices of schooling, help teachers to change within an environment that is often hostile to change, and involve teachers in defining the purposes and activities that take place in the name of professional development. (Shanker 1996, 223)

General Topics of Exploration			
Assessment	*Theory to Practice*	*Teaching*	*Leadership*
Observation of children	How Children Learn	Reading events	Working with adults
Using data to make teaching decisions	Reading and Writing Processes	Writing events	Teacher education
Plan/monitor progress	Oral Language/ Linguistics	Oral language	Literacy plans for schools/district
Accountability for outcomes	Visual Perception	Working with letters, words, and sounds	Collaboration
	Phonology/Orthography	Organizing and managing an engaging classroom	Evaluating literacy programs
	Comprehension	Selecting and introducing texts	Evaluating materials
	Fluency	Engaging children in learning	Selecting materials, resources, schools
	Diversity	Grouping for instruction	Change process
	Social/Cultural Contexts	Meeting needs of individuals	Managing a program
	Literacy Difficulties		Working with administrators
	Concept of Prevention		
	Special Populations		

FIGURE 3–8   *General Topics of Exploration*

If we accept Shanker's premises for professional development, we must abandon the traditional transmission model and learn to co-construct the experiences needed for our professional learning. For both the teachers and the university faculty, it proved to be quite a challenge to construct learning experiences collaboratively. Starting a semester without a detailed syllabus and without a sense of "I know what we need" was uncomfortable. It took time, trust, and a system for problem solving to enter a process of learning. This journal entry from one CLF during the second week of the school year reflects her frustration:

> I am very anxious and frustrated with our new program. I realize the CLF program is a pilot this year and there will be several areas that will be planned as we go, but that does not ease my frustration with not having a scheduled year.

Yet at the end of the year together, CLFs voiced appreciation for the opportunity to co-construct a project with university faculty. They commented that the process made them feel like professionals and enabled them to be more flexible in their own thinking and in their work with teachers and children.

There Is a Tension Between Assessment and Time

As faculty and CLFs were building extensive plans for collaborative study, reality settled in! The first challenge was the assessment of all children in these six classrooms, which was a district requirement and a requirement for project evaluation. In addition, a tenet of the project was to use data to drive instruction. Although classroom facilitators realized the value of information about the literacy performance of children in their classrooms, the classroom facilitators' frustrations mounted because time for assessment competed with time for establishing routines and classroom environments.

CLFs began the year administering Clay's (1993) *An Observation Survey of Early Literacy Achievement*. In addition, they were administering school district assessments and project tests. One CLF expressed the tension in this way:

FIGURE 3–9
Description of Teacher Classes During Implementation Year

Description of Teacher Classes During Implementation Year			
District	*Size of Class*	*Grade Levels*	*University Credit*
A	12	1	weekly for 2 semesters; 6 semester hours credit
B	21	K–1	biweekly for 2 semesters; 3 semester hours credit
C	28	Pre-K–2	biweekly for 2 semesters; choice of credit or stipend

Most of the "good" assessments take such a long time to administer. This is something that I will really need to look at this year. Assessment is such an important task. That is what drives the instruction. I really want to help teachers see that connection.

As the year progressed, the CLFs commented on the importance of initial and ongoing assessment. In class, we began discussing running records of text reading and the implications of those records for tomorrow's teaching. CLFs also explored ways to manage time for assessment and considered how to help teachers understand the value and possibilities of assessment used to inform instruction. These leaders were becoming "assessment literate" (Hargreaves and Fullan 1998), which involves:

- the ability to examine student performance data and make sense of it;
- to act on this understanding by developing plans to make changes to increase performance;
- to participate in the accountability arena by being able to join the debate about uses and misuses of achievement data in a time of high-stakes testing (Fullan 2001).

Classroom Organization Takes Time, Too

As the school year began, we thought we could simply plunge into the study of heavy theoretical issues and sound classroom practices. Again, the CLFs brought us back to reality; they reminded us that organizing and managing a classroom is crucial from the start. Even experienced and highly successful teachers must attend closely to organizing the class environment for efficiency and maximum learning.

I have spent some time this week looking at my classroom organization. Realizing that the students having difficulty with independence in learning stations could be the result of the organization. . . . Reading the chapters in *Word Matters* and *Apprenticeship to Literacy* redefined my thinking and gave me some ideas for implementing additional tasks.

Wide Reading from Multiple Perspectives Is Crucial to Future Problem Solving

We used multiple texts throughout the university course work. Readings on specific aspects of literacy acquisition represented a variety of authors and perspectives. For example, readings related to guided reading came from at least five different authors. The views of authors provided stimuli for discussion and evaluation of ideas presented. The CLFs indicated that the depth and breadth of the professional reading throughout the year was a critical aspect of the project. They also stressed the importance of the materials, supplies, and professional resources that were provided for them, enabling them to experience what was possible with adequate resources. The following journal excerpts demonstrate the premium placed on professional reading.

> The reading for this week was great. I really think all the books so far should be a part of a teacher's "stuff." The schools should provide them. For a beginning teacher the chapters on organization are invaluable. For an experienced teacher it causes one to evaluate and reflect—which is always good.

> I'm reading *Tools of the Mind, The Vygotskian Approach to Early Childhood Education*. So much to think about, so many applications. It's hard to decide what to focus on here. As I read, phrases and descriptions bring to mind specific children in my class and help me to understand them better. First there is Marcus. I thought of him while reading about emotional communication. . . . Charles, what does this mean for you and me in our classroom? Am I setting correct expectations for you? This requires further thought. . . . Susan, you were in this reading assignment also.

> The readings of Dandy's *Black Communication* and DeStefano's "Variations of Language" have opened my eyes to a whole new way of thinking about how language, specifically dialects, affect literacy. I know from personal experience that school environments are not accepting of children with different dialects.

> Chapter 16 in *By Different Paths* and Chapter 1 in *Stirring the Waters* on diversity gave me a lot to think about concerning children and adults as learners. Each case has its own understandings that need to be dealt with by support and acceptance. The hard-to-teach learner, whether adult or child, needs to be approached in the most supportive way through interaction that moves the learner to just enough challenge in order to move their understandings forward. It is going to be very challenging to remember next year while working with adults that their learning needs to be scaffolded, starting with where they are, not where I would wish them to be. I'm hopeful that I can help them to construct their learning through positive interaction and support.

Reading Is Not Enough: We Need to Talk About What We Read

Class discussions of articles and books became more spirited and challenging across the year. CLFs insisted on time to talk about and debate the readings, arguing that the oral interactions enhanced their understandings and perspectives. These journal entries reveal their commitment to interaction with colleagues.

I am so excited to have this help building my professional library. I enjoyed this opportunity to sit and share ideas with colleagues. Classroom teachers need this same kind of support. Most of our chances to talk come at the end of the day when we are all so tired that more complaining happens than helpful dialogue.

We have spent a lot of time discussing oral language development in class. I must admit that it is something I haven't given much thought. . . . These readings have made me much more aware of the important role oral language plays in literacy development.

Allowing time to talk about the readings gave the CLFs an opportunity to expand their understandings, and uncover the edges of their learning.

Critiquing Videotapes Helped Us Connect Theory and Practice

We used videotapes of classroom practices to keep the focus on teaching and learning (Lyons and Pinnell 2001; Sherin 2000). Discussion of videotapes linked the theory and practice constructed across separate courses. CLFs found that videotapes offered common experiences that led to shared understandings among the group. As they talked about teaching, they used language in new ways, becoming more confident in articulating their observations and building hypotheses about teaching and learning. That talk led to further discussions that revealed multiple perspectives.

Each CLF accepted responsibility for videotaping her own teaching or that of her classroom partner several times during the year. Because we were unable to replicate the teaching session model used in Reading Recovery (which employs a one-way glass screen), we used videotapes. We all quickly learned the frustrations related to the logistics of videotaping—quality of picture, sound, etc. In time, however, those videotapes enabled us to view and talk about teaching and learning opportunities. We discovered that we needed a framework to help us focus on the processes involved in teaching and learning rather than simply discussing "how to do to it." Collaboratively, we created a protocol for our talk during and/or after videotape segments that proved very useful (see Figure 3–10).

Protocol for Analyzing Videotapes

- What did the children have an opportunity to learn?
- Were the children actively engaged? How?
- Was there just the right amount of challenge for the children? Evidence?
- Comment on the pacing of the activity/lesson.
- Could you determine the teacher's objective/agenda?
- Was there evidence of the teacher's understanding of the practice/task?
- What else?

FIGURE 3–10
Protocol for Analyzing Videotapes

The first three questions in the protocol focused on the children's *learning*, which is often overlooked when observing teaching segments. We were concerned about opportunity, engagement, and challenge. The decision to focus on the child's learning changed our conversations and always took our talk about teaching back to evidence of learning. The next four protocol items allowed for discussion of teaching and instructional decisions.

Visiting Classrooms Brings Theory to Life

Observing "live" teaching in the real context of classrooms is highly valued by teachers (Lyons and Pinnell 2001). It is possible to predetermine the focus for each visit, which leads to more productive discussion afterwards. For example, early in the year, the CLFs visited classrooms to focus on management and organization and the effect of the classroom environment on student engagement.

We had limited opportunities for visits to exemplary classrooms; however, CLF comments such as the following indicated that classroom visits were valued and should be part of the training in the future.

> [Teacher's name] room was absolutely incredible. I was very impressed with the amount of reading they are able to do. What impressed me even more was the conversation they were having comparing two different stories that had been read. A child initiated the discussion, which I thought was great. I took many pictures of the print in this room and the first grade room. The first graders were little ants all working on their own with [teacher] pulling a few at a time. All were on task and knew exactly where to go if they needed help.

> The visit to the two classrooms at [name of school] was very inspiring, informative and refreshing. What I observed inspired me to make some changes in how we handle guided reading and literacy centers. I really admired how they utilized the space in their small classrooms.

The Relationship—and the Tension—Between Theory and Practice Must Be Reconciled

Because these CLFs were to become literacy leaders in their districts, we knew that they should be grounded in theories about learning, about teaching, and about teacher education. CLFs were therefore involved in weekly theoretical course work throughout the academic year. These leaders would need grounding for their decisions about classroom practice and professional development.

So often teachers say they aren't interested in theory—just their own practice. Yet these facilitators found an invaluable link between the two. These acknowledgements came across time and required reading, discussion, and opportunities to go from practice to theory and theory to practice. This excerpt from a CLF's journal says it all!

> Our recent study of David Wood's book on *How Children Think and Learn* was very difficult but rewarding. I am beginning to see how the theoretical understandings of how children learn can directly affect instruction. I always felt that such theories were just on the fringes somewhere in the teacher's background knowledge. But, the teacher's theory of learning can directly impact how she interacts with her students, her expectations, and what she deems important to teach her students.

An interesting discussion among CLFs at the end of their initial year of training was about the role of theory in the classes they would teach the following year. They hypothesized that much of the theory would arise from classroom practices rather than from formal assignments or intensive readings.

Preparing for New Roles and Negotiating Classroom Change Is Challenging

As the year progressed, so did the facilitators' anxiety about their future roles. They would be teaching classes to cohorts of about 15 early grade classroom teachers for an academic year. Their concerns ranged from course content and sequence, to working with colleagues, to scheduling their time for the most successful outcomes. This interesting use of tennis as a metaphor is representative of the CLF's understanding of adult learners' anxieties and the decision they will have to make to overcome them.

> I used to be a tennis player (this really will relate). It was my passion. I played four to five times a week. I was extravagant and shelled out the money for lessons with a pro as often as I thought I could afford it. But then I moved to Texas, and without all my usual tennis buddies to call, I didn't play for two or three years. Wanting to get back into it, I decided to sign up for a class and sharpen my rusty skills. With great excitement I went to my first lesson, wanting to get my strokes and footwork tuned up. When the coach corrected my backhand I told her that was how I had learned. She said, "Oh, we don't teach it that way anymore. This way is more aerodynamically correct." I had always worked so hard to have my feet sideways to the net. Wrong! Now we know that a 45 rather than 90 degree angle is more effective. I like to learn new things. I went to the lessons to learn new things about my tennis game. But

I didn't want to start all over and learn everything new! . . . I don't play tennis anymore. . . .

I hope that when I work with teachers I can appreciate what they do well. I hope I can help them see how the things they have been doing will fit right into what is perhaps a new system for them. My goal is to fine tune and not overhaul. With young learners we find strengths and build on them. I desire to be as sensitive to adult learners as well.

CLFs expressed their own understanding of adult learners; for example,

- teachers need to see immediate results
- adults are working against a history of failed ventures
- there is a need for focused impact rather than being spread too thin
- adults need a wide base of support
- teachers must see a need for change
- the magnitude of the "content" to be covered is huge

Collaboration Makes Learning Possible

"Networks, collaboratives, and partnerships provide teachers with professional learning communities that support changes in teaching practices" (Lieberman 1995a, 596). CLFs came to recognize the value of collaborative efforts throughout the academic year. They particularly realized the need for collaboration when they began to plan the course syllabi for their teacher classes the next year. They began the process in the spring of their training year and continued throughout the summer. The following quote from a CLF indicates the value placed on collegial support.

We have started working on our syllabus for next year's class. What a major undertaking. I am so glad we are doing this together. There are so many decisions to make and it really helps to be able to discuss ideas with peers who will be working in similar roles next year or who already have some experience in similar situations.

As Fullan (2001) reminds us, "it is not collaboration per se that counts" (254). Perhaps the collaboration among this team worked so well because it was focused on student performance and the practices that facilitate improvement for previously disengaged students.

As year 2 approached an end, the CLFs and faculty faced two realities: *Our intensive time together was soon to end* and *our learning was just beginning.* We had much to consider in planning for work with teachers during the next year, considerations that we had discussed but were now eminent realities. We worked collaboratively throughout the summer to plan and pre-pare tentative course syllabi, recognizing that each cohort of teachers would need to co-construct the learning community in each unique setting. The initial training of CLFs drew to a close, and we began the next phase of learning as we implemented initial training for classroom teachers.

WHAT WE LEARNED FROM TRAINING CLASSROOM TEACHERS

We learned about the training of classroom teachers from listening to CLFs. Conversations between faculty and CLFs during this implementation year revealed a match between project experiences and the six characteristics of successful professional development outlined by Darling-Hammond and McLaughlin (1995). CLFs used these characteristics as a framework to dis-cuss their observations and experiences.

Successful Professional Development Is Experiential

I have always believed that all children can and have a right to learn. This class has helped me develop an awareness of my role in that learning.

Because the year-long course work engaged classroom teachers in tasks of teaching, assessment, and observation, the course content was comprehen-sive. CLFs faced the challenge of organizing experiences across many issues and topics. There was so much to cover, and making decisions about sequence, duration, depth, and breadth proved puzzling. They recognized the need to revisit issues across time at differing levels of consideration. A syllabus could provide only a general "big" picture; specifics had to change based on needs of learners. CLFs began to define course syllabi as merely works in progress!

CLFs verified that teaching, assessment, and observation led to better understandings about learning and development. They noted that teachers formed theories by watching children, assessing children, and working with children. Readings with theoretical explanations worked well after discus-sion of experiential learning, when teachers had some concrete examples of how those theories did or did not support their experiences with children.

All CLFs agreed that the most striking change over time was related to observation and assessment of children. Assessing achievement and progress of individuals using controlled and systematic observation required time, skill, and new understandings. Many teachers initially resisted this type of assessment. But as the year progressed, they com-mented on the power of systematic assessment and how it informed their teaching. Some remarked that it was the first time "testing" had made a difference in their classrooms.

Teachers in the classes commented on the practical nature of the experience. They liked talking about issues and practices in class, experimenting with practices in their own classrooms, and returning to the next class to discuss these practices. All learning was based on children's behaviors. This quote from a classroom teacher at the end of the year demonstrates the practicality and the long-term influences of the experience.

> I have incorporated practices which I knew nothing about prior to this class. I have refined existing practices. I'm continually evaluating the effectiveness of literacy practices in my classroom.

Successful Professional Development Is Grounded in Participants' Questions, Inquiry, and Experimentation

"I am the teacher to my students but a student to the profession."

CLFs discovered an initial tension between *their* "agenda" for what the teachers needed to explore and the construction of the courses based on *the teachers'* questions and perceived needs. Some thought they gave too much leeway to the "constructive" process at first, losing momentum. They continue to struggle with the notion of when to construct as a group and when to dictate what is nonnegotiable. After the implementation year, they concluded that university credit was important in providing legitimacy to the teachers' work and served as a reminder of teacher commitments to the inquiry process.

CLFs viewed the reflection journal as an essential vehicle for identifying teachers' questions and perceptions. The journals were open-ended and invited teachers to reflect on weekly/biweekly classes, on assigned readings, and on experiences in their own classrooms. Entries revealed understandings, confusions, frustrations, and questions. This information provided invaluable information to the CLF. For example, one teacher revealed her initial frustrations by saying, "All you do is spout educational jargon." When the CLF entered into discussion with the teacher, she discovered that terms she considered to be generally understood were not part of every teacher's educational repertoire. The journals, then, provided a feedback loop.

In addition to grounding course experiences in the teachers' work, CLFs found wide reading to be an essential component of teacher development. Assigned readings provided multiple perspectives and helped teachers to find reasons for the practices they took on. Just as the CLFs reported during their training year, the teachers found value in sharing the articles they had read through discussion. Frequently, small groups discussed the readings before reporting to the larger group.

This quote from a classroom teacher demonstrates the lasting effects of inquiry and experimentation on professional lives:

> As a teacher with 23 years experience, I am embarking on a journey which will last the rest of my life. Nothing has had a greater impact on me as a learner.

Successful Professional Development Is Collaborative

> This week's observation really made me realize how much I have changed. What a boost to have peers come in and understand your teaching and objectives. I wasn't nervous, just anxious for you all to see my progress.

CLFs found that a collaborative environment had to be nurtured and supported along the way. Teachers generally have approached university courses by waiting to be told what the syllabus includes, what the requirements are, and what the assignments will be; the *instructor* is in charge. As an example of this traditional view of learning, many teachers were initially concerned about how long their journal entries needed to be.

But this was a different experience! Not only did the teachers have a voice, they were *obligated* to share their practices and their understandings with colleagues. Therefore, developing trust was crucial early in their collaborative work. CLFs reported that they were able to be flexible with their own teachers in training because they had experienced the model in their own training during the preceding year. They did, however, suggest two ways to enhance collaboration: limit the size of the class and limit the range of grade levels.

CLFs recognized several requirements for building the collaborative environment: building trust, scaffolding of the adult learner, and providing validation for ideas and attempts of the teachers. They had to create opportunities and provide vehicles for interactions that were both productive and supportive.

CLFs also encountered an unexpected challenge: working with former peers. They found that when they changed roles, they didn't "belong" anywhere—to the classroom or to administration. Their role was not clear to teachers and there was some apprehension about their potential role as evaluator. They struggled with this identity crisis and realized that it is an ongoing challenge to work alongside classroom teachers in a spirit of true collaboration and trust. In fact, CLFs have requested additional study on working with adult learners for their own professional development.

In spite of these challenges, classroom teachers expressed appreciation for having the collaborative experience and for having the CLF as a colleague and as an advocate for both children and teachers. They requested ongoing updates for next year, citing their need for continuing growth and development. At the end of the year, one teacher commented, "So this may be our last class, but it is really the springboard for the next stage of our journey in the foundations of literacy."

Successful Professional Development Is Connected to and Derived from Teachers' Work with Children

> All assignments were directly related to my classroom. The readings and discussions helped develop and deepen my understandings about literacy. It was also beneficial to be able to apply new learning, receive feedback, and discuss with classmates.

As stated earlier, all work with teachers was connected to work with children.

In addition to going from class study to classroom practice and back to class discussion, many course experiences focused on classroom work with children. Two are briefly explained here.

First, CLFs used videotapes to provide common teaching experiences for observation and teacher talk. Yet they found it difficult to convince teachers to tape their own work. Some teachers were apprehensive about bringing their teaching forward for others to view and discuss. Some wanted the CLF to preview the tape and visit with them before class to ensure a comfort zone.

The CLFs recognized the need for these observation opportunities and sought ways to overcome initial obstacles. In one case, the class met in the school that housed the Reading Recovery teaching room. They often brought groups of children for observation behind the one-way glass screen and reported successful experiences. Some initially used videotapes of teachers not in the class and found this helpful in establishing the process without the tension of "making it personal."

It also became apparent that teachers had to learn how to analyze videotapes. They tended to compliment each other, which was reassuring but did not take learning farther. Protocols for analysis helped (see Figure 3–10) but CLFs reported that more time and trials are needed to increase productivity in using video.

Classroom Literacy Facilitators also connected learning to children through the on-site support they provided to the teachers. Classroom support included: Assistance in organizing and managing their classrooms; Demonstration teaching; Observation of their teaching with feedback; Teaching alongside the classroom teachers; Engaging in face-to-face collegial interactions. Again, after CLFs established trust and clarified roles, classroom teachers considered these visits to be invaluable.

Implementing new learning is difficult. Having the Early Literacy Facilitator observe and provide feedback and having the opportunity for class discussion has helped me successfully implement literacy practices.

Successful Professional Development Is Sustained and Intensive

Yes, I remember reading at the beginning of the year that you should immerse *all* children in texts and books because all students can learn. I completely believe that now.

CLFs reported several arguments for teacher training to last throughout an academic year:

- Assessment of young children changes over time, and it takes time to experience the interactive role of assessment and subsequent teaching decisions. For example, Clay's (1993) *An Observation Survey of Early Literacy Achievement* is intended to examine change over time. And, learning to use running records as an ongoing tool for teacher decisions also takes time. Teachers in some classes analyzed a running record during each class period across the year and discussed implications for tomorrow's teaching of that child. Short-term professional development limits teachers' understandings of the impact of such tools.
- There is a danger in talking about practices at any one point in time. Practices change across time and across levels of performance. For example, examining guided reading practices at one point in time could be very deceiving; attention to change over time is needed.
- Teachers need time to develop trust and to feel comfortable taking risks in their own learning. Trust involves trust in the CLF, in colleagues, and in themselves!
- Changes in beliefs and understandings are the foundation of lasting reform. Yet change in beliefs requires practice and discussion of experience with that practice on a "continuous basis" (Fullan 2001) and that takes time. For example, if teachers have operated from a deficit model in the past, time is needed to shift to a model that works from children's strengths. Shifts in fundamental beliefs about teaching and learning require multiple experiences with children, opportunities for interactions with peers about those experiences, and ongoing exploration and study.
- It takes time to take on the role of decision maker in a classroom. Some teachers were moving from a perspective of "They said . . ." where someone else owns the knowledge to "I am the decision maker in my classroom!" where the teacher takes ownership of her own knowledge and theory. This empowerment of teachers requires knowledge, skill, practice, confidence, affirmation, and time.

- Principals are able to observe changes in teachers across time. They can also look for growth in student behaviors across time as a result of teacher development.
- Last, but certainly not least, is the overwhelming complexity of early literacy learning and the time needed to explore issues as an ongoing professional endeavor. The teachers in these courses did not perceive their learning to end when the year-long course ended. They realized they were just beginning.

Successful Professional Development Is Connected to Other Aspects of School Change

Teaching as a profession does not exist in a vacuum. Nor does professional development of teachers. Change theorists cite the importance of considering the infrastructure and the culture of schools (Fullan 2001; Lieberman and Miller 1984; Sarason 1995). For example, the school principal can be an immediate source of help or a hindrance. CLFs found that principals had varying expectations for the project and their support varied. They recognized the need to communicate closely with principals about the project and to share the experiences of their teachers with them. They proposed adding a "Principal's Academy" to the project. Of course, the infrastructure also includes central office support. It is important to consider how this model of professional development fits into the long-range, systemic strategies for the district.

CLFs cited the following issues connected to aspects of school change:

- Practices of teachers in the project sometimes differed from grade-level colleagues who were not participating in the courses, a situation with potential for either dissension or collaboration within the grade level. Either way, it became apparent that changes in one teacher's practices go beyond her own classroom.
- Some class experiences conflicted with current school practices. For example, in some schools, teachers discovered that required lesson plans were not fostering responsive teaching. As a result, some teachers were completing two sets of lesson plans: one for the principal and one for their own classroom work. This conflict led to a discussion of the school requirements, and in some cases, changes were negotiated.
- Just as CLFs had to learn to negotiate within their role, classroom teachers found a need to negotiate with colleagues in their schools. Some of their new practices involved other faculty members or administrators. Again, they had to find ways to collaborate in resolving potential conflicts.
- Reading Recovery teachers in the project schools expressed delight in collaborating with the participating teachers about children in their classrooms. New opportunities were opened for collaboration about children within the school.

SOME FINAL OBSERVATIONS

As we began our work to construct a model of professional development to support classroom practice, we examined the Reading Recovery training model as an example of long-term intensive teacher development. We constructed a model for developing key personnel leaders in the form of CLFs. These district-level key personnel were successful in their work with classroom teachers and they taught us much. While this model has promise, much more work is needed to ensure successful replication. Also, more trials and careful documentation will be needed to validate the model. In addition, the model will always need to be flexible in order to accommodate specific factors within the context of each setting and situation. One value of the model may lie in the process of collaboratively constructing professional development and evaluating its influence in individual schools.

Ongoing collection of data on children and teacher practice is essential to validate the model's efficiency. Preliminary examination of student outcomes in the project classrooms indicates that the model has promise. CLFs are collecting data on all children during the years they are in project classrooms; plans include following these children as they move through other project classrooms to see the influence of the project in subsequent years. Some CLFs plan to examine teacher practices in years following the initial training year.

Only through ongoing collection of data on children and teacher practice will the project have the validity needed.

We began with a challenge from Linda Darling-Hammond. Now we close with a statement of hope for the future from Ann Lieberman:

> As opportunities increase for professional learning that moves away from the traditional inservice training mode and toward long-term, continuous learning in the context of school and classroom and with the support of colleagues, the idea of professional development takes on even greater importance. For if teacher learning takes place within the context of a professional community that is nurtured and developed both within and outside the school, then the effects may be more than just an expanded conception of teacher development. Indeed, such teacher learning can bring about significant and lasting school change. (Lieberman 1995a, 596)

4 | MAKING A DIFFERENCE WITH PROFESSIONAL DEVELOPMENT

EMILY M. RODGERS
SUSAN KING FULLERTON
DIANE E. DEFORD

Investing educational dollars in professional development opportunities for literacy teachers presumes these investments can make a difference in student achievement. Nearly every public school teacher takes part in professional development every year, testifying to the belief that expanding teachers' skills is the key to greater learning. Yet, these opportunities are often piecemeal at best, with little way of measuring the effect, if any, these experiences have on teaching or on students' learning. We do know from the literature that certain characteristics of professional development appear to be related to greater change in teachers' practice. The fact is, we need to know more about the *impact* of professional development on teachers and students. We need to learn more about what it takes to assure good teaching for every child.

RESEARCH ON PROFESSIONAL DEVELOPMENT

Several themes are evident in current thinking about teachers' professional development. First, taking on new ideas and practices are collegial activities that take place within a community of learners. Professional development is most effective when it is close to the tasks of teaching; that is, we learn about teaching through actually doing it. And the best people to provide professional development are those who are teachers themselves. Effective professional development gives rise to higher order thinking so that teachers continue to reflect on and apply concepts in different ways. Finally, we need to examine the outcomes of professional development, not only in terms of teacher learning but, ultimately, on the achievement levels of the students they teach. A summary of these issues is presented in Figure 4–1.

We found it no easy task to structure professional development opportunities that fit all of these principles, but working with twenty-three teachers in urban schools, we tried to do just that. We involved teachers in a planned, intensive cycle of learning experiences, collected before-and-after perceptions from them about their expertise, gathered achievement data on the children they taught, and held focused interviews with teachers. What we found at the end of our five-month study surprised us and disappointed us, but ultimately informed us.

IMPLEMENTING A COMPREHENSIVE DESIGN FOR PROFESSIONAL DEVELOPMENT

To fulfill its promise, professional development must have an elegant and comprehensive design. No single one of the principles in Figure 4–1 is sufficient to assure success. For example, simply having teachers teach each other does necessarily not assure quality programs.

As faculty members who were working collaboratively with two school district personnel, we set out to construct a comprehensive design. At the end of the study, we understood better the professionalism of teachers and their unrelenting efforts to improve their practice.

All participants in the study taught the lowest-achieving first-grade students in their buildings, working with individual students for half of the day and with either small groups or whole classes for the other half. The focus of our professional development was on their work with the lowest-achieving students. Our plan was to, as much as possible, design experiences that would engage the teachers in problem solving around real examples of teaching, with opportunities to hypothesize with one another about ways to make the teaching even more powerful. We also wanted to ensure that the teachers would experience learning in two contexts:

- working with a group of teachers that was led by a faculty member or school district staff developer

---

Principles of Effective Professional Development

- Professional development should provide "grist" for thinking.
  (Anders, Hoffman, and Duffy 2000)
- Teachers need to learn about teaching through teaching.
  (Broaddus and Bloodgood 1999)
- Learning communities should be formed.
  (Potts et al. 2000)
- Teachers are in the best position to change other teachers.
  (Au 1997)
- Student outcomes should be examined.
  (Baker and Smith 1999)

FIGURE 4–1
Principles of Effective Professional Development

- working individually with one faculty member and one school district staff developer

This structure gave the teachers the benefit of a group experience in puzzling things out and also opportunities for one-to-one time for more customized professional development. In short, we tried to develop experiences that would embrace the principles described earlier by incorporating problem solving on actual teaching along with collegial interaction.

A CYCLE OF LEARNING EXPERIENCES

Figure 4–2 outlines the cycle of professional development experiences that teachers participated in over a five-month period.

As evident in this figure, we structured three ways of examining practice:

- viewing and discussing videotapes of lessons taught by teacher participants with other teachers
- observing, with other teachers, a teacher's lesson through a soundproof one-way mirror (a process called "talking while observing")
- teaching a lesson in a school setting while a faculty member and staff developer observe; and following the lesson, debriefing with the observers

The initial experience for each cycle was an all-day group meeting during which teachers shared and discussed videotapes of their teaching. Since all teachers were providing tutoring for individuals using the same lesson framework, there were common factors to observe and discuss across lessons. Yet every lesson was unique because it was tailored to meet an individual child's needs.

The teachers took turns teaching lessons behind the one-way mirror in order for their colleagues to have a shared experience to discuss teaching

FIGURE 4–2
*A Professional
Development Cycle*

A Professional Development Cycle	
Week 1	*All-Day Group Meeting* • Working in groups viewing videos of their lessons • 2 individual lessons taught behind a one-way mirror • Discussion about the 2 lessons
Week 2–5	*Individual School Visit from Faculty and School District Staff Developer* • Teach a lesson • Feedback and discussion
Week 6	*All-Day Group Meeting* • Working in groups viewing videos of their lessons • 2 individual lessons taught behind a one-way mirror • Discussion about the 2 lessons

practices. They were encouraged and guided by the faculty or school district leader to talk aloud about the teaching as it was going on behind the mirror and to question each other about effective teaching decisions. Often, at the end of the lesson, either the faculty or school district person would also work with the student behind the mirror in order to demonstrate a teaching procedure or try out a hypothesis that the group had developed together while watching the lesson.

Over the following five weeks, each teacher received an individual visit from the faculty member and staff developer, during which time they had the opportunity to receive personalized coaching on their lessons. The final phase of the plan provided for another all-day session for discussion of video and behind-the-glass teaching.

The cycle of experience was repeated three times, for a total of six all-day meetings and three individual visits to each of the twenty-three teachers.

TEACHERS' PERCEPTIONS OF THE IMPACT OF PROFESSIONAL DEVELOPMENT

To help guide our work, we asked the teachers to rate their effectiveness on twenty-one teaching practices using a 5-point scale (5 = very effective). The items on the survey included detailed teaching behaviors, characteristics of good instruction, and the complex combination of practices related to teaching for strategies. We gave the same survey again at the end of our five-month study and compared their average responses before and after the professional development cycle. Results are displayed in Figure 4–3.

Teachers who completed the post-surveys at the end of the study (without access to their previous self-ratings) consistently expressed slightly higher confidence in their teaching across a number of factors related to effective teaching. They had an overall average rise of +.31 on the 5-point scale across all items. Their self-ratings decreased on two items:

- using records to inform instruction
- analyzing running records to inform instruction

The familiarity of these items leads us to hypothesize that teachers may have come to greater awareness of the value of records and running record analysis, but had not yet increased their analytic skills to a point of greater comfort.

On two other items, teachers rated themselves noticeably higher:

- teaching the hardest-to-teach students
- planning and executing effective experiences with linking sound sequence with letter sequence

These results were not surprising given the direct focus of professional development and the need of many low-performing children to learn to connect letters and sounds and use this information while reading.

This group of teachers worked diligently; and while they were modest about their own claims of increased expertise, we, the faculty and staff developers, observed important changes in their teaching practices. These shifts were documented in our field notes across school visits to individual teachers and in our analysis of shifts in understandings during the group sessions. It is not sufficient, however, to simply bring about shifts in teaching practices. We wanted to discover whether such changes made a difference where it counts—in student achievement.

Pre- and Post- Self-Evaluation of Teacher Effectiveness					
Teaching practice (23 teachers reporting)	*Fall mean*	*SD*	*Spring mean*	*SD*	*Gain/Loss*
Teaching for phrasing in fluent reading	3.5	.7	3.7	.7	+.2
Teaching for independence in reading	3.4	.6	3.9	.6	+.5
Teaching for independence in writing	3.3	1.1	3.6	.7	+.3
Using teacher language to get shifts in learning	3.2	1.1	3.7	.7	+.5
Getting independence in hearing and recording sounds	3.6	1.2	4.0	.6	+.4
Selecting new books appropriately	3.8	1.2	4.0	.5	+.2
Using records to inform instruction	3.3	1.2	3.0	.7	−.3
Achieving daily shifts in each lesson component	2.6	1.0	3.0	.5	+.4
Teaching the hardest-to-teach students	2.7	1.0	3.4	1.0	+.7
Helping students learn letters	3.4	1.2	3.8	1.0	+.4
Helping students build a reading vocabulary	3.4	.6	3.9	.5	+.5
Helping students build a writing vocabulary	3.6	.7	3.9	.6	+.3
Teaching for strategy use in writing	3.5	.7	3.7	.8	+.2
Analyzing running records to inform teaching decisions	3.5	.7	3.2	.8	−.3
Planning and executing effective experiences with "linking sound sequence with letter sequence"	2.8	1.0	3.8	.9	+1.0
Having a genuine conversation prior to writing	3.7	1.0	3.8	.8	+.1
Making good teaching decisions about where to cut up a written sentence	3.4	.9	3.9	.8	+.5
Providing appropriate book introductions	3.9	.7	4.0	.7	+.1
Making good teaching decisions during first reading of a new book	3.5	.6	3.7	.7	+.2
Teaching for independence in visual analysis of words	2.8	.9	3.3	.8	+.5
Teaching for strategy use during reading	3.5	.6	3.6	.8	+.1

FIGURE 4–3   *Pre- and Post- Self-Evaluation of Teacher Effectiveness*

Students in the first-grade cohort made better gains than the previous year's cohort of students taught by the same teachers. In 1999, the year of our study, forty-four percent of the students that they worked with individually (*n* = 320) made enough progress to be considered in the average reading group in their classes, even though they had started out as the lowest-achieving students in the lowest reading groups. This figure represents a five percent increase from the previous year's cohort of first-grade students, when just thirty-nine percent of the students (*n* = 486) made similar progress.

Another indication of the students' progress was obtained by examining changes in their reading group placement. Considering only the students who progressed from the lowest in the class to the average, we could see that these students' reading group placement had shifted remarkably (see Figure 4–4).

The students' progress is all the more remarkable when one considers that it is rare for low-achieving students to change their rank in class; those at the bottom tend to remain at the bottom of their class (Juel 1988).

LOOKING CLOSER

Despite the evidence that students had made greater gains after our intensive professional development experiences, and our own notes showing that the teachers' instruction had improved, the teachers ranked themselves only slightly more proficient on the twenty-one teaching areas compared to their perceived effectiveness at the outset of the study. We decided to closely examine our videotapes of focus group interviews with the teachers gathered

Comparison of Changes in Reading Group Placement for Students Who Made Progress and a Random Sample from Fall to End of Year (EOY) in 1998–99 and 1999–00

			n	*Low*	*Low Middle*	*Upper Middle*	*High*
1998	Students Who Progressed	Fall	181	90%	9%	1%	0
		EOY	185	3%	17%	53%	27%
1999	Random Sample	Fall	68	41%	29%	13%	16%
		EOY	58	26%	17%	24%	33%
1999	Students Who Progressed	Fall	137	92%	8%	0	0
		EOY	143	9%	20%	58%	13%
2000	Random Sample	Fall	84	26%	27%	20%	26%
		EOY	68	21%	15%	24%	41%

FIGURE 4–4   *Comparison of Changes in Reading Group Placement for Students Who Made Progress and a Random Sample from Fall to End of Year (EOY) in 1998–99 and 1999–00*

at the end of the study to determine what changes, if any, had really occurred in their teaching practices. When we studied the transcriptions of these interviews, several themes emerged. We coupled this information with our field notes from school visits and found that changes in their practice could indeed be discerned—changes that not only were unexpected, but more complex—beyond our expectations.

What Changed: Extending Theoretical Understandings About Teaching Procedures

During semi-structured focus group interviews at the conclusion of the study, teachers were asked to talk about if and how the professional development experiences impacted their teaching. Even though the teachers were very experienced, they talked mainly about teaching procedures. We noted, however, that these conversations went beyond a discussion about how to carry out a procedure. Teachers also linked the procedures to new theoretical understandings. For example, they not only talked about how to build a core of sight words for reading, but they also discussed the need for a student to become fluent with everything that he knew, from sight words in reading, to writing words he knew, to recognizing letters quickly.

One teacher, as described in the following, said that she was getting better at providing book introductions:

> A teacher who did fourth grade work on summarizing helped me to recognize the potential of making book introductions more concise. Then [the school district person] came to visit, and gave me a better perspective on what I was saying, and thinking about who is telling the story rather than just giving an overview. Then, in continuing contact [group professional development sessions], we talked about *Pat's New Puppy*, talked about how there are two different things going on: the description of the dog and what happened in the park [knowing] that helps the child read the text. (Focus group interview, March 30)

According to their self-reports, the teachers extended their theoretical understandings about teaching procedures as they tried new techniques. These self-reports were confirmed by our field notes taken during the individual school visits and during the group sessions. For example, the entry below, taken following a school visit, suggested that we (the school district person and university faculty member who conducted the visit) saw evidence that the teacher was linking knowledge about a teaching procedure (building a sight vocabulary for reading) to a theoretical understanding of how it would impact the child's processing:

> The teacher analyzed that by using known words in writing and building a reading vocabulary, the child could read more fluently

and would not need to reread so much to self-correct—this was getting in the way of the child's fluent reading. (Field note entry, School visit, Oct. 18)

Extending Theoretical Understandings About Instructional Language

Teachers also stated that these professional development experiences helped them learn how to use specific language to teach more effectively. Again, this discussion went beyond what to say when teaching to focus on *why* and *how* to use language effectively. They felt that they recognized the importance of being more explicit with their instructional language and that this in turn helped their students make links across the lesson components. For example, when a student came to a difficult word in the text while reading, one teacher supported his visual analysis by telling him, "This is just like what we were doing with the magnetic letters on the board [looking for known parts, substituting onsets and rimes]." In concert with this awareness of the need to use more explicit instructional language, teachers demonstrated a growing ability to put this into practice when we worked with them during subsequent school visits and the group sessions.

Extending Theoretical Understandings About Teaching

The teachers also felt they had become more effective in linking theoretical understandings to their teaching practices. For example, rather than teaching word families (phonogram patterns), they were now teaching their students how to manipulate onsets and rimes to derive new words. They were teaching in a more generative way; that is, they were teaching word patterns as items and moving their students toward a flexible and analytic way of understanding how words work.

Teachers also indicated confidence that, consistently and early in the child's lessons, they were teaching for early reading behaviors such as achieving one-to-one correspondence in reading and monitoring known words while reading. They linked this emphasis to a theory that children need to secure these behaviors before they can take on strategies such as searching for more information at difficulty or self-correcting. One teacher noted that she thought these early behaviors were already in place for a child; it wasn't until a school visit that she realized the child did not have the level of control she had previously thought.

These findings confirmed what we had already suspected: that the professional development sessions did have an impact on teaching practices. The experiences even provided grist for thinking, as Anders, Hoffman, and Duffy (2000) said good professional development ought to do. We wondered what the essential features of these experiences were—how did the teachers explain the changes in their instruction?

CHANGES IN TEACHING—HOW THE CHANGES OCCURRED

Teachers reported their instructional language had become more explicit. They also reported changes in how to use procedures more thoughtfully and effectively, and how to make learning more generative for children by making their teaching decisions more powerful (addressing what the individual child needs most in daily lessons).

Demonstrating

Overwhelmingly, teachers found collegial demonstration to be the most powerful tool as they struggled with new ideas or tried to redirect their own practice. They valued the conversations they had during professional development sessions and the help they gained from contact during school visits with other teachers who were more expert than themselves. School visits were often mentioned for their strong contributions to their work with children. School visits helped them to become more effective with their children and make powerful teaching decisions. As one teacher stated, "So many of us are alone. There is no one to bounce ideas off of. If someone is in the building working with you, they teach, you watch; you teach, they watch." Teachers noted that demonstrations provided by either the school district leader or university faculty were important, whether given during school visits, during group sessions when lessons were taught behind the one-way mirror, or while topics were revisited after lessons in the professional development sessions. These demonstrations helped the teachers reflect on their own teaching in light of their observations and conversations.

Teachers considered opportunities to *see* as well as *talk* about teaching around real examples of their students as an important dynamic in their own learning. As one teacher reported, "Behind the glass [when lessons] cleared up ideas we might have had about procedures, I thought you had to do it THIS way. Something always gets sorted out!"

Seeking Improvement

While these teachers felt they had made shifts in their teaching, they were always seeking more ways to improve. They wanted to get better. They asked questions like "How can we get more links across the lesson?" Areas for growth seemed to emerge even as they reflected on their own growth: "It's a problem getting down notes, knowing what to get down, what things should we be watching for? How do we note it to help our teaching?" As one teacher noted, "Teacher talk! I can't stress it enough. The hardest thing to get is language! There are still words in my vocabulary that I'm trying to purge!"

Dialoguing

At the end of the three cycles of professional development, teachers talked about how the year had provided more professional contact than ever before. They expressed the view that having the faculty member as well as the school district leader on school visits and during the group sessions enabled them to truly reflect on their practice and on their students. One teacher said, "The dialogue was sometimes 1:1 or 2:1. However it happened, all of the talk focused on YOUR student and how to achieve gains and that was invaluable to us!" (Focus group interview, March 30). In all instances, the teachers reported shifts in learning while simultaneously talking about critical moments in their work with children and the value of problem solving with other teachers.

For these teachers, the power was in demonstration and conversation. They viewed and also provided demonstrations that were surrounded by talk that helped them in taking on new theoretical understandings and integrating new learning with their previous experiences and practical theories. They observed teaching-in-action and simultaneously talked with peers; they learned to reason through the processes of teaching. Critical learning moments (usually occurring as a result of a demonstration by a more expert other) seemed to provide momentum for their growing understanding. Teachers tied their new knowledge to these powerful moments, which continued to serve them as exemplars. As teachers revisited the topics most critical to teaching in professional follow-up conversations and engaged in additional cycles of use, they gained greater theoretical understanding. In this way, they extended their own practical theories, created more complex experiential networks, and understood new theoretical constructs.

DISCUSSION

Professional development for teachers, though a common enough experience, is usually a piecemeal enterprise, without concerted efforts to ground the professional development in real teaching examples or to relate student achievement to changing instructional practices. In this model of professional development, university faculty, district staff developers, and teachers worked together to collaborate for learning in a variety of contexts. We incorporated individual, paired, and group demonstrations; and we provided opportunities for teachers to analyze, problem-solve, and reflect on shared examples of actual teaching. Evidence collected from our work suggests that professional development can be effective and that fundamental change to instruction can occur along with improvements in student performance. The key is bringing together teachers in schools, staff developers in districts, and faculty in universities around real teaching examples.

No claims can be made from our study for systemic change or long-term effects. Clearly, for the teachers, learning was ongoing. While the data suggest changes in student progress, the changes were small, and we recognize that continued collaboration might be needed to maintain the impact on instruction and have a greater impact on student progress. Our results do suggest that the multi-faceted professional development model that we implemented probably represents the *minimum* effort needed in school districts to create significant change for teachers and students. We are learning what it is going to take.

5 | ACQUIRING CONCEPTUAL UNDERSTANDINGS AND KNOWLEDGE

GAY SU PINNELL

Guiding twenty-six five-year-olds to literacy is a highly complex mission. In a sense, every one of those twenty-six students is a mystery because, even at the age of five or six, individuals bring such varied experiences to school. As teachers, we want to help all of them acquire the important understandings they need. All can learn; some will require more intensive effort and a great deal of problem solving.

The search to improve literacy teaching and learning has taken many different forms, but usually centers on the best teaching methods or new programs and projects that promise big results for the least amount of effort. Here are some examples of those simple solutions that we often hear about:

- Send teachers to an intensive training course. We hear about "phonics boot camps" as the solution to the problem. Once teachers find out what and how to teach, the problems will be solved.
- Select master teachers and put them to work teaching and coaching others. Those who know will show those who do not, and the problems will be solved.
- Purchase a new program that promises the best of systematic instruction. Provide a day or so of training for teachers on how to follow the curriculum, and the problems will be solved because everyone will be delivering good instruction as written by publishers.
- Establish standards and give schools the ultimatum to improve or suffer the consequences such as removal of all staff.

It is pretty easy to see that none of the above solutions is truly a simple answer. Each would be quite complex to implement successfully. For example, coaching has promise but it takes a great deal of expertise (beyond being an excellent teacher) to train others. What about the intensive courses? Teacher education developers know courses have never guaranteed payoff in terms of more effective results in the classroom. Scripts, as included in published material, provide a lift in instruction only if they replace truly weak, disorganized programs; the improvement is usually limited and temporary. Standards without the means for change result in only superficial improvement, if that.

Even if full-range solutions, like the ones above, are implemented in a district, they often conflict with each other. For example, often, the intensive in-service trains teachers to do something that master teachers disagree with and that also conflicts with the prescribed program materials. Many teachers throw up their hands as if to say, "Which is it?" Others may simply not participate. That's how well-meant initiatives work against themselves and standards are not achieved.

On the other hand, a thread of possibility exists within initiatives that are carefully implemented. Reformers must assure that

- a central core of understandings guides selection and implementation of solutions;
- philosophies work together instead of against each other; and
- the actions are strategically planned to make the most of dollars.

One component that must be carefully designed and implemented with the highest quality is professional development. We are only beginning to learn how teachers best develop the complex skills that comprise their craft.

WHAT DOES TEACHER DECISION MAKING MEAN?

A researcher who has devoted an entire career to examining how children become literate argues that good readers have arrived at approximately the same place in that they have developed an *integrated range of cognitive strategies that make up a dynamic reading process* (Clay 2001). This learning system incorporates within it the ability to constantly expand reading strategies and use them with flexibility. At the same time, Clay has said that learners may take different paths to these "common outcomes." Good instruction meets the individual readers where they are and takes them where they need to go in the development of a reading process. Consider these two children, who are in the same first-grade classroom:

- Kristen enjoys stories and joins in enthusiastically when adults read to her. She notices illustrations, makes predictions, and reproduces even tricky language structures while pretending to read. In her approximated rendition of "The Three Billy Goats Gruff," she copes admirably with, "On went the middle-sized Billy goat. Trip, trap, trip, trap," and she reads with good expression. When faced with reading simple, one-line texts, she freely invents the story and pays little attention to the conflicting visual information in print. She does not point to words or attend to letters. She relies heavily on remembering language patterns. Although she can say the alphabet and identify the letters, her writing consists largely of strings of letters, mostly *k*s, *s*s, and *t*s.

- Jack knows the alphabet and some related sounds. When faced with reading simple, one-line texts, he tries to sound out each word. He often substitutes words that start with the same letter as a word he is trying, but his substitutions often don't make sense. His reading is slow and choppy; he points to each word. He frequently skips words he doesn't know. He sounds robotic; and, afterwards, he doesn't seem to have made much sense of the story.

These two children represent extreme examples, yet these descriptions actually fit a good many children. Just about every first-grade class will include readers like Kristen and Jack. Both children are capable, although confused; both are highly at-risk. Both need specific instruction on letters, words, and how they work, but their needs are different. Kristen needs to learn how to look at print, to acquire more knowledge of letter-sound relationships, to learn to build a small core of high-frequency words that can serve as anchors, and to take words apart by noticing letters, sounds, and word parts. Most of all, she needs instruction in *how to use* this information within the context of reading continuous text.

Jack needs to continue developing his ability to take words apart by learning about word structure and patterns of letters that are connected to sounds within words, but he also needs to learn to check his word solving against meaning and language that sound right to him. He needs to monitor his reading using meaning. Right now, Jack may seem to have more knowledge than Kristen; but if he continues to solve words without thinking about meaning, his reading skills will be limited. The core literacy program must provide an organized strata of whole class, small group, and individual instruction to assure that all of the twenty to thirty children are making acceptable progress as they develop in their own individual ways. Instruction must account for these different paths and do so within the parameters of the school day and group teaching.

The complex skills and understandings that teachers require are impossible to develop within one or two university courses. Publishers' materials and curriculum guides offer a ladder of support for teachers as they engage in this complex process, but ultimately, good teaching decisions regarding individuals and groups of children are required for effective teaching of all children. Fast, effective adjustment of instruction is especially needed for the teachers of children who depend primarily on school for their literacy learning.

Effective instruction in reading depends on teachers' abilities to continually think and learn from teaching. Given the complexity of the reading process and of the way literacy is learned, teachers must know

- the complex nature of the reading process
- how reading is *learned*, including many paths to literacy development; that is, how children acquire and relate understandings about literacy
- the strengths and understandings of the children they teach
- how to determine what children *need to know next* in building a reading process

At the same time, teachers must be good organizers and managers of the life within a classroom where twenty to thirty children must learn to work together. Moreover, they need to teach students routines for learning, working, and social interaction.

A DEVELOPMENTAL LEARNING PROCESS

Teachers' theories of the reading process are usually tentatively held, and they are learning constantly through careful observation and teaching. Guiding that learning is, in itself, a daunting challenge for teacher-educators, administrators, and staff developers. At any given time, within a particular instructional approach, and with different individuals and groups of children, teachers can select for attention only a few of the myriad of competing variables. When trying out a new approach, for example, teachers tend to focus on management and materials. They are concerned with performing a set of behaviors, and this focus is hard to change at first.

As the approach becomes more familiar and automatic, techniques and routines actually become transparent. Moving easily through these routines, teachers are able to give more attention to students' behaviors. They can notice evidence of learning or confusion and make the subtle adjustments that maximize learning on the part of individuals. They not only learn the ins and outs of a set of teaching procedures; they learn how to make sure the instruction works for *all* students.

The implications of this developmental process are profound, especially since so many new teachers are now entering education. Initial teacher education tends to focus on philosophy and theory first, turning to specific techniques later as participants move into student teaching and then take their first positions. As they enter the profession, many new teachers immediately demand scripted materials because they fear that they won't be able to make it all up, and they are right on that score. Management is a real issue; theory and philosophy are usually shoved aside or forgotten. In fact, a common recommendation for a good graduate class is that it "has no theory."

This trying-out stage is normal; but expert teachers go well beyond it. The process gets easier as they develop systems for learning from their teaching. It is generally recognized that teachers need support to fully develop as professionals; every year workshops and in-service sessions are directed toward that goal. Such sessions are considered valuable if they provide a collection of specific techniques, but they often fall far short of helping teachers reflect on, analyze over time, and adjust these techniques to assure learning. It is not at all unusual for teachers to do the teaching of several activities, for example, without building bridges between them so that children see how the building blocks of literacy are linked together. They may look skillful in using a technique, but still not meet the needs of this group of students. Professional development is the key to instruc-

EFFECTIVE PROFESSIONAL DEVELOPMENT

Clearly, extended time is needed for teachers to take on and become expert in new ways of teaching. Also, they need support of a particular kind. In Figure 5–1, I outline some of the characteristics of effective professional development that we have learned through our work and research on literacy development. I will explain my involvement in professional development and use these characteristics as a reference throughout this chapter.

With colleagues at The Ohio State University, I have worked for a number of years on the development of comprehensive approaches to developing schools with effective literacy programs. We have tried and refined approaches that are consistent with recommendations for effective programs (for example, Lieberman and Miller 1999). We created a network of schools to implement our staff development program and named it the Literacy Collaborative (see Figure 5–2). Administrators and teachers who joined our network were expected to implement ten features of a comprehensive school development program.

To increase effectiveness at the building level, we provided training and ongoing support for a school-based teacher-educator, whom we call a literacy coordinator. Schools were expected to find uninterrupted time for teaching and learning, establish a strong leadership team to pay attention to implementation, collect and examine data, provide adequate materials and

---

Characteristics of Effective Professional Development for Literacy Teachers

- Is part of a comprehensive and systematic plan that coordinates many different actions designed to work together to promote literacy learning.
- Is provided by an individual who continues to work with children, who has use for the particular approaches over time, and who continues her/his own professional development.
- Is grounded in the practice of teaching children, so that real problem solving as well as useful and practical suggestions are constantly available to teachers.
- Involves exposure to complex ideas within a variety of learning contexts and provides for ongoing conversations about those ideas.
- Over an extended period of time, involves a combination of class sessions, examples of teaching, reflective discussion, analysis of teaching, observation, and coaching.
- Is supported by a learning community who share a language they can use to communicate about complex ideas.

FIGURE 5–1
Characteristics of Effective Professional Development for Literacy Teachers

supplies to support learning, and create a parent/family outreach program to promote home reading. As an early intervention safety net, schools were also expected to provide one-to-one tutoring in the form of Reading Recovery. We conducted in-depth interviews with teachers and staff developers to determine their perspectives on learning. At the conclusion of the program, we observed changes in teaching and documented the results. We have learned much from these practicing teacher-educators.

Documenting the Effectiveness of Professional Development

We investigated the effectiveness of our professional development initiative by looking first at the results in terms of students' achievement gains.

FIGURE 5–2
What Is a Literacy Collaborative School?

What Is a Literacy Collaborative School?

1. Teachers in classrooms implement the range of research-based approaches that are included in a language and literacy framework, either at primary grades or at all grades of the elementary school. The framework includes instruction in reading, writing, language, and word study.

2. A high priority is placed on time for teaching and learning, with at least two-and-one-half hours daily designated for the language and literacy framework in all classrooms. One hour of uninterrupted time is available for reading and one hour for writing.

3. The school has a literacy coordinator who has successfully completed the initial training program at a Literacy Collaborative university or district-level training site.

4. The literacy coordinator is based in the school and provides professional development for teachers. The literacy coordinator also teaches children for part of the day.

5. There is a school-based literacy team that includes the principal, the literacy coordinator(s), and teachers representing the grade levels involved.

6. Teachers in the school participate in intensive training and are coached in their classrooms by the literacy coordinator.

7. After initial training, teachers participate in a variety of ongoing professional development opportunities, including but not limited to, regular meetings, coaching, study groups, and action research.

8. Sufficient materials and supplies are provided to support literacy instruction, which includes a school book room that houses an extensive collection of leveled books for guided reading, as well as rich classroom collections of children's literature.

9. Reading Recovery is provided as a safety net for first graders who need extra, intensive tutoring in addition to good classroom instruction; other services are provided at various grade levels.

10. There is a parent outreach program that includes books to promote home reading.

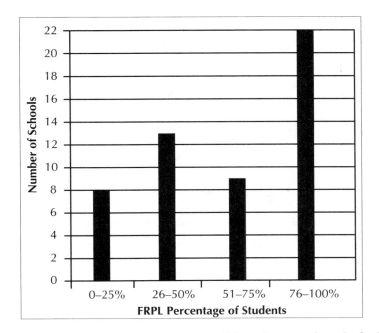

FIGURE 5–3
Number of Schools
Grouped According to
Percentage of Students on
Free or Reduced Price
Lunch Status During
2000–2001 Year

Recently, Scharer, Williams, and Pinnell (2001) reported results for fifty-one schools that participated in the comprehensive program for four years. These schools were representative of others in the network in that they included diverse ethnic and economic populations; for example, twenty-two of the schools have populations with more than fifty percent Caucasian students; 124 have more than fifty percent African-American students; five schools have more than fifty percent Hispanic students. As shown in Figure 5–3, only eight of the fifty-two schools have twenty-five percent or fewer students with Free and Reduced Price Lunch (FRPL).

In contrast, fifty-one percent or more of the students are receiving free or reduced price lunches in thirty-one of the fifty-two schools, and twenty-two of those schools have at least seventy-six percent of their students with FRPL status.

Second-grade students in the fifty-one schools were administered the Gates-MacGinitie Reading Test every fall for four years. NCE scores were analyzed for each cohort over the years.[1] The teachers in our schools wanted to

---

[1]An NCE is a statistical transformation of percentile ranks in which reading achievement is divided into 99 equal units with a mean of 50 and a standard deviation of 231.06. NCEs are generally considered to provide the truest indication of student growth in achievement because they provide comparative information in equal units of measurement. An NCE score of 50 is equal to the mean (average) score for the general population, which indicates where a student is expected to be for his or her grade level. Consequently, an NCE score of 60 is above the average. For a student's NCE score to remain the same at post-test as at pre-test does not denote a lack of absolute progress. On the contrary, it means that the student has maintained the same relative position in terms of the general population. Even a small gain in NCEs indicates advancement from the student's original level of achievement.

compare each cohort of children to determine whether greater learning occurred over time as they expanded their skills in teaching. For each cohort, measures of phonological awareness and text reading were administered upon entry to kindergarten. When we looked at these entry scores, it was clear that children's knowledge and skill level at the beginning of kindergarten did not change over the four-year period, although scores at the beginning of first grade revealed that the cohorts increased in strength over time.

In Figure 5–4, I present a graphic that summarizes performance of the four cohorts on the Gates-MacGinitie, administered in fall of second grade. This test measures the combined effectiveness of the kindergarten and first-grade literacy programs. The average NCE results for second-grade cohorts demonstrate increasing means from 36.00 to 48.70 NCEs.

What Makes a Difference in Implementation?

In Figure 5–5, I present a second analysis, examining average NCE scores for each of the fifty-one schools.

The overall average NCE gain across all fifty-one schools was 6.8. The average NCE gains for the forty schools with increasing results was 9.4 and ranged from 0.8 to 18.9. No NCE change was found in three schools, and eight schools revealed a pattern of declining average NCE results; the average NCE change across these schools was –2.6. This analysis revealed that seventy-eight percent of the schools showed a moderate-to-dramatic upward trend; six percent of the schools stayed the same; and eleven percent had a

FIGURE 5–4
Second-Grade Student Performance

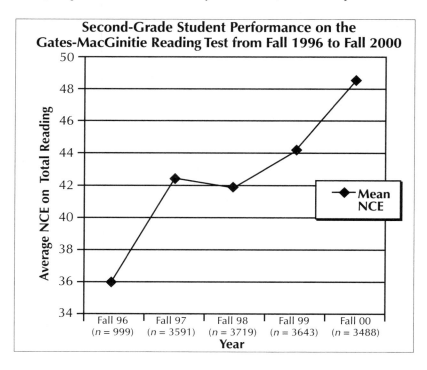

minimal declining trend. Schools within each quartile of FRPL status demonstrated a wide range of changes in achievement. Further analysis revealed that
the average NCE performance was much higher for students who experienced the school's program in full; that is, students who remained in the same
school for kindergarten, grade 1, and fall of grade 2 performed at an average
NCE performance on both Reading Comprehension and Total Reading
(50.10 NCEs), which is where students are expected to be for their grade
level. In other words, most schools were highly successful in improving
achievement. A comparison of schools that did not make progress (twenty-
two percent of all schools) with the high-progress schools (seventy-eight percent of all schools) revealed some interesting differences (see Figure 5–6).

High-progress schools had strong literacy teams that met regularly and
provided support for implementation; these literacy teams provided leadership for data collection and supported the staff developer. In high-progress
schools, there was higher coverage for first-grade students in Reading Recovery; that is, a larger proportion of the cohort received intensive tutoring to
help them make accelerated progress and move into average levels so that
they could profit from classroom instruction. The schools were therefore
able to substantially reduce the number of children in the lowest quartile of
achievement, bringing up the "tail enders" as well as the average. The average performance increased from one cohort to the next across time and the
number and percentage of children in the lowest quartile (as defined by the
Gates-MacGinitie Total Reading Test) decreased.

In high-progress schools, there also was more uninterrupted instruction
time for language and literacy teaching, a higher level of classroom teachers'

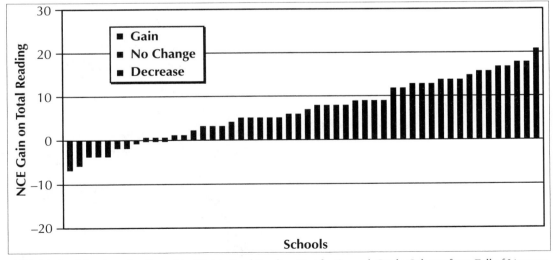

NCE Gain by School on the Gates-MacGinitie Total Reading Test for Second-Grade Cohorts from Fall of Literacy
Coordinator's Training Year to Fall 2000

FIGURE 5–5 *NCE Gains by School*

support for the philosophy and practices of the program, more concentrated time for coaching of individual teachers, and more ongoing professional development beyond the initial course. These results support our focus on professional development.

Building Success: An In-School Staff Developer

The key component of the Literacy Collaborative is a dynamic professional development program. A literacy coordinator is trained for each school. This full-time staff developer is available to teachers on a daily basis and continues to teach children daily in regular classroom settings. He or she has a multi-faceted role that includes

- providing an on-site initial training course of 40+ hours for classroom teachers in the building
- teaching children on a daily basis
- providing in-class coaching for teachers
- interacting informally with teachers to answer questions and provide advice and support
- working with the principal and leadership team
- supervising the data collection and helping the staff look at evaluation results
- assuring that the school has sufficient materials, including a shared leveled book collection

Many Avenues to Excellent Professional Development

We have learned over time that a variety of learning settings are essential for effective professional development. Research-based approaches are introduced to teachers in after-school classes. Literacy coordinators take care to provide videotaped examples of teaching and engage participants in reflective discussion. These sessions are followed by coaching in classrooms, which may then move from demonstrations to support and feedback. Concepts that are encountered in course settings come alive as the literacy coordinator and teacher work together with children. The idea is not perfect

FIGURE 5–6
Characteristics of Implementation in High-Progress Schools

Characteristics of Implementation in High-Progress Schools

- Strong literacy teams that provide oversight and support for implementation.
- More uninterrupted instruction time for language and literacy teaching.
- A higher level of service by Reading Recovery teachers.
- A high level of support for the philosophy and practices of the program by the primary teaching staff.
- More concentrated time for coaching sessions with individual teachers.
- More ongoing professional development beyond the initial course.

teaching, but collegial problem solving. The content of the course is thus grounded in the practice of teaching children, insuring the availability of complex concepts because teachers are building their understandings over case after case of actual child behavior.

An Example of an Integrated Series of Professional Development Activities

In the following examples I will provide a series of professional development activities that are typical of the way literacy coordinators work with teachers.

Robin, the literacy coordinator in an elementary school of 540 students, had been working with her colleagues on creating an effective minilesson for word study. Over a couple of sessions, she helped them understand some important concepts.

Introduction of the Concept

First, she showed the teachers some examples of minilessons (brief, clear explanations of a principle related to letters, sound, or how words work) and the application activities that would help first graders acquire important understandings. Through reading, discussing, and playing with words themselves, she also helped the teachers to develop some important theoretical understandings about the linguistic system. She taught them to use a comprehensive continuum of concepts that are important in learning to read and spell. She involved them in practicing how to state principles clearly in the words that children could understand, and she helped them plan some good lessons related to their students' needs.

Observation and Coaching

Next, Robin scheduled in-class coaching sessions with teachers in the group. With Sheila, a first-year kindergarten teacher, she demonstrated a lesson on initial consonants and connections to letters that the two had planned together. With Rick, a first-grade teacher with several years experience, she observed a minilesson and provided coaching. Rick's lesson was on word structure, specifically plurals. Children had participated in previous lessons and were showing good knowledge of making plurals by adding -*s* to nouns. Rick thought of some clear examples that his students could understand. He added examples while working with the children.

Rick began by reviewing the plurals you make by adding -*s* and referred to a previous chart. Then, he said, "You know that for most words you add -*s* to make it more than one. Today we are going to look at some words that are different. I'll say the word for one thing and you try to say the word for more than one—one bus." He wrote *bus* on the chart. Children responded by saying, "Buses."

Rick: "That's right—two buses. Now, I am going to write *buses* and you think about what I am adding. Here is another one–*dish*." He wrote *dish* on the chart. Children orally produced the plural, *dishes*, and Rick wrote it on the chart. He then asked children to tell what we add to make more than one. Several children noticed that he added -*es*. **Rick:** "What about the word *box*?" (He wrote *box*.) "What do you think I need to add to *box* to make it more than one?"

Sara predicted *-es*. **Rick:** "You can hear the *-es* at the end of these words. Let's read them." He then guided children to read the words one at a time and listen for the *-es* at the end of the words. Allie and Juda observed that it sounded like a *z*.

Rick: "You can hear the parts of these words, too. Clap *bus*." Children responded by saying and clapping *bus*. Rick said, "How many parts does it have?" Children responded by saying "one." **Rick:** "Now say and clap *buses*." Jeremy noticed that the plural words had two parts. Rick continued writing singular words on the chart and asking children to say and predict the spelling of the plurals. He then instructed children in an activity to help them apply their learning. Using word cards, they had previously matched the singular and plural forms of twenty-five nouns that add *-s*. He added the *-es* singular/plural forms and mixed up the words. Then children matched singular and plural forms in a pocket chart. He also showed them how to put clear yellow highlighter plastic on the *-es* ending of words. This activity would be undertaken independently by individuals as Rick worked with small groups in guided reading. At the end of the instructional period, Rick brought children together in another community meeting and reviewed the principle he had taught.

Robin observed the lesson and noted the strengths of Rick's lesson, including the following characteristics:

- stating the lesson principle clearly
- building on what children had already learned
- using time well so that the lesson was brief
- providing an active way for children to explore the principle
- involving children conversationally

She also noted that the lesson, while effective, was almost totally teacher directed. She knew that Rick had a goal to encourage children's exploration of words.

She opened the coaching session by asking Rick to think about his lesson and what children learned. Rick was articulate in providing examples of children's comments that indicated understanding. He also said that he had observed the word sorting and highlighting and felt that most children grasped the idea.

Robin then suggested that he probe deeper to see what children had taken from the setting. Since Rick would be reviewing this lesson the next day, she suggested that he ask them what they had noticed as they sorted words.

The next day, Robin visited again and Rick invited children to talk about what they had noticed about words that are plural. Here are some of the comments generated:

"You add *-es* to some words to say more than one."

"You can just add -s to some words to make them more than one."
"All of the -es words have two parts in them."
"Why do words have plurals different ways?"
"The -es words sound like -z."
"The -es words have x or z, or s."
"Some of them have sh or ch."

By opening up his lesson to children's observations, Rick learned that he needed to gather more information about what his students were noticing and the structure of words. While his first-grade students were not ready for sophisticated rule statements, they were internalizing important understandings. The structure of words has logic; the more children can notice and discuss about this structure, the more likely they are to form useful categories that will help them build understandings about the way words work.

As a coach, Robin had to think fast. She had to use her observation to help her determine the most effective change that Rick could make to expand his teaching skills in this particular area.

STUDYING TEACHER DEVELOPMENT

As previously mentioned, we have learned a great deal from working with literacy coordinators, the school-based staff developers who help teachers with their practice. In 1999, ten teachers and five literacy coordinators agreed to participate in a two-year study that focused on the complexities of learning to teach (Lyons and Pinnell 2001). We were interested in how teachers and staff developers conceptualize their work in the teaching of literacy to young children, as well as how their understandings change and expand over time. Our ultimate goal was to gain insights into the kinds of experiences and support systems teachers need to develop the characteristics of effective teaching. Data collected over the two-year period included

- entry and exit interviews, that were tape-recorded, transcribed, and analyzed
- lesson observations, in ten-spaced intervals over the two years, that were documented by field notes
- coaching sessions after lessons, that were tape-recorded, transcribed, and analyzed
- interviews about lessons, that were tape-recorded, transcribed, and analyzed
- written plans for improvement of teaching, that were collected and analyzed

The results of this research indicated that coaches were more effective when they focused on the one or two most important points that would help teachers move forward in their instruction.

Analyzing Lessons for Important Coaching Points

Analysis of these data led to the creation and validation of several scales we compiled for analyzing teaching. Scales represent categories of observation and rubrics for assessing teacher performance during lessons. The scales originally emerged as research tools to analyze lessons in relation to results. Scales were considered to be specific to instructional techniques; for example, a scale was created for guided reading (small group instruction) as well as for interactive writing (group instruction of a piece of written text). Scales evolved into a tool for staff developers that was quite complex in nature. We realized that coaches needed to observe lessons and then, with an economy of action, decide on one or two suggestions that would be *most* helpful to the teacher.

Originally, when we first observed literacy coordinators, we noticed that they tended to make fifteen to almost thirty coaching points to the teacher. Teachers could not cope with this array of suggestions and tended to remember only one or two points. In problem solving with coaches between year 1 and year 2 of the study, only a few decided to focus attention on targeted points; however, that focus proved to be more effective as indicated by teacher and literacy coordinator interviews. Scales were first designed as a tool for analyzing lessons. They proved to be related to student achievement. They also proved to be useful in helping literacy coordinators quickly organize their thinking about the teaching they have observed. Scales for guided reading and interactive writing were verified by the research; a proposed scale for minilessons that we have found useful is presented in Figure 5–7.

Any group of teachers and staff developers can create a scale like this one. In fact, the process involved in creating the scale is an excellent training session for staff developers. The idea is to analyze instruction so that the most important next steps emerge. Robin, the literary coordinator, *did not use the scale in the classroom.* That action would have created distrust on Rick's part. She used the scale to sharpen her own observations of minilessons of all kinds and she applied it to her own teaching. In doing so, she learned how to quickly select one or two coaching points that would make a difference.

Conversations About Teaching and Learning

When we look at the series of events described previously, we are talking mostly about planned, intentional professional development; but we should not neglect the information learning that flows through a school that has become a learning community. Our research project revealed a great deal about how literacy coaches and teachers can work together to sharpen their observations and refine teaching. Interviews with teachers and literacy coordinators brought forward some informal factors that we had been ignoring. Our idea was to build strength at the school level by having professional development right there as part of the teaching day. We wanted support for learning to be continuous and to take place alongside daily teaching; accessibility and engagement were paramount goals. The model would be substantially different from the district staff developer who drops into five or six different schools to offer in-service sessions.

Teachers and literacy coordinators at every school assured us that it was very important for the literacy coordinator to be a staff member in that school. They liked the convenience and accessibility of the support, but they offered some additional reasons. We heard comments like this:

"I can just stick my head in and tell her, 'It went great today!'"

"I can ask a quick question any time I want to, even just walking down the hall."

"I can share a piece of writing to let her know a student is making progress."

"She can ask me how it is going without making an appointment."

"I can get advice on a difficult student right away."

"Having a literacy coordinator makes our discussions at lunch so interesting. We are all talking about our teaching."

"We are having book clubs during lunch once a week—just information talks about books but it helps since I haven't read as much as other people have."

"I can look at the charts in her room to get ideas."

These teachers highly valued the quick, informative interactions they had with literacy coordinators. We found that sentiment to be true across our network of schools.

Scale for Analysis of Minilessons			
Use Clear, Explicit Language and Demonstration 0 1 2 3	**Connect to Students' Current Knowledge** 0 1 2 3	**Engage Students in Inquiry** 0 1 2 3	**Connect to Curriculum** 0 1 2 3
Statement of Principle • Select a *single* principle or procedure for the lesson. • State principle in one or two sentences. • Write principle on chart.	• Select principle that students *need to know next* and already know something about. • Ask students what they already know. • Ask students for examples.	• Provide opportunities for students to make hypotheses related to principle. • Test hypotheses in a clear, interesting way.	• Make connections to observations of reading, writing, and spelling. • Make connections to students' spelling.
Specific Points Related to the Principle • Provide examples that clearly demonstrate process or principle. • Make a few clear points that break down the process to make it understandable.	• Select examples that students will recognize. • Ask students for examples. • Write examples on chart or easel.	• Promote new hypotheses as points are made. • Ask students to test one another's hypotheses.	• Connect points to texts students read, their writing, or content curriculum. • Draw examples from texts students read, their writing, or content curriculum.
Discussion • Engage students in active discussion. • Encourage students to use precise language that will help them internalize principle or procedure.	• Invite students to restate principle. • Invite students to share discoveries. • Invite students to ask questions. • Ask students to respond to each other.	• Promote new learning through shared examples and ideas. • Be open to questions.	• Invite students to make connections to texts they read, their writing, or content curriculum.
Summary • Provide a clear summary statement at the end of the lesson.	• Promote active listening to summary statement. • Ask students to assess their own understanding and ask questions if needed.	• Be sure students understand summary as a basis for discovering more.	• Be sure the summary statement is one students can connect to examples they find in reading and writing.
Application • Demonstrate application activity. • Provide clear directions for application activity. • Provide directions in writing at center or for each student.	• Be sure students know they are to use what they know in application activity.	• Ask students to connect the summary statement to what they will be doing: "As you are . . . think about . . ."	• Expect students to draw examples from reading, writing, and content curriculum during application activity.
Sharing and Discussion • Restate principle in summary form.	• Invite active sharing of discoveries.	• Teach students how to learn from one another's examples. • Promote new learning through discussion.	• Invite students to describe connections to reading, writing, and content curriculum during discussion.

FIGURE 5–7   *Scale for Analysis of Minilessons (Lyons and Pinnell 2001)*

Literacy coordinators, on the other hand, were constantly gathering information that made their own jobs as teachers and teacher-educators easier. They knew the names of children across the grades; they could bring attention to successes teachers were having. They could focus course sessions on problems people were having or areas of real interest. Many of us know the difficulty in walking into a school where you have little knowledge of what the teachers care about or their concerns. Even the best session can lack focus for the participants. This would not be the case with literacy coordinators. They have content to impart, but they do so within an environment that they know. They have daily evidence of teachers' struggles and learning.

SYSTEM THINKING ABOUT PROFESSIONAL DEVELOPMENT

Our experience and research has led us to what we call "system thinking." Rather than a day, a week, or a scattering of in-service sessions, a professional development system consists of a series of interrelated actions, all of which are essential in creating an effective professional development plan with lasting effects. Here are some important points that will be helpful in moving from one-shot approaches to system thinking. A professional development system:

1. Is based on information about the school, about the teachers, and about the students; that information goes well beyond a pencil-and-paper needs assessment.
2. Creates a culture that encourages reflection, honest feedback, mutual support, and collaborative problem solving.
3. Has an overall design with compatible and coordinated components.
4. Focuses time, people, and materials where they will make the greatest difference.
5. Provides for a balance of informing and encouraging constructive thinking.
6. Provides a range of learning contexts—classes, discussions, demonstrations, in-class assistance, coaching, and collaborative research.
7. Takes place over a long period of time, with monitored and supported application of concepts.
8. Monitors the impact of professional development in the school—is it making a difference in teaching?
9. Monitors the outcomes of professional development in the school—are students learning more?

Professional development exists with a larger vision and is the key component for making that vision real.

6 | TEACHERS' REFLECTIONS AND MEANINGFUL ACTIONS

Linda S. Wold

In this chapter I tell the story of three literacy teachers who engaged in ongoing "deep-level" learning, so-called because it results in substantial changes in teachers' knowledge as well as in their practice. Deep-level learning means more challenging intellectual work for teachers and the result is improved student achievement (Newman, Lopez, and Bryk 1998). Deep-level learning requires analysis of instruction before, during, and after teaching; and it must be supported by long-term professional help both outside and within the context of the classroom. Teachers who have this support can strategically use a combination of procedural and conceptual knowledges while teaching; and in the process, learn from their teaching in a consciously developing way (Lyons and Pinnell 2001; Wold 2000).

This strategic decision making about literacy practice requires:

- honest reflection (Yost, Sentner, and Forlenza-Bailey 2000);
- action to revise pedagogical beliefs that we hold dear (Dewey 1933); and
- continued focus on targeting instruction to improve student achievement (Lyons and Pinnell 2001).

A total of eight teachers engaged in this two-year study of literacy teachers' development. This chapter focuses on three of the eight teachers and the way they used two instructional contexts to support their teaching in three different urban school settings. I briefly describe the two-year study, the teacher sample and contexts for implementing literacy instruction, the findings, and conclusions. Highlights include stories of teachers who show that deep-level learning and action-based reflective practice improved their teaching and their students' growth as readers and writers.

CONTEXT FOR THE STUDY

All three teachers were profiled working in primary grades in schools that were part of a network supported by the University of Chicago's Center for

School Improvement and The Ohio State University's Literacy Collaborative. That connection meant that the teachers were expected to participate in ongoing professional development and had access to a "coach," called a literacy coordinator, who would provide support for their learning as they went about their teaching. Both universities were located in urban settings; the Center for School Improvement in particular, has worked extensively in the urban area where the three teachers in this study taught. I briefly describe the Literacy Collaborative and the schools as important contextual factors.

Literacy Collaborative Model of Professional Development

The Literacy Collaborative model of consistent, ongoing professional development provided training and mentoring for teachers by an on-site literacy coordinator throughout the study. The literacy coordinator played a central role in advancing teachers' literacy concepts and skill development by coaching teachers to help them reflect on and refine their practice. The comprehensive goal of the project was to improve the quality of literacy implementation in guided reading (Fountas and Pinnell 1996) and interactive writing (McCarrier, Pinnell, and Fountas 2000) in kindergarten through grade 2 classrooms.

See Chapter 5, this volume, for a fuller description of the Literacy Collaborative. Also see Lyons and Pinnell (2001).

Instructional Contexts

Guided reading and interactive writing were selected as the literacy components to emphasize because they provide strong instruction with the goal of building a literacy knowledge base for students.

Both required a particular set of instructional procedures as well as observation of student behavior. In both components, instruction is adjusted to address student needs. For example, during guided reading, teachers worked with small groups of students who were reading the same book at a level matched with their current skills (see Figure 6–1).

Teachers used texts in ways that would support students in applying effective reading strategies. Teachers explicitly taught comprehension and word-solving strategies during and after students read the text (Fountas and Pinnell 1996).

FIGURE 6–1
Characteristics of Guided Reading Instruction

> **Characteristics of Guided Reading Instruction**
> - Grouping children for efficient instruction
> - Selecting texts using levels
> - Introducing texts
> - Explicitly teaching
> - Focusing on comprehension and word-solving strategies

Interactive writing instruction took place in both whole class and small group settings. Teachers guided children to compose and write an authentic text—a message, story, summary, letter, or other nonfiction text. Teachers "shared the pen" with students as they composed and constructed meaningful written texts on charts or on the board. This "sharing the pen" had high instructional value.

I served as one of a five-person team of researchers who collaborated with the literacy coordinator and several researchers. My role was to explore the interplay of knowledges that support developing expertise as a teacher of literacy. "Knowledges" is a plural term because teachers must constantly conceptualize and adjust instruction based on knowledge of reading strategies and how they are acquired, knowledge of the routines and management of instruction, and knowledge of their particular students and their current understandings.

Urban School Settings

The urban schools participating in the study included populations in which 96% to 99% of the students were eligible for free meals. In School 1, the entire student population was African American, while the enrollment in Schools 2 and 3 was mainly African American and Hispanic. These schools were committed to instilling values consistent with the comprehensive reform initiative at The University of Chicago Center for School Improvement. This reform initiative centered on literacy development. Literacy coordinators at each school site were involved in a two-tiered process of literacy support:

- daily improvement of literacy teaching
- bi-monthly training of staff

The coordinators supported, nudged, and at times, cajoled teachers to reflect on and analyze their teaching. Literacy coordinators coached teachers to raise the quality of their instruction. They also provided training sessions that focused on reflective practice and the use of assessments to inform future instruction. Each school had a long and discouraging history of low student achievement; flowing through the discourse was the idea that students had many strikes against them and found it hard to learn. Literacy coordinators by no means found their roles easy. They found themselves

---

Characteristics of Interactive Writing

- Whole class or small group instruction
- Group composition of an authentic written text, fiction or nonfiction
- Construction of the text by writing words and sentences
- Use of "sharing the pen" to draw children's attention to any aspect of the construction of written text
- Explicit teaching of conventions, skills, and the craft of writing

FIGURE 6–2
*Characteristics of
Interactive Writing*

constantly challenging the prevailing patterns of discourse as they attempted to improve the quality of teaching and learning.

TEACHERS IN THE STUDY

Each literacy coordinator, using subjective judgment, selected one teacher out of approximately three participating teachers from each site, who had made the most change in her literacy instruction. Literacy coordinators' selections were based on their continuous, systematic, documented observation of teachers as they worked in classrooms over the two-year period. The sample included two kindergarten teachers, Kara and Beth, and Peggy, a first-grade teacher. I confirmed literacy coordinators' selections by looking at researchers' ratings of teachers' videotapes of lessons using rubrics, or "scales" for evaluation (Lyons and Pinnell 2001). Students' achievement gain scores (Figure 6–3) were also examined to confirm this selection assuming that greater gain scores were related to improvement in teaching. These gain scores were the result of the average two-year achievement data compiled from *An Observation Survey of Early Literacy Achievement* (Clay 1993) and the Degrees of Reading Power Comprehension assessment using a Rasch analysis (Wright and Masters 1983). Composite student scores from these measures created a common metric scale for analyzing students' reading ability in kindergarten through grade 2. Average gain scores reported in Figure 6–3 indicate the highest composite achievement scores of each classroom. These results validated the teacher sample by indicating a visible gain in student achievement.

An examination of the information in Figure 6–3 reveals interesting differences in teaching experience and training among the group. While Kara was a novice teacher and newly involved in the introductory Literacy Collaborative training, Peggy and Beth were both practicing literacy educators with at least three years of specific training and coaching. We might expect more experienced teachers' literacy instruction to result in higher achievement gain scores, but the average achievement gain scores were actually similar. The teaching experiences and literacy training varied at each of the sites, yet all three teachers were expected to reflect on their work and continuously improve instruction to meet the diverse needs of their individual students.

Sample of Teachers Who Shifted Most in Literacy Implementation					
School	*Teacher Code (Pseudonyms)*	*Teaching Experience*	*Literacy Collaborative Training Experience*	*Experience Level*	*Average Achievement Gain Scores*
School 1	Kara	1 year	1 year	New	26.1
School 2	Peggy	7 years	3 years	Moderate	28.4
School 3	Beth	25 years	3–5 years	Experienced	28.2

FIGURE 6–3 *Sample of Teachers Who Shifted Most in Literacy Implementation*

I will briefly describe each of the teachers in the following sections. All three were volunteers, who elected to participate in the research project as a way of improving their teaching.

Kara

Newly trained in the Literacy Collaborative framework and a second-year African-American kindergarten teacher, Kara taught African-American children at School 1. One would not expect a new teacher to demonstrate the most visible change in practice, but Kara did just that. As a novice teacher, Kara was perceived as an extremely capable educator and assigned a large block of special-needs students. She was determined to improve her teaching while providing her students with the educational opportunity they would need to achieve in spite of the constraints of the high poverty neighborhood in which the school existed.

Peggy

A seventh-year Caucasian teacher at School 2, Peggy taught first grade to mostly Hispanic and African-American students. These children, too, lived in a neighborhood with high poverty, crime, and gang warfare. Peggy was upbeat and positive, handling disruptive students well and coping with the various student services they required. She constantly worked to improve the quality of her teaching. She often talked about what she would do to improve the effectiveness of her teaching in the very next lesson. She initiated meetings with the on-site literacy coordinator for daily support.

Beth

Beth, a twenty-five year veteran kindergarten teacher, was a Caucasian teacher at the predominantly Hispanic and African-American School 3. Beth's principal referred to her as a gifted teacher whose classroom served as a literacy demonstration site for others. Beth's students lived in a high poverty neighborhood that was also termed "activist" in that the community and school supported and worked for drug reform. Beth was a soft-spoken teacher who worked to create a positive learning environment; she also provided additional literacy support for children who needed it.

DATA COLLECTION AND RESEARCH PROTOCOL

I used the interactive analysis method (Miles and Huberman 1984) to guide the data collection, data analysis, and conclusion-drawing verification. This systematic method allowed me to cluster patterns in the data collection, providing evidence upon which I could base conclusions. Next, I describe data collection, the research protocol, and the analysis.

Our research team used an action-based reflective protocol to improve literacy teaching and learning. The protocol for each data collection included the following component: a videotape of a 30- to 60-minute guided reading and/or interactive writing lessons for K–2 teachers in October, November, January, February, and March. During observation and taping, each researcher took written field notes documenting teacher-student language and interactions. After the observation (within a time span of one hour), the researcher conducted teacher interviews. Videotapes of lessons and interviews for each teacher were transcribed. During the interview/debriefing session, a five-minute video segment was used to highlight an important teaching point and the teacher was asked to reflect on this particular point in the lesson. The literacy coordinator coached the teacher and helped her plan for future instruction. Their debriefing sessions after teaching were intended to facilitate deep-level learning for teachers in the study. In these sessions, knowledge was constructed and refined through reflection and analysis of the experiences (Jadallah 1996). At the end of the session, teachers wrote action plans, including one or two self-selected targeted areas for improving instruction. Literacy coordinators encouraged teachers to act on these explicit plans as the next step in improving teaching.

In year 2, the protocol was changed to provide additional information. Before the lesson the researcher asked the classroom teacher: "What do you hope children will learn in guided reading or interactive writing today?" And, "Where in the lesson do you anticipate learning will take place? Why?" These questions helped to focus teachers' thinking toward strategic literacy instruction and also provided interesting data.

ANALYSIS PROCEDURES

Over the two-year data collection period, I used the "clustering patterns" strategy to discover patterns in the video transcripts, teacher interviews, and field notes (Miles and Huberman 1984, 245). First, I analyzed the transcripts of teachers' interactions with students during the teaching of guided

FIGURE 6–4
*Guided Reading and
Interactive Writing Scales*

Guided Reading and Interactive Writing Scales

In **guided reading,** the teacher helps children:

- Read for meaning
- Monitor their reading for accuracy and comprehension and self-correction if necessary
- Read fluently with phrasing
- Solve words by taking them apart (using letter-sound knowledge)

In **interactive writing,** the teacher helps children learn to:

- Plan and decide what to write
- Learn how print works including directionality, features of letters and words, the use of spaces, etc.
- Solve words by using sound-letter relationships to spell

reading and interactive writing at six points in time. I looked for consistent patterns in the conversation surrounding reading and writing. Next, I reviewed records of field observations and teacher interviews, again looking for patterns. Finally, I analyzed video scale functions within the data collection to document how teachers made changes in their instruction in response to reflection (Lyons and Pinnell 2001).

Each part of the data helped me to search for patterns of teachers' actions and to draw conclusions and verify findings in multiple ways. Mathison (1988) uses the term "triangulation" to indicate patterns that are consistently validated by multiple measures. When findings emerged, I triangulated the data in the documentary evidence by confirming the pattern in at least two video transcripts of different teachers and varied teaching contexts. I wanted to understand the complexities of teachers' behaviors as inseparable from what goes on in the classroom; that is, I was working for "interpretation in context" (Cronbach 1975, 123). To verify results, I replicated patterns again, checking findings against outliers or extreme cases in the body of data. For example, conclusions were triangulated in the documentary evidence by confirming the recurrent patterns in multiple video transcripts and field notes, as well as in different literacy contexts.

The guided reading and interactive writing scales (Lyons and Pinnell 2001) that were developed for literacy educators to analyze literacy lessons provided a standard format for analyzing teachers' behaviors. I was looking for visible changes in teaching that indicated deeper levels of understanding and awareness. I used the individual functions of each scale to compare and contrast lessons using transcripts and video footage.

The scales for analysis of guided reading and interactive writing were developed and tested over the two years of the research projects (Lyons and Pinnell 2001). Researchers analyzed lessons in great detail; emerging from the process were lists of characteristics, for which observers could find behavioral evidence. These characteristics could be categorized under areas related to the reading and writing processes. Scales were related to student achievement.

For guided reading, the scale provided a way to assess the extent to which the teacher helped students gain meaning from the text, self-monitor their reading for accuracy and understanding, read with fluency and phrasing, and solve words using a range of strategies to take words apart while maintaining a focus on meaning.

The interactive writing scale enabled researchers to reliably assess the extent to which teachers were helping children learn to compose and plan a text, use the conventions of print, and spell words they want to write as part of an authentic message. The researchers considered these characteristics (or "functions") separately although recognizing that they are integrated during authentic teaching situations. For each function of the scale, observers were to rate lessons as shown in Figure 6–5.

The video rating scale indicated the level of literacy implementation and provided a way to think about patterns in the data. I categorized these ratings into three patterns: A "positive trend" was indicated when the analysis patterns indicated an upward or increasing level of literacy implementation; a "stable trend" showed no real change; a "regressive trend" revealed a downward or decreasing trend.

Analysis using the scale on Peggy's guided reading lessons over the two-year period revealed her ability to help children self-monitor their reading. Initially, Peggy's lessons were evaluated as demonstrating "some evidence of supportive teaching and learning." By the end of year 2, analysis of Peggy's guided reading lessons indicated important "high evidence of supportive teaching and learning." It is important to note that analyses of lessons took place at the end of the study and were performed by trained, objective observers who did not know Peggy. These trends were validated in multiple literacy contexts to provide additional evidence for conclusion-drawing and verification (Miles and Huberman 1984). The guided reading and interactive writing scales provided an effective way to think deeply about teacher development and learning.

FINDINGS

Each teacher addressed the question: "How can I improve literacy instruction?" Each, with support, reflected on practice, engaged in planning for self-improvement, and documented the process through individual written plans. As I reviewed what they taught, how they taught it, and how they acted on coaching sessions, I found two consistent patterns that revealed teachers' literacy thinking and action patterns. First, as teachers reflected on practice, action was built on action in incremental ways. Second, they began to teach for deeper-level student processing while at the same time they continued to express concern about and to improve their use of procedures. Let me explain these with examples.

First, significant change builds on itself over time. It may not, at first, be dramatic; but the smallest change is real when it occurs within actual teaching contexts and results in teachers' adding up information and improving practice over years of teaching. Second, even after two years of support, teachers were consistently concerned about procedural issues, such as the timing of the lesson and the steps required to teach more effectively.

FIGURE 6–5
Video Rating Scale of Teacher's Literacy Implementation

Video Rating Scale of Teacher's Literacy Implementation	
1	No evidence of learning and supportive teaching
2	Some evidence of learning and supportive teaching
3	Moderate evidence of learning and supportive teaching
4	High evidence of learning and supportive teaching
5	Model for excellence in teaching

Teachers were willing to participate in the study, believing that more effective teaching of guided reading and interactive writing would help their students succeed. Some changes in behavior may have seemed small, yet, taken over time, step by step, they were significant. For example, teachers might adjust interactive writing to provide small group instruction focusing on students' needs. They might work for quite some time on providing quality book introductions rather than "picture walks." In fact, these incremental changes represented patterns that occurred in all three classrooms.

What seemed unclear to teachers, initially, was the distinction between attempting to teach children and facilitating children's attempts to teach themselves (Cashdan 1976). Teachers in this study had to learn how to help children become agents of their own learning. I noticed that once teachers began to focus on learning how to teach for student processing—to teach students to use their "in-the-head" strategies to help themselves—they built on those routines to improve practice. Even though I discovered that Kara, Peggy, and Beth were acutely aware of the need for students to "do the work," it was difficult for them to consistently act on that concept.

It was clear that teachers were acting upon their own guided reflections to make changes in teaching, but they did so selectively. For contrast, I asked myself: What didn't teachers act on from their reflections and coaching? I found several patterns that suggested the tension between teachers' development of conceptual or theoretical knowledge and their use of procedures and routines. For example, teachers were developing the idea that meaning was central to all reading and writing instruction, yet even when providing explicit instruction on decoding words, the teacher would not forget to support comprehension. In addition, across both instructional contexts, teachers were inconsistent in supporting students' construction of meaning.

EXAMPLES OF INCREMENTAL CHANGE

In this section, I will describe examples from each teacher's story to illustrate shifts in behavior as teachers were helped to reflect on practice.

Peggy

At the end of year 1, Peggy was encouraging her first graders to read for meaning and with fluency. In her coaching interview, she had stated that she formerly focused almost solely on letters and words but her comments in the interview indicated a change: "I review and make sure that the word in the story makes sense. We make sure that it makes sense." Peggy's guided reading group was eager to read *Henry and Mudge* (Rylant 1996). Here is an excerpt from their introduction of the text.

Peggy: This is a story about a little boy who lives on a block and has no brothers or sisters. He wants to move and his parents say, "Sorry." So he asks for a pet. Do you know the name of a pet?

Danny: A dog.

Peggy: Now I want you to whisper read this story. Read the pages to see what happens. If you come to a tricky word, I want you to help yourself—check the pictures to make the story make sense.

After the guided reading, the literacy coordinator and Peggy discussed the lesson.

Literacy Coordinator: I liked the way you modeled what kids were doing for the other kids—like the hard part and then they fixed it. You told everyone what they did to help themselves—to show what good readers do, even when students were silent reading.

Both the teacher and literacy coordinator were struggling here. This somewhat vague compliment did not help Peggy know how to shift her behavior.

Peggy was working hard to help her students reread text to make sense; but students in this guided reading group need further instruction to help themselves in using decoding in combination with meaning. It was not enough to reread parts of the story. They needed explicit instruction on using visual and letter-sound information while at the same time maintaining a sense of the whole story. When the action plan was discussed, the literacy coordinator encouraged Peggy to adapt her instruction to provide more support for students in using multiple sources of information. "Students run their fingers under the beginning of the word and ask, Does it look right? And, does it make sense?"

Peggy reflected and later adapted her interactions with students to use this more explicit language to promote students' use of independent word-solving strategies. She modeled the process in a way to help students use that model when reading other books. This minor adaptation in instruction helped Peggy to focus on teaching for increased independent student processing because she acted on reflection.

Kara

In her first year of interactive writing instruction, Kara learned that she was doing most of the talking in her lessons. She was modeling the process of saying the words slowly to hear the sequence of sounds, meaning that she was pretty smooth with the procedures, although students were not very active in the process. Her literacy coordinator reported that Kara "used routines wisely," but she also said that Kara had a difficult time reflecting on her work and deciding what to change. Over the course of two years, helping students to "say the words slowly and listen to the sequence of sounds" repeatedly appeared in Kara's action plans. One plan stated, for example: "Students know the routine so make them independent." Over time, Kara learned to help children do the work for themselves; that is, she transferred the task so that they could learn to segment words for themselves. It is not a new idea that children become active or passive participants in knowledge construction based on the way we support learning (Piaget 1955; Vygotsky 1978), and it is a highly theoretical one. Kara's ability to make a small but critical change in her teaching routine opened the door to playing out this important theoretical concept.

Beth

At first, Beth did not think she would learn much from her participation in the study. In her interview, she said, "I thought I knew everything about literacy." In the excerpt below, Beth focused on the purpose for interactive writing as she helped students to compose and construct a group story.

Beth: We're going to do our own writing. . . . let's do something today that you can go home and show your moms. We can do that and your mom is going to say, "I am so happy. You are wonderful. You are so wonderful and you work so hard in school!" We know our color books about red. We've been reading about red. And we know how to write about red.

During the composing and planning process, Beth invited students to brainstorm ideas about red.

Beth: O.K., let's talk about what color we are going to write about today.

Lilly: Red!

Beth: Now what do you think we should say on this page [interactive writing chart paper]?

Lionel: Fire truck

Beth: You'd like to say—fire trucks what?

Lionel: They take fire away.

Beth: O.K. That's a good thing to say, and fire is red. What would you like to say Eddie?

Eddie: Stop signs are red.

Julie: Hearts are red.

After collecting several sentence ideas, Beth asked her students, "Do you love red?" Her students chimed in, "Yeh!" After discussing Clifford the big red dog and a few other contributions, Beth invited the children to plan their interactive writing.

Beth: How should we start our story about red? What should we say?

Jerold: Fire trucks.

Beth: Fire trucks are red. O.K. That's it. We're going to write: "Fire trucks are red." And on another day, we'll write "Clifford is red," and we can use everybody's ideas. They are great ideas!

After the lesson, Beth reflected: "I was taking too much time . . . [interactive writing] definitely should be a lesson where they bring back something for their independent writing. I definitely have a mindset on what I want them to achieve each day . . . and that goes back to their independent writing." It helped Beth to talk with others as she worked toward improved practice, but she also needed explicit coaching and specific suggestions from a literacy coordinator who could show her how to make interactive writing more effective.

Beth changed her thinking in year 2 as she began to follow her literacy coordinator's suggestions, which could be summarized as: "be less supportive and more of a guide so that students are able to problem-solve and start to understand the writing process."

Beth reported, "I have really learned a lot: that I didn't pay attention to, I may not have been concentrating on the exact preciseness of what I should have been teaching. So, I feel that I've changed this year. I'm more aware of what the target should be . . . , teaching pieces more specifically. Before, I was more casual . . . [and students had to] catch the ball I'm throwing. Now, I make more of an effort that they do catch the ball and I perhaps double check more . . . I'm more aware of what they bring with them to the independent writing." In her exit interview, Beth stated that she began the study fully confident that she knew literacy practice well, but she surprised herself with this discovery: "There is always something important to be learned from every lesson."

DISCUSSION

From this study, I learned that literacy instruction requires flexibility and adjustment to meet students' and teachers' changing needs. Teachers base these decisions on a foundation of understanding that deepens over time. Reflection assists teachers in developing knowledge, and coaching is essential to making changes in behavior. Finally, change may be small but become significant over time.

Regarding my first point, I discovered that teachers were most successful when they adapted set routines in guided reading and interactive writing to focus on what students needed to learn. As they grew in comfort and knowledge, rather than thinking only about procedural steps, teachers began to adapt their own internalized routines, to have impact more on student learning. It seems that teachers need to know the procedural steps very well, as they continually develop the conceptual knowledge base. Then they must be able to use those knowledges flexibly in differing contexts. Also, as teachers learned more, each appeared to shift her thinking about who "does the work." They began to notice students' levels of independence and adjust their own behaviors to promote it. All three teachers came to understand that they could demonstrate routines, for example, saying the words slowly during the interactive writing session. When the teacher continually performed the task for them, however, students were not able to use that knowledge in their independent reading and writing. Direct coaching helped these teachers shift their understandings and behaviors over time. Important change requires long-term literacy support, and we cannot expect sudden and dramatic change. These teachers made a series of small changes that accumulated over two years. Such gain is authentic. To multiply effects, teachers need continuous support (Lampert and Clark 1990).

CONCLUSIONS

These three teachers consistently demonstrated reflection on their practice as well as response to coaching; of the eight teachers in the study, these three changed the most over time. Their stories suggest the need for further research and development. I conclude this chapter with three proposals.

Provide Long-term Support to Deepen Teachers' Learning

Deep-level literacy implementation requires strategic decision making and action. The process of becoming an exemplary literacy practitioner requires deliberate, long-term attention to and reflection on practice. Frequent and ongoing professional development must focus on the goal of improving learning for all teachers, including veteran, pre-service teachers and support staff (Teitel 2001, 62). Moreover, this development must focus on both specific procedures and conceptual understanding of "in-the-head processing" strategies (Clay 1991).

A Critical Teaching Culture

Implementing reflective practice doesn't just happen. Teachers who participated in the study were generally reflective practitioners, who were willing "to explore, be curious, and be assertive to gain self-awareness, self-knowledge, and new understandings of the world" (Eby 1997, 10), a stance most of us do not take easily and one that requires time to develop. Teachers were encouraged, even "nudged" by literacy coaches; in the process they continued to develop the base of knowledges to inform their practice. Teachers like

---

Principles Emerging from the Study

- Effective literacy instruction requires flexibility and adjustment to meet students' changing needs.
- Teachers base decisions on a foundation of knowledge that changes over time.
- Reflection and coaching support teachers in deepening knowledge and changing behavior.
- Change is incremental, with small adjustments accumulating over time.

FIGURE 6–6
Principles Emerging from
the Study

Peggy, who immediately acted on her reflections, shifted more in their thinking.

For teaching to contribute significantly to the development of thoughtful, reflective practitioners, Zeichner (1980) suggests that educators begin to focus on the quality of implementation of instruction in pre-service field experiences. This study confirmed experienced teachers' needs as they struggled to improve literacy teaching. These three teachers believed that they would learn from their ongoing participation in the research project and this was confirmed as they noticed changes in their own behavior and evidence of learning on the part of their students. The school culture supported teachers' beliefs that quality teaching matters.

Schools also create cultures in which "learning is a continuous and a self-renewing process" (Lyons and Pinnell 2001, 170)—learning from teaching while teaching. Literacy principles matter most when educators act on the belief that "All students deserve teachers who are primarily guided by student needs and interests and who are both willing and able to construct and examine their practice in conscientious, principled and judicious ways" (LaBoskey (1997, 162). Principles, such as these, were developing within the relationships that literacy coordinators and teachers had established over time.

Complexity of Professional Development

Professional development must honor time and teacher commitment, as well as school/site limitations. Teachers' engagement is also essential in raising school standards for quality teaching (Ben-Peretz 2001). Clay (1991) poses generic learning as a way to develop "a network of competencies which power subsequent independent literacy learning" (1) for emergent readers. Professional development might benefit from a discussion of a similar principle. We can think of teachers and students building knowledges in cycles as they advance, regress, and stabilize learning. The process is clearly nonlinear. On-site developers like literacy coordinators can play an instrumental role in accelerating teachers moving from a technical prescriptive approach to a reflective practitioner stance. Why? Because reflective professionals "generate student learning that far exceeds that of teachers who function from a mechanical stance" (Boyd et al. 1998, 62).

What does this research mean? Foremost, I believe this long-term study reveals that teachers' reflections and actions truly matter. Teaching is complex and requires "moment-by-moment adjustment of plans to fit continually changing and uncertain conditions" (Lampert and Clark 1990, 21). Teachers adjust how to teach and act on new literacy understandings slowly as they develop expert knowledge (Lyons and Pinnell 2001). Lampert and Clark (1990) suggest that the accumulation of such expert knowledge must also be linked to teachers' capacity to use developing expertise toward "desirable growth" (23). Making that growth possible means that literacy educators must nurture a positive stance toward long-term professional development.

7 | BECOMING AN EFFECTIVE LITERACY COACH
What Does It Take?

Carol A. Lyons

Research clearly has shown that the key to improved student learning is a competent teacher (Costa and Garmston 1994; Darling-Hammond 1996b). There is also growing support that the most powerful way to increase teachers' knowledge and improve practice is through coaching and collective problemsolving around specific practice (Darling-Hammond and MacLaughlin 1995). Additional research has demonstrated that coaching sustained and embedded in the real work of teachers' practice results in increased student achievement (Costa and Garmston 1994, Lieberman and Miller 1999).

Our research and experience over the last sixteen years in Reading Recovery (Lyons, Pinnell, and DeFord 1993) and the Literacy Collaborative (Fountas and Pinnell 1996) have convinced us that the most effective way to improve instruction is to develop teachers' conceptual understandings about the reading and writing processes. And the most efficient and effective way to improve teachers' knowledge base, analytical skills, and expertise is through one-to-one coaching that is informed and based on students' behaviors. We have learned that the key to teachers' growth, development, and improved practice is the ability to reflect on one's learning, to change practice based on that reflection, and to develop a theoretical frame of reference or set of understandings that takes into account one's experiences and the experiences of students. Our research has also shown that the greatest shifts in understanding and practice occur when the teacher is engaged in the reflective process with a more knowledgeable and experienced coach. Therefore, we designed a professional development program for literacy educators with a focus on coaching (Lyons and Pinnell 2001).

Studies of literacy coaches reveal that teachers whose students have shown the greatest pre-test and post-test gains on informal and formal assessments have been coached by literacy coordinators who have developed a set of interrelated coaching skills (Lyons and Pinnell 1999; Pinnell and Lyons 1999). These coaches learned how to effectively work with teachers to bring about real, fundamental change to instruction. Figure 7–1 illustrates what we have learned about effective coaches.

As teachers and coaches continue to work closely together in a coaching context, they become colleagues, engaging in collaborative problem-solving and inquiry-oriented conversations. They begin to rely on and trust one another to provide support and skills they may need and can be shared with others. Effective coaches learn how to work alongside different teachers in different classrooms. Together they reflect, analyze, and interpret students' work, building personal and collective theories of literacy learning that enable every child to become a more competent reader and writer (Lyons and Pinnell 2001).

In this chapter, I discuss the six components of an analytical coaching model which we designed as the result of a two-year study conducted in five high poverty schools in Chicago (Lyons and Pinnell 2001). We designed experiences embedded in the act of teaching to help literacy coordinators learn how to become more effective coaches. Each component will be described with a vignette of a hypothetical coaching session conducted by Patty, an effective coach, working with Mary, a first-grade teacher.

AN ANALYTICAL MODEL OF COACHING

The analytical model of coaching represents six differentiated, recursive, and systematic series of actions that coaches engage in every time they observe a lesson and coach the teacher. Each component is described separately.

PREPARING TO COACH

There are three important actions literacy coaches must do before they think about scheduling time to coach a teacher: gather information, listen for the teacher's agenda, and generate hypotheses. Each action is critical to gaining

FIGURE 7–1
*What We Have Learned
About Effective Literacy
Coaches*

What We Have Learned About Effective Literacy Coaches
Effective Coaches:
• analyze teacher and student interactions
• call attention to critical parts of the lesson that have potential for shifting teachers' learning
• engage teachers in constructive conversation
• select powerful coaching points that will lead to deeper conceptual understanding and new learning
• engage teachers in the reflective process to improve their teaching
• create a trusting relationship within which critical feedback is valued
• establish a trusting environment
• set a positive tone for conversation
• create a stress-free context in which teachers feel comfortable sharing their ideas, struggles, and concerns

insights into teachers' strengths, conceptual understandings, and skill level. Unless coaches pay attention to the subtle details teachers reveal through actions and conversation, everyone's time will be wasted and coaching will be ineffective.

Gather Information

First and foremost, coaches must develop the capacity to systematically think, assess, and record multiple sources of information that make sense to them. It must make sense to the coach so that he/she can see learning patterns of student behaviors that are refined, change, and shift over time. Effective coaches learn how to do this by routinely collecting information

---

Steps in an Analytical Model for Coaching

Preparing to Coach:
- Gathering information
- Listening for teacher's agenda during pre-conference
- Generating hypotheses about teacher's perceptions

Observing a Lesson:
- Assessing generic aspects of teaching
- Analyzing the reading and writing process
- Analyzing teacher and student interactions
- Thinking about coaching while observing

Reflecting After the Observation:
- Synthesizing analyses of teaching (generic and reading and writing processes)
- Determining positive aspects of lesson
- Selecting one or two coaching points

Coaching for Shifts in Teaching:
- Establishing trust
- Initiating the conversation
- Listening for the teacher's perspective
- Providing constructive feedback
- Writing an action plan to strengthen teaching

Reflecting After Coaching:
- Did you (the coach) accomplish your goal? How?
- Was the teacher's agenda met? How?

Coaching for Self-Analysis and Reflection:
- Working alongside the teacher
- Developing contexts for collaborative inquiry

FIGURE 7–2
Steps in an Analytical Model for Coaching

Adapted from a Spiral of Learning (Figure 2.1) in C. A. Lyons and G. S. Pinnell (2001), Systems for Change in Literacy Education: A Guide to Professional Development, p. 12

about students' and teachers' strengths. They use multiple sources of data, collected over time during reading and writing lessons with groups of students representing varying ability levels. These data include samples of students' work, teachers' written records, videotape and audiotapes of teaching, teachers' written reflections in journals, and notes taken while observing lessons. As shown in Figure 7–3, the coach has specific questions in mind while analyzing data before the observation.

Examples from students' work are used as evidence to draw some tentative answers to these questions. By grounding hypotheses in student data, the coach learns how to use specific examples to point out students' learning rather than teachers' behavior. Coaching should never focus on what the teacher is doing right or wrong, but how the students' are learning as a result of teaching.

Vignette

The Coach Gathers Information Before the Lesson

Mary, a first-grade teacher in the study, had been teaching interactive writing for six weeks. Patty (the coach) was making her fourth visit to the teacher to observe a lesson. While observing the students during independent writing, Patty was puzzled by two kinds of student behaviors. First, the majority of children were copying words from the word wall to use in their stories. She noticed only two students attempting to hear and record the sounds in the words they wanted to write. Patty wondered why most of the students were not using a technique such as "say the word slowly, what letter do you expect to hear at the beginning of *cat*?", that is demonstrated during interactive writing lessons? Second, Patty noticed that three of twenty-four students in the room did not have control of spacing between words. She wondered why. Are these children new to the classroom? Are they second language learners who do not understand this concept? Did the teacher realize that the three boys needed more specific instruction? Was she not attending to their spacing because something else was more important?

FIGURE 7–3
Gathering Information Before the Lesson: Guiding Questions for Coaches

Gathering Information Before the Lesson: Guiding Questions for Coaches

- What does the teacher know about student learning?
- What does the teacher understand about literacy learning?
- What does the teacher do well?
- What are the students' strengths and needs?
- What have the students learned about the reading and writing processes?
- What do the students understand about how to read and write?

Patty decided to discuss the children's independent writing during the pre-conference. She knew Mary wanted her to observe an interactive writing lesson and that discussing the students' writing would give them an understanding of the children's writing strengths. Patty hoped that by discussing the writing samples, she might better understand the teacher's perspective about what the children know and can do when writing independently.

Listening for the Teacher's Agenda During the Pre-conference

The coach has a brief discussion with the teacher before the lesson observation to ascertain her/his goals or focus of the lesson she is to observe and areas in which she/he would like some help. The conversation helps the coach to identify the teacher's priorities and expectations for students' learning, level of understanding about procedures for teaching a specific element (e.g., guided reading, interactive writing), and skill level in adapting a specific technique (e.g., book introduction) to meet individual or group needs. Effective coaches learn how to listen for the teacher's agenda. What does she/he hope to gain from the observation and follow-up coaching session? What can I do to help her?

When teachers know you are listening for their ideas, concerns, and opinions, you validate their thinking and teaching. Dismissing the teacher's thoughts and holding to your agenda diminishes the impact of the coaching session on teachers' learning and may prevent the teacher from taking a risk to try something else. When this happens, children are denied an opportunity to learn.

Vignette

Patty, the Coach, Talks with the Teacher Before the Lesson

Patty and Mary examined the independent writing samples that had been collected earlier in the day. They looked at several students' work and Mary pointed out that they knew the high-frequency words on the word wall. Patty agreed but wondered why the children did not write words that were not on the word wall? Mary replied because they cannot spell many words and they know they are not to interrupt her during guided reading groups to ask how to spell a word. So she told them to guess how to spell the word, but most of the children did not want to write the word spelled wrong because it could not be read. So they only wrote words that they knew were spelled correctly. Patty said she did notice two children saying a word slowly and then writing the letter they heard. She wondered why more students did not use that technique. Mary said during interactive writing, she asks the children to say the word slowly and predict what letter they hear and she did not know why they did not try to use the technique when they wrote independently. The teacher hoped Patty could answer that question. Patty made a mental note to watch the students' behaviors when the technique was used during the interactive writing lesson.

Patty then focused Mary on several pieces of writing that had good spacing between words and the writing of three boys who did not leave spaces between the words. The teacher commented that they had difficulty sitting still and were easily distracted. Their sentences were short and sloppy because they did not like to write and wanted to get writing over with. Mary commented that the boys usually acted out during the group interactive writing lesson and asked Patty to observe the boys and provide some suggestions for getting them to behave better. The spacing problem did not come up.

Patty summarized the pre-conference by noting that Mary asked her to do two things: (1) to observe the children's behavior when she asked them to say a word slowly and hear the sound of the letters in a word and then when they come to the easel to write the letter in the sentence, and (2) to observe the three boys who misbehaved often and help her develop better management skills.

Generating Hypotheses About Teachers' Perceptions and Skills

Finally, in the pre-conference, the coach must use the information he/she has gathered to decide what to look for during the observation of teaching. Patty organized her thoughts by asking the following specific questions:

- What do the children's writing samples and running records reveal about what the children have learned about the reading and writing process?
- What did I learn when I asked the teacher to discuss the running records or writing samples for a specific group of students that I will be observing?
- What are her/his perceptions of students' strengths and weaknesses? Does the data support the teacher's observations and conclusions?
- What does the students' work reveal about their understanding of the reading and writing process?
- What do the children need to learn next?
- How is the teacher helping children develop a strategic processing system of strategies?
- Where in the lesson would you expect to see the teacher teaching for a specific strategy?
- What does the teacher want me to observe?
- Does her/his request make sense based on the student and teacher data?

Not every question needs to be addressed during every observation, but the idea is that the coach hypothesizes about what may support and/or interfere with students' processing and identifies a few places in the lesson that might reveal specific evidence to support or confirm these hypotheses.

Vignette

The Coach Generates Hypotheses Before the Lesson

Patty knew that Mary was expecting feedback about how to manage the misbehaving boys during the lesson. She wanted to focus on calling the teacher's attention to the importance of helping the "disruptive" boys learn how to write a sentence word-by-word with a space between each word. Patty also wanted to observe how the students were learning to construct words they did not know, letter-by-letter. Perhaps then, she would be able to help Mary understand why they were not using the hearing and recording sounds in words technique during independent writing. With a clear focus in mind, Patty was ready to observe the lesson.

OBSERVING THE LESSON

Unless coaches know what and how to observe, analyze, and assess what they see, they will not know how to direct the teacher's attention to facilitate the coaching conversation. Observation and fine discrimination skills (and the ability to ignore unimportant information to focus on essential demands of the task while teaching a particular instructional approach) is critical to creating a context to coach effectively. And when guided in an analytical process about key teacher and student behaviors to look for, literacy coaches can acquire the skill. In order to become an astute observer of teaching behavior, however, the coach must learn how to distinguish and separate generic teaching practice (e.g., timing and pace of the lesson) from practice that focuses on teaching an instructional technique (e.g., teaching strategies for reading and writing text).

Assessing Generic Aspects of Teaching

Generic factors are important and highly related to effective teaching (Senge 1990). I have described ten generic aspects of teaching, each of which can be used to analyze any lesson at any grade levels, with students of different abilities (see Lyons and Pinnell 2001).

- *Materials:* Are the basic materials needed to teach the lesson accessible? Or does the teacher have to stop a lesson and find a specific book, the magic marker, or pointer?

- *Organization*: Is the teacher prepared? Do the parts of the guided reading lesson, for example, fit together in an orderly, coherent way?
- *Time*: Does the teacher have sufficient time for each part or component of the literacy lesson? Does the teacher implement the procedures and techniques in a timely way throughout the lesson?
- *Pace*: Does the lesson move along?
- *Intensity*: Is the teacher actively teaching in an energetic and persistent way throughout the lesson?
- *Feedback and Praise*: When the teacher responds to children, is the response constructive, specific, and grounded in students' behavior?
- *Interaction*: Does the teacher actively interact with all students? Does she encourage every student to participate?
- *Engagement*: Are all the students engaged in the lesson? Does she/he hold every child's attention?
- *Enthusiasm*: Does the teacher show enthusiasm through language and actions? Does the teacher appeared bored?
- *Rapport*: Does the teacher connect with the children in a meaningful way so that they feel successful?

The preceding questions are designed to address generic characteristics of effective teaching. They are not content specific.

Vignette

During the Lesson, the Coach Assesses Generic Aspects of Teaching

Patty noted that Mary was organized and materials were easy to reach, but the lesson was forty-two minutes long and slow moving. The teacher seemed to have good rapport with two thirds of the children, actively engaging them in conversation while negotiating the text. These same children came up to the easel to write words. The other third of the children were not engaged and some students were only engaged when the teacher asked them to behave. Feedback and praise was limited to "O.K." or "good." The teacher appeared anxious and was distracted because several boys (which she had identified in the pre-conference) were misbehaving.

Research shows that generic aspects of teaching must be in place in order to have an effective lesson (Lyons and Pinnell 2001). Furthermore, the generic aspects may override and cloud a coach's judgment as to the effectiveness of a lesson. When generic factors are not working well, that is, in a consistent and effective manner, teachers struggle. But effective coaching also involves analyzing and assessing instructional approaches and moves related to the reading and writing process (the content) and strategies for learning how to read and write.

Analyzing the Reading and Writing Processes

According to Clay's theory of reading and writing instruction, all readers, from five-year-old children reading their first book to proficient adults, must monitor and integrate information from multiple sources and check one source of information against another (Clay 1991). Four types of information sources are available to read text: semantic (text meaning), syntactic (sentence structure), visual (graphemes, orthography, layout and format), and phonological (sounds of oral language). The goal of early literacy instruction is achieved when children have acquired a self-extending or self-improving system of behavior that enables them to become more proficient every time they read and write. The teacher's role within the literacy lesson is to create a scaffold, within which she/he supports emerging skill, allowing for the student to work with the familiar, introduce the unfamiliar in a measured way, and deal constructively with partially right responses (Clay and Cazden 1990).

Using the preceding definition of the reading process as a guide, a series of questions are provided in Figure 7–4 to guide literacy coaches' thinking about the reading process while observing a lesson.

The reading and writing processes must be understood well before a coach can pinpoint parts of the literacy lesson that are interfering with student learning and provide specific guidance to help the teacher construct a rationale for changing her/his behavior. Listed previously are some general questions that effective coaches have used to analyze the reading and writing processes. A more comprehensive series of questions, along with a guided reading and interactive writing scale and descriptions of this analysis, are available (see Lyons and Pinnell 2001).

Guiding Questions for Coaches to Analyze Reading and Writing Processes

How is the teacher helping readers:
- construct and extend meaning of the text?
- monitor and correct their own reading?
- maintain fluency and phrasing while reading continuous contexts?
- problem-solve words on the run while reading continuous texts?

How is the teacher helping writers:
- establish a purpose for writing?
- engage in conversation to compose a precise text?
- inscribe a composed message?
- write the actual words letter-by-letter?
- by providing opportunities for the children to connect reading and writing?

FIGURE 7–4
Guiding Questions for Coaches to Analyze Reading and Writing Processes

The Coach Takes Specific Notes While Observing the Lesson

While observing the interactive writing lesson, Patty recorded the total time for each component of the lesson, noting how much of that total time was used to manage the class. Patty also included comments specific to the generic aspects of teaching and teacher actions that facilitated children's understanding of the writing process.

Figure 7–5 on page 104 displays Patty's notes.

Analyzing Teacher and Student Interactions

While observing any lesson, literacy coaches should be thinking about and noting how the students are responding to the teacher and instruction.

- How does the teacher use observation to infer students' understandings?
- Are all the children engaged?
- Are books selected appropriate for this group of students?
- Do the children negotiate the text (sentence)?
- Which children are not participating in the lesson? Why?
- Does the teacher follow the children's behavior?
- How does the teacher alter instruction to meet individuals' learning needs and strengths?

The coach writes specific teacher and student behaviors to provide evidence to support responses to the preceding questions.

The Coach Observes and Records Examples of Student/Teacher Interactions

Patty indicated that total lesson time was forty-six minutes; of that time, sixteen minutes was used to manage the group. Approximately seventeen of twenty-four children were engaged. Children who were not behaving in the expected way were not called on. The three boys who did not know how to space were looking out the window or down at the floor. The child who was considered most disruptive was kicking another child. Approximately one third of the students could not read the text and stopped reading. The teacher and students did not negotiate the text or work together solving how to write unknown words. Mary did most of the work. Patty noted the following routine for writing the text.

- Teacher says the word; the children repeat the word.
- Teacher repeats word. Does anyone have a name that begins with that sound?
- Students look at the name chart and find the name of someone whose name starts with the sound of the first letter of the word that the class wants to write. (Teacher does not ask children what sound do you hear when saying the word *wave*).
- The child whose name begins with that letter comes up and writes the letter.
- Wilfrado wrote the letter *w* in the word *wave*, Antonio wrote the *a*, Violet wrote the letter *v*, and the teacher put in the silent *e*. The same routine was used to write the remaining words in the sentence.
- After the word is written, a child comes to the easel, places two fingers on the chart paper, puts spaces between the words.
- If no one has a name that beings with the word, the teacher gets the magnadoodle out.
- Teacher: What word are we trying to write?
- Student: *clap*
- Teacher: Listen to how the word starts. [T says *clap* slowly] Now you say it.
- Student: *c-l-a-p*. [saying word slowly]
- Teacher: What letter do you hear at the beginning of *clap*?
- Student: *c*
- Teacher: Watch me write the *c*. Teacher writes *c* on the magnadoodle. The routine continues until the sentence is completely written.
- Teacher: What is at the end?
- Students: Responding together "a period."
- The teacher says the word slowly and asks the children what they hear. The children call out the letter they hear and the teacher writes it on the magnadoodle. Once the word is written correctly, the children orally spell the word while another child writes each letter on the chart paper.

Thinking About Coaching While Observing

Armed with information gathered in the ways previously described, the coach thinks about how to address the teacher's agenda, expressed during the pre-conference, while extending his/her conceptual understanding to improve instruction. The coach tries to pinpoint a specific part of the observed lesson to bring to the teacher's attention. Effective coaches learn how to carefully select several coachable moments during a lesson that may have potential for shifting a teacher's perceptions and improving instruction. They circle these potential parts of the lesson in their notes and make a final decision when the observation is over. This is important because you want to be able to select one or two memorable interactions (coaching points) to

Patty's Observation Notes

Establishing the purpose: Total time: 4 min. Management: 3 min.

After the children were seated on the rug, the teacher determined if each child was ready to listen and raise their hands to speak.

T: I can see Jacob sitting tall and hands folded. Jacob is ready; Michael is not ready etc.

T: Today we are going to write a story about something all of you do. Can you guess what it is? Many responses but not what the teacher wanted. No purpose was established for writing the text.

The writing process: Negotiating the text.   Total time: 11 min. Management: 3 min.

T: What can you do with your hands? Many students raised their hands. Suggestions included open jars, wave at cars and trucks, clap, shake other peoples hands, wash, pick things up, touch stuff, feel how cold or hot it is outside, make stuff. Every student in the group is attentive.

T: I will call on students who are behaving.

Patty noted that the text did not emerge from children's experience and was not negotiated with the students. The teacher had the idea. Patty noted that the three boys who did not leave spaces between words had raised their hands to participate but were not called on. The most behaved students' comments were considered.

Composing the text   Total time: 8 min. Management: 3 min.

The teacher wrote the stem . . . "With my hands I can . . . " Different students were called to complete the sentence. Sentence was: With my hands I can wave, clap, wash, and write. The teacher had the idea; students filled in the rest. The teacher accepted words that she wanted the children to write. More complex words or sentences (shake hands with my friend) were ignored.

Writing the sentence; how print works; word solving: Total time: 18 min. Management: 4 min.

The teacher said the word slowly and used the magnadoodle to write the word herself. Teacher also relied on name chart to find a child's name that began with the letter of the word they were to write. Teacher did most of the work. Children did not reread to keep the whole message in mind. When rereading does occur, the teacher rereads herself.

Reading/writing connection: Total time: 5 min. Management: 3 min.

The children reread the sentence in unison six times. Some children had difficulty reading the words. Different children pointed to the words. Only children who were well behaved were called on.

use to initiate the coaching conversation. Patty circled negotiating the text, writing the words (specifically the use of the magnadoodle to teach hearing and recording sounds in words), and rereading the text.

REFLECTING AFTER THE OBSERVATION

Sharpened, systematic observational skills are the tools that enable coaches to organize, synthesize, and reflect on what they observed over time and determine how to most effectively assist and extend teachers' learning. In order to be effective, the coaching conversation should be characterized by shared intentions (teacher and coach) in search of some answers to improve students' learning outcomes. This process involves a conversation where both individuals reveal their ideas and information and engage in respectful listening. The reflection should not take any more than three or four minutes. When the lesson is over, the coaches sort, organize, prioritize, and select the points that they want to make during the coaching conversation in a systematic way.

Synthesize Information Using Generic Aspects of Teaching and Reading and Writing Process Questions

First, the coach examines his/her notes. The idea is to synthesize information and look for patterns of teacher behavior and student responses that may indicate that an important generic and reading/writing component of instruction is present and/or absent. For example, if the teacher tells the children what they are going to write (interaction), what impact does that have on helping students reread the sentence, engage in word solving, and understand how individual words are put together to express something meaningful? Or, if the introduction of the new book takes less than one minute (time), what impact will that have on children's ability to gain meaning and predict using language structure and visual information to predict what is written? In each case mentioned above, a generic aspect within teaching a specific component of the reading and writing process was not being addressed.

Vignette

The Coach Writes a Synthesis of Her Observations

Mary does not have a clear understanding of the writing process. No purpose was set for writing the sentence. The sentence stem was decided by the teacher. Patty did not think the text grew out of a meaningful experience but she was not sure. The children did not negotiate the text. The teacher put up a stem "With my hands I can . . . " This stem was not within the children's natural language patterns. No attention was given to print conventions;

where to start, which way to go, spacing between words. Punctuation at the end of the sentence was attended to but since the teacher wrote the first word of the sentence *With*, the capital *w* used to begin the sentence was not discussed. Writing samples collected at the beginning of the lesson revealed that approximately half the class did not understand how to begin the sentence with a capital letter.

The only problem solving that occurred involved helping the children to think about how the word would start and naming the letter, and finding the name of a child in the room that begins with that letter. No attention was given to saying the word slowly and connecting the sound to letters, attending to letters after the first letter, making connections between words they know and new words, solving words using analogy, or visual patterns. The children read the sentence orally while someone pointed to each word. It appeared to be a word recognition task; not a text that could be connected to anything they were reading or writing. The syntactic patterns were not natural and the words were not in children's listening or speaking vocabulary.

Determine Positive Aspects of the Lesson

It is important to set a positive climate for the coaching session so that the teacher feels support, encouragement, acceptance, and safety. Specifically, the teacher must feel that his/her ideas will be honored and valued and failures will not be met with ridicule or shared with others. Therefore, it is important to recognize the teacher's strengths. Think about the generic aspects of teaching. What does the teacher do well? Are her materials well organized and assessable? Is the book choice and introduction appropriate for the group of children you observed? Did the lesson move along at a good pace? Were the children engaged? Was the teacher interacting in a positive and encouraging way?

Next, think about the instruction. Was the teacher teaching children strategies for predicting the first letter of a word? Did he/she adjust questioning to meet individuals' need, during guided reading? Did the teacher help the children negotiate the text? Was the teacher sensitive to what a child could contribute to the interactive writing lesson and why?

Vignette

The Coach Notes the Teacher's Strengths

Patty decided she would mention how well organized Mary was and that materials were available for use when needed. (This had been a problem for the teacher when she observed the lesson two weeks ago). Mary also helped the students compose a text that required problem solving at the word level. There were opportunities for children to make connections between the first letter of the student's name written on the name chart and the first letter of words written on the word wall.

Selecting One or Two Coaching Points

Our research (Lyons and Pinnell 2001) has revealed that the most powerful and efficient way to initiate a conversation and call the teacher's attention to a specific part of the lesson is to select a snippet of a videotape to share with the teacher. Patty reviewed the videotape of the lesson and selected a segment that showed the "disruptive" boys with their hands up to be called on while the text was being written. She thought by showing this one-minute snippet, the teacher would realize that if she called on the boys to make a contribution, they would feel successful and attend when she wanted.

A second two-minute snippet of videotape was selected to illustrate how Mary used a magnadoodle to teach the children how to hear and record sounds in words. Patty thought this snippet of video would help Mary understand why the children had not been able to use this strategy to write unknown words while writing independently. Patty selected two snippets of teacher/student interactions to make her coaching points. She was ready to begin the coaching session.

COACHING FOR SHIFTS IN TEACHING

The primary goal of coaching is to assist the teacher in observing, analyzing, and reflecting on teaching in order to become more sensitive to children's behavior as evidence of learning, and shift her/his teaching to support students' learning. This goal is accomplished through a scaffolding process (Bruner 1978) during coaching. The scaffolding structure is described by Vygotsky (1978) as the zone of proximal development. The coach (or more knowledgeable colleague) initially guides the teacher's actions. Gradually the two begin to share the problem solving, with the teacher taking the initiation and the coach guiding when the teacher falters. Through this experience, a teacher learns how to observe students' behaviors to determine their competencies and shift her/his teaching to expand and further develop students' knowledge and skills. The coach helps the teacher come to understand the rationale (that is, reasons *why*) and how specific teaching moves promote student learning.

Research conducted during coaching sessions reveals that through coaching, teachers learn how to refine procedures to meet individual needs and acquire deeper understandings of the impact of their decisions on student learning (Lyons and Pinnell 2001). A teacher commented,

If I didn't see the snippet of videotape, I would have never believed I was doing all the work. Now I see that I am not helping the kids become independent, I talk and do too much. If you did not point this problem out, I would have continued doing too much work. Now I can see that it is through the kids' responses that I will know if and when my teaching is effective.

Effective coaches, from the first time they are involved in a coaching session, provide rationales for why teachers are doing something and how the action will support student learning. As teachers learn how to think in *why* terms (e.g., "I am giving a more supportive introduction because the language structure in this book is more complex and may interfere with second language learners' understanding") they gain a clear and deeper understanding of the underlying theory. Effective coaches are always discussing teaching decisions and actions in terms of *why* this is critical to student learning.

Establishing Trust

Trust is crucial to the creation of powerful and effective coaching conversations. Even if the coach and teacher believe in the beneficial outcomes of coaching, they cannot develop trust in just one coaching session. Only over a period of time in which trust and subsequent respect are established can a teacher feel secure and confident in developing a collaborative partnership with his/her coach.

Initially, the teacher and coach must have enough trust to be willing to begin the coaching sessions. If teachers feel that the coach listened to and respected their point of view, responded to questions in a positive and sensitive way, and valued their experiences, trust will grow. One teacher, when asked why she trusted her coach, replied:

I was really worried about my first coaching session. I didn't know what to expect and I thought I was going to be evaluated. But (the coach) immediately put me at ease by asking me what I thought happened when one of the children couldn't respond to a question. Her response was that she didn't know the boy as well as I did and perhaps the two of us could figure out what had happened. That one comment showed she valued my experience. Another thing she did was listen. It was not just a courteous kind of listening, but really active like she thought about what I said and added to it. She asked me a question to help me clarify my thinking and also helped her to better understand what I meant. That one question made me think differently about my idea and I knew she really wanted to know, she wasn't just asking to be polite. I ask her to visit me as much as possible. I trust her completely.

Conversely, trust is most fragile when the coaching relationship is relatively new. Unsuccessful coaching experiences, in which the teacher feels threatened, judged, or inadequate, destroy the possibility of building a trusting relationship.

As teachers and coaches examine student behaviors together, they are able to build trusting relationships, which are the backbone of effective coaching sessions. By making meaning together, both the teacher's and coach's growth is fostered. Through reflection and shared dialogue, teachers and coaches can begin to construct new and improved understandings about the teaching and learning process that they probably would not have developed alone. But how do you get started?

Initiating the Conversation

Trust and active listening are not the only characteristics of effective coaching conversations. To initiate the conversation, discussion around and about explicit student behaviors must be brought to the teacher's attention. Grounding the discussion in student behavior provides a safe context in which coach and teacher can exchange ideas, ask provocative questions, provide data to be examined through another viewpoint (lens), exchange comments, and give feedback.

Many of the actions being described here as part of initiating and sustaining a conversation can also be found in the current term "inquiry act." Inquiry acts, according to Judith Wells Lindfors (1999), are:

> conversational turns that turn toward the partner (both teacher and coach) for help in going beyond present understanding. Like all language acts, each inquiry utterance provides whatever the speaker deems sufficient for the partner to respond to and each is non-neutral, resonating with mood and tone and feeling—curiosity perhaps or puzzlement, reflectiveness or tentativeness. (51)

Effective coaches see themselves as inquirers. They understand how reciprocal processes of conversation evoke a trusting context, focus on construction of meaning, and help to engender new behaviors and learning for the teacher and themselves. One coach commented: "I certainly do not have all the answers. I must rely on the teacher's understanding, analysis, interpretation, and perspective in order to offer informed ideas to support and improve the teacher's practice."

Listening for the Teacher's Perspective

It may not be easy for the coach to put aside his or her own views and listen for the teacher's ideas about student/teacher interactions, but it is essential to establishing trust and rapport . . . conditions necessary for a collaborative relationship. Accepting the teacher's point of view encourages the teacher to consider others' point of view. The very act of asking for the teacher's opinion establishes cooperation. Cooperating means striving together for a common goal by individuals who regard themselves as equals and treat each other with respect and honesty. Respectful listening establishes a cooperative partnership in three ways.

First, in listening to the teacher's analyses of an interaction, the coach has an opportunity to look for and establish common ground . . . integrating the teacher's analyses and perspective with his/her own. Second, listening to the teacher's assessment of students' behaviors provides a guide to his/her perceptions of student learning by virtue of what the teacher observes and discusses. The coach uses specific evidence from which to infer the teacher's understandings and a basis for framing questions and suggestions. The coach now has an opportunity to support, add to, clarify the teacher's assessment and/or offer an alternative point of view, and an opportunity to use observation and analyses grounded in student performance to help the teacher design and implement a more powerful teaching technique.

Finally, in listening for the teacher's perspective, the coach is showing respect for his/her knowledge and right to speak up. Listening establishes a certain psychological equality in the relationship. The motive for cooperation begins in a feeling of mutual respect for each others' opinions because the coach and teacher are working for the same goal . . . that is to support and enhance student learning. The following comment by a teacher in our study makes this point.

> I knew Melissa wanted to know what I was thinking because she always started out asking what I saw when I watched the snippet of my lesson. Sometimes she totally agreed with my analyses and other times she added to my observation. I became more analytical and started to ask myself how I was supporting student learning. I became more responsible for what I was doing even when I wasn't being observed. I was also more willing to take her advice because she confirmed what I said and was really interested in helping me make better teaching decisions to make my kids better readers and writers.

Providing Constructive Feedback

First and foremost, effective coaches understand that they must strive to attain a common goal while coordinating one's own perspective with a consciousness of the teacher's perspective. They consider the teacher's point of view and encourage the teacher to consider their point of view. With this in mind, the coach gives constructive feedback. In my view, constructive feedback occurs when the coach initiates a dialogue in which the teacher can reshape his/her knowledge and understanding through interaction with others. And the coach's responses to teacher's comments particularly affect the kind of learning that takes place; nonjudgmental responses are more likely to facilitate learning.

Effective coaches generally begin the coaching session by addressing the teacher's agenda, which is uncovered in the pre-conference, focused on during the observation, and most likely revealed in the snippet(s) of videotape that are selected to view, analyze, and discuss. The following dialogue between Patty and the teacher demonstrates how these ideas unfolded in their coaching conversation.

Vignette

Patty and Mary's Coaching Conversation

Patty: During your pre-conference you mentioned two things you wanted help doing: how to manage the three boys who were disruptive during total group interactive writing sessions and how to encourage your children to use the hearing and recording sounds in words technique to write unknown words during independent writing. Is that right?

Teacher: Yes, you're right. I wanted to know if I was doing something wrong.

Patty: What I observed you doing was a lot of right things, but this isn't about you but about how the children are learning. Generally speaking, how well are they doing in writing?

Teacher: For the most part really well. I am pleased with how they can think about the words they want to write and come up with the first letter of a word. Some are even coming up with the ending and middle letters. With the exception of those three boys, most of my kids are attentive during interactive writing.

Patty: Well I did select a snippet of videotape that showed the boys so we could find out what is going on.

(Patty and the teacher watch a one-minute snippet of videotape of the teacher and children negotiating the sentence. Mary immediately comments that the three boys she was concerned about were raising their hands and she did not notice them.)

Patty: Could the three boys have contributed something?

Teacher: Of course, everyone can contribute. You do not have to say anymore. The picture was worth a thousand words. I will call on them tomorrow.

Patty: If I showed you more videotape of your lesson, you would see that these boys were not attentive throughout the lesson.

Teacher: I know you are right. I had to stop the lesson several times to get them on task.

Patty: So what do you think may be going on?

Teacher: They do not understand how to write a sentence. Even in their writing that was collected today, you could see that.

(Patty and the teacher examine samples of the boys' writing. Mary points out that none of the boys leave spaces between words.)

Patty: How can you get them involved in the interactive writing lesson and help them understand the importance of spacing?

Teacher: They can be the spacers. Great idea. I will do that tomorrow, too.

Patty: Do you think that will work?

Teacher: Yes, because they will have a job to do and they will have to listen to what is being said to decide when to get up and space.

Patty: You are absolutely right. How will that help their independent writing?

Teacher: They will start to think about leaving a space between words.

Patty: Good. We have taken care of your first concern, now for the second one. How to help the children use the hearing sounds in words technique demonstrated in an interactive writing lesson when they write independently. What specifically do you want the children to know how to do?

Teacher: To think about the word they want to write, say the word slowly so that they hear each sound in the word, and then write the word. I want them to focus on beginning and ending sounds and even sounds in the middle of a word.

Patty: Good. You said you want to teach them how to think about a word, say the word slowly and think about the beginning, middle, and ending sounds. How are you teaching them to do that?

Teacher: I use the magnadoodle so that they can all see what I am writing.

Patty. Let's look at this snippet of writing and think about what you just said.

(The snippet shows the teacher using the magnadoodle to write unknown words and then the children copying that word from the magnadoodle to the chart paper.) What do you see?

Teacher: I am saying the word slowly. Some kids are following?

Patty: Who said the word slowly first? Who is taking the lead?

Teacher: I am. For some reason, I thought I should say it slowly so that they could imitate me and not mispronounce the word.

Patty: Is the word *wave* in their speaking vocabulary?

Teacher: Of course it is, so the children can say it slowly. I get it.

Patty: How will that help them?

Teacher: They will know immediately what to do when they want to write an unknown word during independent writing.

Patty: Absolutely. You need to teach them the process for word solving; saying the word slowly and listening for the sounds is the first step. Now what happens after the word is said slowly. What did you see?

Teacher: I asked them what sound did they hear at the beginning of the word *wash* and they said *w* and I wrote the *w* on the magnadoodle.

Patty: Who is doing all the work?

Teacher: I am.

(Patty and the teacher discuss the possibility of having the children [not the teacher] write the word on the chart paper instead of using the magnadoodle.)

Teacher: And just let them write it on the chart! We tried that once and they left so much space between the letters.

Patty: Could you use that incident as an opportunity to teach them to put letters close together to make a word and leave a space between words? Then you would be teaching them the idea that individual letters make up a word. They understand the concept of a word when they read a book; don't you think that they need to understand a concept of a word when they write?

Teacher: I see what you mean.

Patty: You said that in independent writing you are not seeing them say the word slowly and writing the letter they hear. And you want them to do that.

Teacher: Right.

Patty: What would happen if the children were doing all of that and writing the letters they heard on the chart paper as they were going through the process of hearing and recording those letters to write the word *wave*?

Teacher: It would be sloppy.

Patty: That is what you have the white tape for. Ask them if the letter looks O.K. and some will probably say it is written sloppy. Then take the magic tape and cover the letter and voilà, they have another chance to make it look better. What would the children get out of the experience?

Teacher: They would get a lot more out of it. They would learn the importance of writing the letters neatly. And by going to the chart paper they would write the *w* and know that it begins the word *wave*. They would have to say the word *wave* and listen and figure out what sound they hear at the beginning of the word and what letter goes with that sound.

Patty: And then how could they use that strategy in independent writing?

Teacher: Well once they got used to hearing the sounds and writing the letter on the chart paper, they would do it on their own paper. That is pretty good. I have to give up control and not worry about sloppy writing.

Patty: Yes, I agree, you need to relinquish control. Do you think they would use more words than what is on the word wall for independent writing?

Teacher: Yes, I was already thinking that. It would free them to write more interesting sentences. Be more creative.

Patty: Do we have both your issues solved?

Teacher: Yes, thank you.

Patty: You answered your own questions. You made my role easier because through your good observation and reflection, YOU found your own solutions and answered your own questions about how best to support your children's learning. Thank you.

Teacher: Now I need to write my action plan so that I do not forget.

As the preceding coaching conversation reveals, when the process of constructive feedback is working well, the teacher and coach do not dismiss each others' comments but listen attentively, show respect for each others' opinions, are sensitive to the feelings and knowledge base of others, and disagree without attacking.

Writing an Action Plan to Strengthen Teaching

The action plan is a commitment, written by the teacher, to set goals and priorities and to try something new to support students' learning. The plan represents next steps she/he needs to take to create more opportunities to improve students' learning. Mary wrote two goals on the carbon copy pad of paper.

Interactive Writing

1. Pay particular attention to the three boys who are having difficulty with spacing between words. Call on them to contribute words to write; call on them frequently to be the spacer.
2. Reteach how to hear and record sounds in words. Make sure the children say the word slowly first, let the children write the letter they hear on the chart paper. Let them continue to write the word letter-by-letter.

Patty and the teacher each had a copy of the action plan. The teacher mounted hers on a bulletin board near her desk. Patty kept hers in a notebook to refer to when she visited the teacher the following week. The action plans provide a record of shifts in teachers' learning; it is a rewarding and fulfilling documentation of teachers' learning captured over time. The entire coaching session took nine minutes.

REFLECTING AFTER COACHING

It is critical that coaches take time to think about what happened during the two hours she/he spent with the teacher. Thinking reflectively about your role, as well as the teacher's role throughout the coaching process (from the pre-conference to writing the action plan) helps coaches in three important ways. First, they will learn to appreciate the complexity of the coaching task without becoming overwhelmed by it. Second, in carefully analyzing one piece of the puzzle, they will find that other pieces fall into place. Finally, they will learn how to approach future coaching situations more systematically and be reassured by that ability. To that end, the coach must ask himself/herself several questions.

Did You (the Coach) Accomplish Your Goal? How?

Patty's first goal was to call the teacher's attention to the fact that the three children in the room did not space between words (evident in the writing samples). This goal was met. She accomplished the goal through conversation with the teacher about one of her issues—how to manage the disruptive boys. In showing the video snippet of the teacher ignoring the three boys raising their hands, she had an opportunity to suggest that they would be attentive if they come to the easel to space between words. Patty wanted to bring to the teacher's attention the fact that the boys did not space between words, but the teacher did not recognize the problem. The teacher's idea to keep them attentive by serving as spacers provided an opportunity for Patty to show the teacher their writing samples. Mary then realized they needed to learn how to leave a space between words and the importance of spacing, concepts they are more likely to learn if they are personally involved in the writing process. This was an unexpected outcome. One piece of the puzzle solved another issue.

Patty's second goal was to help Mary understand the importance of not doing all the work for the children. Although the focus of this particular lesson was having the children, instead of the teacher, hear and record sounds in words, a bigger idea was addressed: How to relinquish control of the lesson and give the children more responsibility? Patty believed that the teacher took the first step in understanding how to teach the process, not *do* the process for children. Patty's agenda was met.

Was the Teacher's Agenda Met? How?

It was clear from the coaching conversation that the teacher's two concerns were addressed. Most importantly, Patty knew that coaching points she made during their conversation had an impact on the teacher. The teacher's action plan is a record of the effectiveness of the coaching session. Patty will look for evidence that the teacher has acquired new skills (e.g., encouraging the children to hear and record sounds in unknown words) and conceptual understandings revealed in the action plan when she visits the teacher next week.

For both teacher and coach, reaching shared understandings depends on learning to be proficient at the practice of engaging in a coaching conversation; that is, to convey through words and actions what they are thinking and doing. The coach must learn ways to reach a teacher by being attuned to the particular characteristics and qualities of the teacher, learn how to read the teacher's potential and struggles revealed through practice, and discover what the teacher makes of this practice.

The teacher must learn how to listen, think about what the coach is saying and doing, and try to understand the coach's meaning conveyed through actions and words. I believe the coaching conversation between Patty and the teacher reflect this stance. How long will Patty be coaching for shifts in the teacher's practice? It is hard to tell, but over time they will move to another level of coaching—coaching for self-analysis and reflection.

COACHING FOR SELF-ANALYSIS AND REFLECTION

The last phase of the analytical model for coaching emerges when the coach and teacher are true collaborators in the coaching experience. By true collaborators, I mean that the stance they take is that only by working together will they be able to improve their practice. They become colleagues, engaging in collaborative problem solving and inquiry-oriented conversations. They begin to rely on and trust one another to provide support and skills they may need and that can be shared. Before one can reach this level, teachers have to learn how to be good analyzers of their own practice.

Working Alongside the Teacher

As teachers continue to learn more about procedures (e.g., the components of a guided reading and interactive writing lesson) instructional routines become automatic. They begin to discuss how to focus instruction to meet the changing needs and demands of a particular group of students. Examining student work and behaviors in relation to the reading and writing process revealed in the guided reading and interactive writing scale (see Lyons and Pinnell 2001) helps teachers to gain understandings about the strategies and approaches students bring to their learning. The teacher's ability to do this is contingent upon the kind of opportunities the coach provides during coaching conversations.

The coach's role is to switch between listening for understanding and adding to what the teacher is saying, to analyzing and inquiring to help the teacher become more analytical and explicit. Through the coaches' questions and probes, the teacher learns how to analyze, evaluate, explain, justify and determine the impact of teaching on students' learning. The following comments illustrate these points.

> I asked my coach to visit me working with a very low guided reading group. I had analyzed my videotaped lessons several times and tried several different approaches to reach Carlos, but did not see improvement. I was at a loss for what to do. After observing a lesson, my coach and I discussed what we saw. She asked me what the running records revealed about Carlos's processing and then to compare the running record with what he did and said during guided reading. There was a big mismatch. When she asked me why, I came up with one answer . . . he didn't use visual information. Then she asked me to think about as many explanations for Carlos's behavior as possible. I revisited the snippet of tape and thought of other possible reasons. I would not have asked myself those questions or analyzed how Carlos was responding to my teaching without the coach's input. I found our problem solving sessions the most critical and beneficial learning experience I have ever had because I was part of discovering possible solutions. I also understood the solution on my own terms, not by doing something someone else said was important.

The teacher's reflection shows that the coach's questions were meaningful. Questions probed the unknown and could not be immediately answered. They also stayed with the teacher long after the coaching conversation and were with her until answered. The coach had the following comments about the collaborative conversations she had with the teacher.

> I would not have known there was as big a problem without watching the lesson with the teacher and asking her possible rationales for the students' behaviors. In analyzing this lesson together, other problems emerged that needed to be resolved. The teacher had in-depth knowledge and skill teaching very low children how to read and still found difficulty teaching one child. As we picked each other's brains, possible solutions emerged. She learned how to observe, analyze, and monitor her behavior more closely. I learned that I have to encourage teachers to think more about *why* they are doing something, not what else can they try. What she taught me will be incorporated into my professional development classes.

These comments help us better understand the power of a coach working alongside the teacher. Both individuals learned because they both owned the problem, were part of the process of discovery, and owned the solution. The "ah-hah" they felt was a result of working together, not alone. As partners in learning, teacher and coach expect that by working together they both gain deeper understandings.

Developing Contexts for Collaborative Inquiry

While the preceding coaching conversation was collaborative, the coach's probes and questions facilitated the process. In creating collaborative communities, several teachers and the coach are colleagues. Members of the group are analytical and reflective and use each other's idiosyncratic expertise to focus on a common issue. They provide one another with additional possibilities for examples, hypotheses, and strategies. Group members' thinking is challenged and elaborated on as they explain to one another the sources and reasoning behind their hypothesis. When an answer is not known, they negotiate to find answers that satisfy the group.

Members of the group learn to move outside themselves and to listen attentively to the perspectives and thinking of others. This conversation is a mutual and dynamic exchange of ideas and concerns. No one has the "right" answer, there are many plausible explanations. It is in the context of collaborative inquiry that knowledge is constructed and personal and group meanings are created.

CONCLUSION

Coaching is an important and complex undertaking that has great potential to improve teachers' and students' learning. Research has demonstrated that coaching is effective when teachers develop conceptual understandings of the reading and writing process and how to engage students in powerful ways to learn how to learn (Lyons and Pinnell 2001).

The very act of coaching implies an interdependent relationship to the development of concepts. Understanding a concept requires complex thinking. It involves developing astute observation skills grounded in student and teacher behaviors, as well as the ability to analyze and critique those behaviors.

Developing conceptual understandings is not only an intellectual goal but also a social goal. When coaching is viewed as a cooperative partnership, teachers are willing to extend their understandings by adding the thinking and ideas of others. It is within the coaching context that teachers and coaches have an opportunity to develop mutual respect for each others' point of view and in the process, extend and elaborate their thinking and practice. The analytical model for coaching, described in this chapter, may provide the needed structure to begin the process.

8 | TEACHER RESEARCH AS PROFESSIONAL DEVELOPMENT
A Study of Teaching and Learning

Susan King Fullerton
Mary Perinis Quinn

As teachers, we want research to help us deal with the complexities of our work, with the daily interactions of teaching, and the changes that occur in children (Clay 1989). Teachers become *teacher-researchers* for the same reasons. As researchers, systematic observation of students and the study of practice informs our teaching (Downhower, Melvin, and Sizemore 1990). In addition, teacher research helps us to better understand, put into perspective, and evaluate the research of others (Milz 1989).

Research projects are typically developed in response to a problem or concern. Johnson (1993) suggests that teacher research is characterized by spiraling cycles of problem identification, data collection, reflection, analysis, data-driven action, and finally, redefining of the problem. Practice is studied as a means of increasing understanding of curriculum, teaching, and learning (McKay 1992). Reflecting on their own practice, as teachers of teachers, Roskos, Risko, and Vukelich (1998) suggest that rather than being prescribed, teacher practice must rest on the professional judgement, understanding, and caring of the teacher, "who must make sense of complex, localized situations" (232). Their statement provides a strong rationale for teacher research as a way to make sense of one's own teaching and learning environment.

In this way, teacher research becomes a form of self-study. Moreover, teacher research (Cochran-Smith and Lytle 1990; Goswami and Stillman 1987; Hubbard and Power 1993) is increasingly viewed as a powerful mechanism for professional development (Tierney et al. 1988) and for implementing school change (Downhower, Melvin, and Sizemore 1990; Goatley et al. 1994; Hoffman and Pearson 2000). Several critical factors gleaned from a number of studies help to explain how teacher research promotes professional development and change (see Figure 8–1).

We wish to thank Jean Frey, Judith Thompson, our teachers-as-researchers group, and the Greater Washington Reading Council for their support of our research.

These factors include

- teacher empowerment (Richardson 1994)
- teachers taking charge of their own professional development within a collaborative environment (see Tierney et al. 1988, as an example)
- increased teacher observation and reflection (Fullerton and Quinn 1996–1997)
- teachers as users or consumers of research (Downhower, et al. 1990)

Reciprocity of theory and practice is at the heart of professional development, as well as teacher research. Researchers at the University of Georgia and University of Maryland recognized this when they wrote the proposal for The National Reading Research Center: "When teachers engage in research, posing problems and examining their own work, there is inherently a bridge between theory and practice. Teacher inquiry develops ownership of the research questions, enhances the credibility of the findings, and fosters dissemination" (University of Georgia and University of Maryland 1991, 5). Within their proposal, there was a major emphasis on the study of teacher research and collaboration between university and school researchers. This endeavor was similar to work done in 1982 by Tierney and others (1988). They conducted a study documenting teacher and student learning and curricular changes through teacher research as a form of professional development. They found that teachers began to take ownership for their professional growth using a problem solving approach similar to that characterized by Johnson (1993).

Over a number of years, we, the authors of this chapter, took much responsibility for our professional growth as we worked together in collaborative roles as teachers, presenters, and writers for several years. In fact, our work as teacher-researchers was so important to us that when Susan, a Title I teacher, was asked to also become a staff development facilitator and was moved to a different school, Mary applied for a position there the following year. So did two other teachers who had been a part of our "teachers-as-researchers group." The contributions that we were making to each other's learning as a collective group were too important to give up.

We have since moved on to different roles, but teacher research has served many important purposes in our professional lives. In this chapter, we

FIGURE 8–1
How Teacher Research Promotes Professional Development

How Teacher Research Promotes Professional Development
• Teachers become empowered as they examine their own practice and look at the data that provides evidence of results.
• Through research, teachers take charge of their own learning because they are engaged in inquiry and theory building.
• Teachers increase their power to observe behavior and reflect on the process.
• Teachers learn about research because they are involved in it; in the process, they can more easily be consumers of research.

choose to focus primarily on the ways that teacher research became a tool for professional development and a means of increasing our pedagogical awareness. We viewed this increasing knowledge as a lens through which we could more skillfully observe the children we worked with and, in turn, improve our practice. A cycle of analysis and reflection mediated our understanding of theory and practice, influencing us to become curriculum creators and avid consumers of research. What follows is a description of change for ourselves and our students as we attempted to implement an in-class model of Title I instruction into a second-grade language arts classroom.

IDENTIFYING THE PROBLEM

We did not set out to be a team of researchers. We set out to be problem solvers and gradually became teacher-researchers. We had worked in the same school for a year. We came together, a classroom teacher (Mary) and a Title I teacher (Susan), because of our frustration with the pull-out model that our district had been using for many years. The district had developed several initiatives to support our school with its large "at-risk" population, but still, many children were reading below grade level. We made a list of our concerns about the pull-out program which we later found echoed the concerns of Allington (1994)—lack of communication and continuity, lost time, methods of instruction that do not connect or actually conflict, and labeling of students, resulting in poor self-concept. We shared them with the Title I coordinator. We were glad to hear that an alternative program of in-class instruction was under consideration as a pilot. We happily volunteered.

We decided not only to pilot the project but to research and evaluate the way we implemented changes. Neither of us had been teacher-researchers up until this point; but we knew that if we developed a model that worked, it would be important to have detailed information so that we could improve, refine, and share our results. We were fortunate that our district was supportive of teacher research and helped us connect to a regional network of teacher-researchers. The group provided us with a list of resources and books to help us begin.

Over the next three years, we conducted research on a number of aspects of literacy instruction. For example, when we started this collaboration, we had not considered using literature discussion groups with Title I students (Daniels 1994; Eeds and Wells 1989; O'Flahavan 1994/95; Raphael and McMahon 1994). Our attention to literature discussion developed from a need to balance all aspects of the language arts program. To ensure that these at-risk students developed into strategic readers, much time was spent on guided reading and one-to-one support, but we knew that these actions alone would not guarantee the development of lifelong readers. We were also concerned about providing a supportive literacy environment for the diverse needs of all our students, not just those in Title I.

In order to develop literate and engaged learners, we recognized that students needed opportunities for social interactions with other literacy learners. Through our own professional readings, we understood that in order for a learner to internalize a behavior, it must first occur on the social level, and then later, on the individual level (Vygotsky 1978). Initially, we viewed ourselves as having the primary responsibility for assuming a regulatory role so that the learners would eventually internalize particular behaviors, but what became clear from our research was that initially this was the case, but eventually more capable peers began to assume this role as well.

Our Questions

The first year of the study provided a broad foundation for our "wonderings" (Hubbard and Power 1993). In subsequent years, our questions changed and became more tightly focused, but initially, we framed our questions as "open-ended enough to allow possibilities the researcher hasn't imagined to emerge" (Hubbard and Power 1993, 5).

1. What tools (planning, communication, and evaluation) would be effective in implementing an in-class model of Title I instruction for language arts?
2. How would an in-class model and our collaboration influence our teaching of language arts?
3. How would we change as teachers through this collaboration?
4. How would the students change as readers as a result of the in-class model and our collaboration?

These questions helped us consider what was most beneficial in our teaching and student learning and to determine changes that occurred.

THE SCHOOL CONTEXT FOR THE IN-CLASS PILOT

As stated earlier, we piloted this in-class model in a second-grade classroom in a school that had a high percentage of free and reduced lunch participants. Because of the large number of at-risk students in first and second grades, the district had implemented a reduced ratio program so there were seventeen students in this language arts classroom, eight students were receiving Title I service and two were second language learners. In fact, even more students were reading below grade level. The range included non-readers (based on inability to pass the lowest level assessment) as well as a number of students reading at a beginning to mid- first-grade level. In addition, even those students who demonstrated strong decoding skills evidenced poor comprehension on the assessments.

Since our project was a pilot, we had no blueprint for how the model should look or what would work. Periodically, during the first year, we met with two or three other teaching teams who were also piloting the model. We learned that each implementation looked somewhat different because of each classroom's and school's particular needs.

EVALUATING THE EFFECTIVENESS OF OUR TOOLS

Looking back, we recognize that the most critical aspects of our collaboration were planning, communication, and evaluation (see Figure 8–2).

Planning not only promoted efficiency and consistency in structuring what we would do, but it gave us time to discuss what we were observing and helped us evaluate the organization of the language arts sessions, our teaching, and student learning.

Planning and Communication

We began planning in the summer before the start of the school year so that we could get a better idea of our philosophies and approaches to teaching language arts. Fortunately, our views were compatible. We began to develop a plan that we eventually referred to as a conceptual framework and as the year continued, this framework became our map in terms of learning content or what Pappas, Kiefer, and Levstik (1990) refer to as an "integrated language classroom." As we examined our district's curriculum or "Program of Studies," we realized that science emphases on animals, insects, life cycles, and social studies content such as communities might allow us to integrate these areas within language arts and coordinate them across a conceptual framework of "Changes." (See Figure 8–3 for an abbreviated version of the framework.)

Thus, this focus became a flexible guide that dovetailed with the required curriculum, yet allowed us to more creatively connect thematically across many areas of learning as we drew upon a variety of sources within children's literature, content texts, and professional articles and books.

We kept a dialogue journal that we shared back and forth to communicate. We also used this journal to keep our notes from planning, teacher research meetings, and our anecdotal records and field notes. We planned briefly (for approximately 15–30 minutes) on a daily basis using lunch periods, planning periods, or after school. Our weekly planning (of at least an

---

Critical Aspects of Collaboration

Planning and Collaboration

- Developing a conceptual framework.
- Using a "road map" of concepts.
- Engaging in dialogue—oral and written.
- Holding weekly planning sessions.

Evaluation

- Engaging in ongoing evaluation to inform the process.
- Engaging in summative evaluation to draw conclusions.
- Using effective tools.
- Redefining problems as results are discerned.

FIGURE 8–2
Critical Aspects of
Collaboration

hour or two) provided an opportunity to examine running records, anecdotal notes/field notes, work products, and assessments that were used the previous week to make decisions about how to support these learners during the upcoming week. Often, we used part of our district's designated early closing period (at 1:00 p.m. on Mondays) or after contract hours, to plan. We also established a period of approximately two hours monthly to focus on long-range planning. During this time we examined our program of studies, revisited and added to our conceptual framework, and reconceptualized how we might work with students individually and in groups based on their literacy progress over the previous month. Early in the year, as we were learning to work together, more time was required.

The time frames mentioned here evolved gradually, but early on in the fall, we recognized that ongoing evaluation of what we were doing and how students were learning would be the key to the model's success and that regular communication was required. The time commitments are approximations and may not adequately reflect all communication. Incidental communication also occurred as we talked over lunch, at meetings (espe-

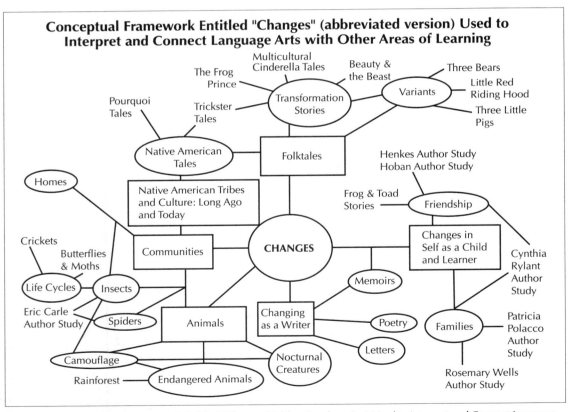

Conceptual Framework Entitled "Changes" (abbreviated version) Used to Interpret and Connect Language Arts with Other Areas of Learning

FIGURE 8–3 *Conceptual Framework Entitled "Changes" (abbreviated version) Used to Interpret and Connect Language Arts with Other Areas of Learning*

cially teacher research meetings), and over the phone. This allotment also does not reflect time spent individually reflecting on student work and assessments, on journal entries, and reading research and professional articles. We suspect that we spent more time than was required, but our engagement and commitment to the project was increased because we valued the model we were implementing, and we were intrigued by what we were experiencing in terms of student growth and our own learning.

Evaluation

We agree with Butler and Turbill (1984, 85) that evaluation is an "inherently continuous part of every classroom activity." Each of our planning sessions supported the spiraling cycle that Johnson (1993) refers to. The following are tools that we used for rereading, reflecting, and analyzing:

- journal entries (Susan's and Mary's)
- anecdotal records
- field notes
- running records
- students' response journals
- transcriptions of audiotapes or notes
- student writing
- classroom artifacts and work products (graphic organizers, webs, cooperative learning projects, etc.)

Through these data sources, we redefined problems (or what we characterized as areas of strength and need) and cycled back through data collection, then further analysis and reflection in concert, and followed up with adjustments in our plans and instructional framework that resulted in data-driven action (Johnson 1993).

THE INFLUENCE OF TEACHER RESEARCH, THE IN-CLASS MODEL, AND COLLABORATION

Very quickly in the fall, we became aware of how effective and efficient it was for students to receive all their language arts instruction in the classroom rather than being pulled out. There was no longer a need for Mary to help students catch up on what had been missed during pull-out time. Since we were planning together and working as a team, there was no need to supplement the classroom curriculum. Now there was one cohesive curriculum! Susan did not have to mesh curricular needs from two or three classrooms from which she was taking students. As a result, we had more instructional time, improved monitoring of student progress, increased and immediate interaction that resulted in strengths and areas of need being more readily identified, and enhanced communication between classroom and Title I teachers. In addition, time was saved because all assessments were coordinated and shared. We worked together as a team to assess students using running records, informal reading inventories, writing rubrics, checklists and other assessments, and there was no longer an overlap of assessments or time spent repeating similar tasks in two settings.

Our learning as individuals was also expanded. Mary had had little experience with running records and became quite skilled in their use. Our theoretical knowledge and teaching repertoires were enriched and strengthened by our research and collaboration. Mary's knowledge of cooperative learning was put to the test with so many Title I students, but Susan learned from Mary's skillful approach to organizing learners.

We each came to value the modeling that was done incidentally. One of us would comment aloud that we valued an idea that was expressed by the other, and we began to see students respond in similar complementary and respectful ways. Without our researcher's lens, we may have overlooked such incidental, yet important learning behaviors, but because we took field notes regularly, we captured changes in responses—both in students and in each other. After read-alouds, one of us might express ideas about a character or book, and the other might agree or disagree. Students picked up on this and began to preface comments with—"I agree with you" or "I have to challenge that idea . . . ." We began to see this internalization of our language as a tool that could be used more intentionally in instruction.

Two other benefits of the model were the absence of labeling and heterogeneous grouping. The Title I students were not isolated from their peers and benefited from more proficient reading models. Interestingly, though students were grouped for guided reading instruction based on reading level and specific individuals were worked with individually, none of the students seemed to question Susan's role. Based on our observations, as well as student interviews, they viewed her as everyone's teacher. No one was identified as qualifying for Title I. Data collected across the year provided evidence of this lack of labeling and suggested that heterogeneous grouping, cooperative grouping, and the camaraderie that developed between us as teachers seemed to positively influence the building of community within the classroom.

Our data also suggested that a factor in student success was the flexible organizational structure that we incorporated throughout the year. This means that we used many of the same instructional elements in the language arts program, but we did not necessarily continue with the same weekly or year-long schedule. As the year went on, organization of instruction changed because the students had changed. We no longer had eight students reading below grade level, so there was less need for working one-to-one, and we could then give more attention to other learning contexts such as literature discussion and cooperative groupings.

Most teachers think carefully about time and organization of the day, but may not give the same attention to how they group students. A colleague, Elizabeth Fasulo, who had studied her own grouping practices

(Fasulo, personal communication, February 1, 1994) shared with us a monitoring matrix (see Figure 8–4) that we adapted to help us evaluate the attention we were giving to whole group, small group, pairs, and individual instruction.

We realized that with so many at-risk students, it was unlikely that we would be able to meet their needs in whole group instruction alone. Initially, we recorded our time allocations on the matrix, which also helped us determine that, at first, we were not providing enough familiar and independent reading time to promote fluency. We recognized that the matrix and time allocations should reflect our belief that students must be given ample time to practice developing strategies (Allington 1994). Attending carefully to the organization and regularly analyzing whether students were being given ample time to practice reading and writing was instrumental to learners' progress.

Grouping Matrix for One Week				
	Whole Group	*Small Group*	*Pairs*	*Individual*
Monday	MM ML Read Aloud SR—Big Book	GR LD	PR	FR DEAR JW
Tuesday	MM ML SR—poem SR—Big Book Read Aloud	GR LD	PR SC	FR DEAR JW
Wednesday	MM SR—poem Read Aloud	IW CG—web GR	R/W	FR DEAR JW
Thursday	MM SW—poem Read Aloud	FL LD	Partner edit drafts PR	FR DEAR R/W
Friday	MM Read Aloud Shared Reading	CG–Venn Diagram GR	PR CC	FR DEAR R/W

Key

CC—Computer Center	JW—Journal Writing	PW—Partner Writing
CG—Cooperative Groups	LC—Listening Center	R/W—Reading/Writing Conference
DEAR—Drop Everything and Read	LD—Literature Discussion Gr.	SC—Spelling Center
FR—Familiar Reading	ML—Minilesson	SR—Shared Reading
GR—Guided Reading	MM—Morning Message	SW—Shared Writing
IW—Interactive Writing	PR—Partner Reading	

FIGURE 8–4 *Grouping Matrix for One Week*

Carefully observing the students and evaluating our management scheme helped us to recognize that early in the year, it was appropriate for us to spend time in whole group discussing routines for individual or paired work such as centers, partner reading, and individual reading, then observing students as they implemented these routines to get them established early and well.

Afterward, we began to incorporate morning message, shared reading, interactive writing, process writing, and guided reading. Figure 8–5 provides an example of this organization. Fairly early, cooperative grouping began, and after ten weeks, we introduced literature discussion groups for some students and gradually incorporated their use with all learners (see Figure 8–6).

CHANGING AS PROFESSIONALS

At the end of that first year of working together, we decided to respond separately in written form to answer the question of how teacher research and this collaborative effort changed us. We then combined responses that were similar in focus and looked back in our journals for corroborating comments and evidence. The following is a summary of our key points.

Responses on Change from Mary and Susan

What follows are reports on changes that we mutually experienced.

Increased Willingness to Implement New Ideas

We both implemented new aspects to our teaching repertoire and organizational framework. For example, we increased our use of cooperative groups, and other groupings became more heterogeneous, or in the case of guided

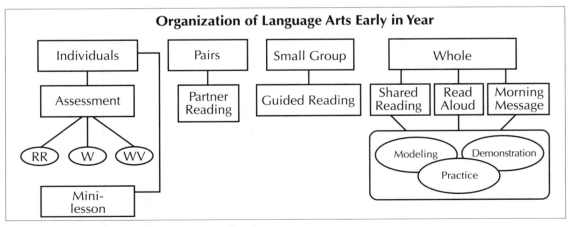

FIGURE 8–5   *Organization of Language Arts Early in Year*

reading, more flexible. For the first time, we incorporated literature discussion groups as an important part of the language arts program.

Changes in Orientation/Philosophy

We developed a more constructivist, process oriented, student-centered classroom. More instructional time was allocated for student reading, read-alouds, whole group and small group discussions, the study of literary techniques and genres, cooperative group projects, and written responses to literature. We no longer spent time on superfluous and unrelated presentations or work products that were cute or showy.

More Time Given to Teacher Reflection and Analysis

Through anecdotal records and field notes, our dialogue journal, and direct communication with each other, we constantly discussed, evaluated, and reflected on our teaching and student learning.

Expanded Knowledge Base

We became more knowledgeable about literature, authors, and students' abilities to analyze and respond to literature. After our first attempt, we have a better understanding of how our own research can inform our teaching. Through our development of the conceptual framework, "Changes," we

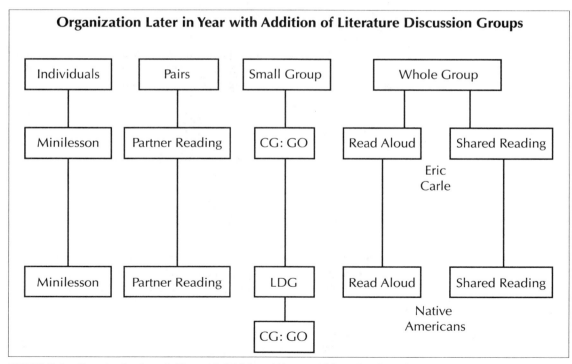

FIGURE 8–6   *Organization Later in Year with Addition of Literature Discussion Groups*

developed innovative ways of integrating across curricular areas and our district's program of studies. In addition, this framework seemed to help students see relationships across ideas and between areas of the curriculum.

Increased Risk Taking

We supported each other's efforts and applauded or commiserated with all attempts. We knew that we had much to gain by trying new things and learning from each other. We developed strong trust and knew that we could count on the other's feedback about our teaching and instructional concerns.

Responses on Change Unique to Mary

Mary had her own unique insights, which resulted in change. These follow.

Enhanced Opportunities for Observation of a Peer

All of us have a desire to see how other teachers approach teaching and learning, but we get few opportunities to observe others in action. Susan, as the Title I teacher, presented new instructional strategies and assessment tools that were unfamiliar to me. Especially in the beginning, she modeled techniques and strategies for me. As time passed, this became unnecessary because I had incorporated them as well.

Less Need for Teacher Control Within the Learning Environment

Much time was spent early on establishing routines and supporting students as they learned to work together in cooperative groups, small groups such as guided reading, interest groups, pairs, and as individuals (during writing, sustained silent reading, or centers). Our observations and data helped us determine that students were capable of independence and control of their learning with guidance and support—so our goal became moving from a stance of primarily teacher-controlled activity to much more community and student-centered learning.

Responses on Change Unique to Susan

As well, Susan experienced changes unique to her own learning. Examples follow.

Stronger Motivation to Seek Out New Ideas

As a result of our collaboration and having a partner to talk with, we gave even greater attention to professional reading and there was an increased desire to bring new ideas and research into the classroom. We were constantly supporting our collaborative efforts through increased knowledge.

Shift in Attitude

While I did not view the Title I students from a deficit perspective, neither was I giving them enough credit. I learned a great deal from the other children—Title I students were viewed differently than in previous years.

Their peers did not know who they were, and we began to see them through new eyes. We were at first surprised and eventually impressed with their capabilities and contributions. I began to recognize how important it was for "low-performing" children (based on one testing situation) to be a part of a community of learners rather than pull-out program students. Such an environment provided much stronger opportunities for them to display the strengths that they had but may not have shown in a pull-out setting.

Perspective on Teacher Research (not a part of the original list, but added later)

Coming from doctoral training and primarily a quantitative approach to research, I began teacher research with skepticism. In short, I had little understanding of its purpose or utility. That changed as I began to read a variety of texts, first Mohr and Maclean (1987), then Cochran-Smith and Lytle (1993), Hubbard and Power (1993), Patterson et al. (1993), and the list continued that year and every year after. Only a few months into this endeavor, I recognized this research as a bridge to connect my interest in theory and research with the practice of teaching that I returned to after my doctoral program.

CHANGES IN LEARNERS

It is hard to adequately capture the spirit of learning that was a part of this classroom, but anyone who spent even a brief amount of time observing recognized that this was an enthusiastic, independent group of learners. The following descriptors attempt to summarize the primary areas of growth and change that occurred within the learners.

Peer Instructors

Through observation of teacher modeling and coaching within whole group, guided reading, and individual instruction, these learners began to coach each other when working together in groups or pairs. One of the most satisfying observations was seeing Jesse, a second language learner who was the only student who had received Title I the previous year and was not quite on grade level, coaching partners who were reading at a higher level (perhaps decoding might be a more appropriate term). Our intent was to pair him with a stronger reader, but we saw that in many ways he was the more strategic reader and prompted partners appropriately to monitor or problem-solve. Through observations and a variety of assessment tools, we saw steady gains in strategic processing for all students.

Improved Readers

As just stated, all students in the classroom became better readers, but the gains were most substantial for the eight Title I students. At the end of the year, six of the students were on or above grade level and no longer qualified for Title I services. The remaining two students also made gains, but were still reading below grade level. The following year, both students were referred by their third-grade teachers and eventually placed in special education.

Literature Enthusiasts

This aspect of change was the most pleasing to us. We knew that our efforts in working with the at-risk learners could help them read and write on grade level, but that we would only achieve success if they freely chose to read and write. Many of the changes in our teaching and organizational framework revolved around stronger incorporation and discussion of literature. As a result of this emphasis, coupled with strong doses of guided reading, our students were able to read independently, enjoyed reading, and were able to make appropriate book choices. They frequently requested more time to read and were upset when time was interrupted or decreased. Most importantly, they responded to and began to critically evaluate literature.

Advanced readers served as role models for others in terms of the books they were reading, and often the Title I students figured out ways to read these books, too. We learned from Donika that it is important to help all readers find ways to read books that interest them, even when the book might be challenging. Donika approached the table before guided reading and asked to read *Ira Sleeps Over*. Since I viewed the book as too difficult for her, I offered to read it to her during DEAR (Drop Everything and Read) time. The next day, when I returned to the classroom, Donika asked to hear it again, and on this day, we arranged for a partner to read it to her. Similar scenarios occurred across a number of days until one day, when I entered the room, Donika announced she had something to show me. She took me over to the table and proceeded to read *Ira Sleeps Over* to me with success and great pride. Why this book was so important remains a mystery, but it is clear that this book piqued her interest. Whether it was the story itself or a desire to be like her peers, Donika was motivated to accomplish the task and greatly enjoyed discussions of the book with her friends. This event became a turning point for Donika, changing her self-perceptions as a learner. It was also a turning point for us. Prior to this experience, we often had more advanced readers participating in literature discussions while the less proficient readers worked with one of us for guided reading. After we learned from Donika, we found ways to use DEAR time, paired reading, older buddy readers, parents, and the listening center so that all of the students had opportunities to participate in literature discussions.

As the year progressed, the influence of good literature became increasingly apparent. Book language began to appear in students' writing. Students attempted to imitate genres (such as mysteries), authors, and styles of writing. They relished book talks and discussions. They learned to challenge each other's ideas using the text as a reference. As discussants, they began to demonstrate the ability to analyze the author's craft, noting repetition of language, colorful descriptions and passages, illustrations, and connections to author's lives and experiences. In addition, they identified genres and made connections to other pieces of literature, including folklore and the Bible, as well as drawing upon experiences from outside school. We did not see indicators of these types of responses at the beginning of the year, but our data indicated increasing growth in the quantity and quality of responses.

Group Leaders and Participants

As the year continued, instructional time was more frequently used for collaborative activities. As students became more proficient readers, the time needed for one-to-one reading instruction and assessments decreased. Early in the year, we began to give students responsibility for cooperative roles or jobs. These roles were frequently reviewed and practiced. Gradually, students demonstrated their ability to take on a variety of roles and responsibilities. For example, throughout the day, table captains managed their table areas, keeping materials organized and their group talk within a quiet range. The table groups were organized thoughtfully and balanced in terms of gender, ethnicity, ability, and leadership qualities. Often, instruction was then organized so that these table groups could work cooperatively. As an example, science or social studies related nonfiction was incorporated into shared reading and students then worked together to create graphic organizers or webs as they interacted in roles such as manager, recorder, editor, and presenter. They worked similarly in their literature discussion groups, taking responsibility for developing and discussing thoughtful questions and conversing about books.

TEACHER RESEARCH AS PROFESSIONAL DEVELOPMENT

Professional development has been regularly criticized for its lack of continuity, its lack of connection to the daily work of teachers, and for reinforcing current practice rather than changing practice. It is regarded as something teachers *do* or that is provided *for* them in the form of activities or workshops (Little 1996)—a "top-down model of knowledge construction" (Check 1997, 8). Counter to these representations, Darling-Hammond states:

> Research says that professional development has to be directly connected to daily work with students, related to content areas, organized around real problems of practice, . . . continuous and ongoing, and able to provide teachers with access to outside resources and expertise. Professional development should take place within a professional community, a team or network, or both. (in Lewis 1997, 4)

Therefore, it seems that schools organized for teacher learning would provide for the systematic study of teaching and learning (Little 1996). Teacher research represents one form of learning that fits the professional development needs just mentioned. It is an outcome of "real problems of practice." At its foundation is the recognition of a question or problem—each teacher is approaching the inquiry from a problem-solving perspective, examining how things can change and improve.

One of the primary goals of professional development is change—change in teacher knowledge, change in instruction, change in student learning, and eventual change in school and district progress. Teacher research is "a powerful, teacher-centered, democratic and pragmatic force for reforming our schools" (Check 1997, 8). We would add that it is also an avenue for developing professionals who view themselves as efficacious problem solvers and change agents. Increasingly, teacher research is recognized and characterized as a valuable source of professional development (AERA's 1996 interactive symposium serves as one example), but there is much learning to be done in order for there to be widespread support for such innovation. We were fortunate to have a district facilitator and a school administrator who supported our work by providing classroom coverage so that we could meet once a quarter during the instructional day rather than always on our own time after school. These individuals encouraged us to present research at school and district meetings, then later at regional, state, and national conferences, often providing small amounts of funds to aid us, but more important than the financial support was the demonstration of collegial confidence in our research.

Someone once suggested to us at a conference that our results suggest a Hawthorne effect. To a certain extent, we would agree, but there is a critical difference. Unlike researchers that come in for a period of time, study the classroom, then leave, teacher-researchers stay in the environment, but the novelty effect doesn't wear off—there is always a new question, a new problem to solve, a new area of wondering or inquiry to investigate, so learning never ends.

9 | OLD ROADS AND NEW PATHS
What Happens When Two Teachers Attempt an Alternative Teaching Strategy Within a Peer Collaborative Relationship

ADRIAN RODGERS

A BRIEF INTRODUCTION TO THE COLLABORATORS

Too often at the secondary level, English instruction can take the "stand and deliver" approach. As a secondary English teacher, I was happiest with some of the extra-curricular approaches that I undertook with an after-school drama club, but I struggled with infusing instructional alternatives into my day-to-day classes. I undertook doctoral studies to help me think more about how professional development could support teachers in taking initial interests in alternative teaching pedagogies and developing them into class-room practices that could work. Change is complex and hard to tackle alone. Too often, teachers find themselves in lonely boxes, attempting, with the best of intentions, to improve practice. It has occurred to many of us, as teachers and students of professional development, that having companions along the way makes change seem easier—even adventuresome. In this chapter, I describe such a partnership.

Shortly after I began my doctoral studies, I met David Kleinman. Dave was a veteran school teacher and adjunct lecturer at the university. He was also a part-time doctoral student and worked as a coach of other teachers in a professional development program. Dave also traveled to national conferences sponsored by the Coalition of Essential Schools and worked on building a team of teachers who attempted to implement the Coalition Principles at his school. In short, I saw Dave as a dedicated professional who had been a leader in his school's reform efforts and a person whom I had come to know, not only professionally, but also personally.

Knowing such a competent professional raised a number of new possibilities regarding professional development. It occurred to me that Dave and I might be able to work together, building on each other's strengths and forging a form of professional development by relying on collaborative lesson planning and teaching. By pairing the expertise of one person's instructional repertoire with the classroom knowledge of another, Dave and I saw the opportunity to realize instructional change. I was excited about our partnership, both because it gave me an opportunity to explore alternative instructional strategies, and because collaborative professional development would have important implications for reform and for in-service teacher education. Instead of bringing teachers together for day-long workshops in large groups, maybe it would be more powerful to pair master teachers with other novice teachers for varying lengths of time so that they could help each other develop as professionals. I was also excited about the opportunity to confront the challenges of such a model firsthand, and to explore the veracity of such a model.

EXPLORING QUESTIONS IN THE RESEARCH LITERATURE

During the time that Dave and I were teaching university courses together, we became acutely aware of an increasingly vocal movement calling for school reform. The political mantra of better test scores, reading guarantees, and more accountability, while important, didn't really help us to do a better job teaching Monday morning's lesson. I found the National Commission on Teaching and America's Future's (NCTAF) publication *What Matters Most: Teaching for America's Future* (1996, vi) to be especially helpful in crystallizing some of the concerns of critics of American education. In addition to painting a picture of educational shortcomings, the NCTAF document also offered a blueprint for reform claiming that "what teachers know and can do is the most important influence" on what students can learn. I also found the writings of the Holmes Group (1986, 3) to be helpful in thinking about educational change. The Holmes Group, a consortium of large American colleges of education with a reform orientation, has published literature claiming, "America's dissatisfaction with its schools has become chronic and epidemic. Teachers have long been at the center of the debates, and they still are today." In fact, the Holmes Group reports that teachers are often the "butt of most criticism" in the talk regarding educational reform, explaining that "paradoxically," although teachers are often the target of criticism, they are also "singled out as the one best hope for reform." There were lots of things that I did not like about these reports, but what I did like was their emphasis on the role of the teacher.

A number of scholars have suggested specific ways for professional developers to work with teachers. Little (1987) and Maeroff (1993) call for us to reinvent professional development by having teachers work together more closely. As the model for reinvention, Little emphasizes closer working relationships that involve collaboration on curriculum and instructional development. For Richardson and Anders (1994), Calhoun (1994), and Atwell (1991), the reinvention of professional development can best be accomplished through establishing collegial relationships that withstand the test of time. Richardson and Anders (1994) believe that these relationships over a substantial time period support teachers in examining their own and others' practices and premises and serve as the key factor leading to significant educational reform. Action research, for example, can be used to support teachers in becoming lifelong learners (Calhoun 1994). Calhoun also believes that the combination of active inquiry conducted over a protracted time period brings about an "essential component of school renewal . . . an orientation to work that means we are willing to accept the discomfort and joy of never finishing our education, of never graduating from our study of teaching." Finally, English educator and classroom teacher Atwell (1991) affirms Calhoun's belief that reform might occur if teachers can become lifelong learners. She explains that when teachers can act as "scholars, closely reading [and] heatedly debating, . . . schools become more thoughtful places" (3).

These scholars are recent contributors to a professional conversation that asks how classroom-embedded professional development can be fostered. Research in peer coaching (Joyce and Showers 1980, 1988), teacher reasoning (Lyons, Pinnell, and DeFord 1993), Wasley, Hampel, and Clark's (1997) "kid's voices" in reform-oriented schools, and the Holmes Group's (1986) emphasis on Professional Development Schools (PDS) are all a part of the now burgeoning literature arguing that large-scale reform initiatives in the area of professional development must be contextualized within schools, and in some cases, within individual and small groups of teachers in their classrooms (see Figure 9–1).

Indeed, Zimpher and Howey (1992) conclude that the characteristics of the new, nontraditional professional development initiatives include teachers

---

Characteristics of Nontraditional Professional Development for Teachers

- Is contextualized within schools
- Is embodied in classrooms
- Includes teachers and students as main voices in reform
- Includes pedagogical and curricular elements
- Includes a variety of strategies such as modeling, coaching, practice, and feedback
- Rests on critical dialogue in classroom settings

FIGURE 9–1
Characteristics of Nontraditional Professional Development for Teachers

and students as the main voices in the reform. Additionally, the nontraditional approach includes pedagogical and curricular elements, engagement over time, and a variety of strategies. In conclusion, the sum total of the literature on collaborative professional development specifically suggests that critical dialogue in classroom settings over time is a very powerful tool for reforming teaching practices. This tool for reform can be further supported with the modeling of instructional techniques that provide opportunities for practice and feedback. These are approaches that teachers cannot do by themselves and that require the support of their colleagues.

These increased calls for educational reform generally are resulting in significant pressures on literacy teachers to change their teaching practices. More potent ways of addressing initial teacher preparation would help, but since most teachers have been teaching for a few years, continuing professional development holds even greater promise for fostering educational change. Also, changing the professional development of in-service teachers offers great promise because alternative educational approaches can be attempted within the classroom context. Contextualized approaches to reform have the possibility of being more successful than the one-size-fits-all approach that is typically offered in a one-day in-service-type workshop.

USING PROFESSIONAL DEVELOPMENT AS A VEHICLE TO ACCOMPLISH CHANGE

With these trends in mind, I was interested in exploring changes in school teaching practices and at the same time examining how changes fit within the framework of educational reform. The National Commission on Teaching and America's Future (NCTAF 1996) explains that the "historical view of professional development" has viewed "professional knowledge" as something "developed by 'experts' who hand it down to teachers." In this traditional view, professional development is viewed as the "delivering [of] simple recipes to teachers working in isolation" (42). Historically, professional development has too often been unconnected to students or teaching and was not supported by groups of teachers approaching problems collaboratively. I liked the idea of working with Dave collaboratively as a way to think about our classroom teaching. In doing so, it might be a way to embrace a different vision of thinking about the kind of professional knowledge that the National Commission (NCTAF 1996, 42–3) talks about:

> These new approaches connect teachers to one another through in-school teams and cross-school professional communities that tackle problems of practice over time. Though different in some respects, all of these approaches share certain features. They are:
>
> - connected to teachers' work with their students
> - linked to concrete tasks of teaching

- organized around problem solving
- informed by research
- sustained over time by ongoing conversations and coaching

In Figure 9–2, I summarize these contrasting views.

EXPLORING RESEARCH QUESTIONS IN A COLLABORATIVE RELATIONSHIP

Dave and I liked that we were trying to think of how we were a part of a different way of thinking about changing our teaching practices; and in a very small way, I liked to think that we were a part of what Fullan (1993) called the "reculturing" of approaches to reforming instructional practices. I felt that the study that Dave and I undertook very much fulfilled the new kind of approach that the NCTAF report talks about. Dave and I examined what occurs when two English teachers

- work in close collaboration
- work over a long period
- use new strategies
- implement a research-oriented focus on our teaching
- maintain ongoing professional development initiatives
- work in a challenging urban school context

With our collaborative relationship in mind, we tried to think of what we needed to learn about our teaching and what would be helpful to report to others about our process. Dave and I agreed to implement a collaborative and peer-supported professional development initiative to investigate our teaching. We would collaborate to plan lessons and at the same time examine the processes in which we participated. Specifically, we wanted to know what happens to lesson planning when two teachers attempt an alternative teaching strategy within the collaborative relationship of peers.

Contrasting Views of Professional Development		
Traditional Views		*New Views*
• Developed by experts	*versus*	Based on research
• Experts hand down professional knowledge to teachers	*versus*	Professional development connected to the work of teachers and students
• Teachers receive recipes	*versus*	Professional development centered on real problems
• Teachers work alone	*versus*	Groups approach problems collaboratively
• Historical culture	*versus*	Reculturing approaches

FIGURE 9–2
Contrasting Views of Professional Development

IMPLEMENTING THE RESEARCH PLAN

Our research plan unfolded through our initial conversations. Dave was a high school classroom teacher; I acted as a researcher and teacher.

Once Dave and I had agreed to collaborate so that we could gain insights into our teaching, we thought a little more about what we would do and how we would do it. In order to understand what alternative teaching methods we would use, we first needed to understand the traditional approaches Dave used in his teaching.

Examining Traditional Instruction

When I worked with Dave in my teacher role, I used a case study approach that employed a "participant-observer" perspective on action research (Patton 1990). We wanted to have a sense of the traditional approaches that Dave used, so that we could place the alternative approach that we wanted to use in perspective.

Participant-Observer Roles

During the parts of lessons based on traditional approaches, I worked as an observer only and Dave was the participant. When we tried an alternative instructional approach, we adopted Glesne and Peshkin's (1992) view that we did not have to act as either participants or observers. Instead, we could both act as observers and as participants, moving back and forth on a continuum of possibilities. That is, taking turns, each of us might be more participant than observer at some point in time, and more observer than participant at others. At times, Dave and I entered both participant and observer roles simultaneously.

Data for the Study

The school instructional plan worked on a two-hour block schedule, trimester format. As a result, we met with the class two hours every afternoon for sixty-five consecutive weekdays during the fall. Data for the study are summarized in Figure 9–3.

FIGURE 9–3
Data for the Study

Data for the Study

- Class meetings recorded on videotape for sixty-five consecutive weekdays
- Transcriptions of selected excerpts from videotapes
- Audiotapes of weekly teacher planning sessions
- Audiotapes of daily fifteen-minute debriefing sessions after each of sixty-five classes
- Assignments and students' written responses
- Printed material available in the school (e.g., textbooks, handbooks)

I videotaped all of the class meetings and transcribed selected excerpts from those videotapes. I also audiotaped the weekly planning sessions when Dave and I planned our lessons, as well as the daily fifteen-minute debriefing sessions held after each class. In addition, I studied printed material that was available at the school (for example, the textbook and the handbooks for both the teachers and the students). Finally, I copied all assignments and the students' responses to the assignments. The result was a large data set, enabling me to look for trends both within each type of data and between different types of data.

Analysis of Data

The nature of the data sources dictated my focus of analysis. For example, when I analyzed transcriptions of Dave's and my reflective sessions, I focused on different ideas, issues, and characteristics than when I analyzed classroom lessons. Once I decided on a focus of analysis for each data source, I needed to develop a system of data organization. Since I was interested in looking at lesson planning, lesson implementation, and reflection on the lessons over a period of time, I arranged all of my data in chronological order. Instead of keeping all videotapes of classes together, I placed the tapes, transcripts, and logs for the first week of field visits together. I then undertook the same process for subsequent weeks of the study.

As an additional step in the segmenting of the data, I examined each planning and class session and then considered each sub-event of the unit planning and teaching. By *event*, I mean a planning session or a class that Dave taught (see Figure 9–4).

By *sub-event*, I mean parts of the planning session such as discussion of the literature to be taught or the writing assignment to be undertaken. Likewise, sub-events could include the parts of a lesson that were taught. It was helpful to organize my data in this way because it meant that I had the capability to look only at a particular kind of session, such as a planning session, or to look at all of the different kinds of sessions that, when added together, became a unit of instruction. After I sorted my data, I undertook further analytic choices including coding and looking for patterns (Miles and Huberman 1984). This kind of sorting allowed me to more easily use different data sources to add veracity to my findings.

Context for the Study

Dave taught at a school that I will call Midwest High School, and that's where I gathered the data. I gathered data about the school from statistics and interviews. According to statistics provided by the school's enrollment

Segmentation of Data	
Event:	A planning session or class lesson
Sub-event:	Parts of the planning session or class lesson

FIGURE 9–4
Segmentation of Data

office, eighty-five percent of the students at the school are African American, ten percent of the students at the school are of Southeast Asian descent, and the remaining students are of European descent who are a part of a larger Appalachian community near the school. Midwest High School has a student enrollment of over 1,400 and a teaching staff of eighty, including ten English teachers. The school, one of over a dozen high schools in the city's public school system, seeks to offer a comprehensive program of studies to the students who attend.

The English department offers only four English courses:

- Grade 9 English
- Grade 10 English
- Grade 11 English
- Grade 12 English

Each course includes a college-bound or challenge track and a regular track. Although Midwest High School is located outside the expressway that loops the city, the teachers and students called it an inner-city school.

The staff, the school, and the district are involved in a large number of professional development and reform activities. During the past five years, they have been active participants in the Coalition of Essential Schools (Sizer 1992). The Coalition is a network of teachers in a few hundred schools who are in the process of reconceptualizing their instruction. Rather than proposing a particular model of reform, the Coalition is based on nine common principles that can be adapted to a particular school's context. These principles include a focus "on helping adolescents use their minds," setting simple and universal goals that can be personalized to each student, emphasizing that the student is a worker, issuing a diploma based on a student's exhibition of her or his work, creating a school with an attitude that expresses high expectations of student work, building a staff with a sense of commitment to the students and the school, and budgeting issues that support reduced student loads per teacher and "substantial time for collective planning by teachers" (Wasley, Hampel, and Clark 1997, 217–19).

In addition to the reform-oriented approaches undertaken by the school's staff, Midwest High School also operates as a Professional Development Site (PDS) in collaboration with a nearby College of Education, affiliated with a research university.

The net effect of the large number of reform initiatives at the school would seem to place Midwest High School at the forefront of educational reform in its district. Yet, in spite of these initiatives, a number of elements necessary for reform were noticeably absent. For example, although the teachers told me that almost all of the students in most of their classes were not college bound and that they "just wanted the kids to keep reading books," they delivered their curriculum from an anthology that seemed more appropriate for college-bound students. Indeed, in spite of the project's focus on developing a curriculum for block scheduling, it seemed as though the curriculum had not changed very much at all.

Dave and I would come to negotiate in very different ways the seemingly inherited traditions of the English program.

Examining Dave's Traditional Instruction Approach

One of the first of our difficulties was Dave's last-minute assignment to teach a Grade 12 class. Although he had requested a Grade 12 teaching assignment, Dave had taught only the Grade 9 English course for the previous twenty years. A Grade 12 English class became available on the Friday before the first day of school. Dave had sufficient seniority to turn the class down, but after so many years of requesting the Grade 12 class, Dave perceived this opportunity as important for subsequent years. I had taught some of the Grade 12 material recently, and the assignment to a new course seemed to complement our desire to try new and alternative instructional approaches. Although Dave felt some awkwardness about my working with him in developing lessons for a new grade and curriculum, he welcomed my familiarity with some of the literary selections. However, even with my previous knowledge of the literature (a silver lining), Dave and I continually struggled with the gray cloud of his change of assignment. Our struggles were compounded by limited knowledge of the textbook's literary selections and lack of the reservoir of materials that a veteran teacher typically builds after many years teaching the same course.

Dave assumed a curriculum and a grade level new to him; he was unsure about the instructional units and types of evaluation that he would use in his Grade 12 English class. Although he had used trimester-long syllabi with Grade 9 classes, Dave did not want to do the same for his Grade 12 class simply because he had not planned beyond the first two weeks of the school year. By not committing to a long-range syllabi, Dave retained flexibility in the planning process for the Grade 12 course. On the other hand, he faced substantial difficulties as he tried to give curriculum and instruction a coherent shape.

In order to remain organized and to communicate course requirements to students, Dave decided to issue weekly syllabi to his students every Monday. Dave did his planning on the weekend immediately preceding instruction. These syllabi summarized the work that he planned to cover during that week and his expectations for the students.

With his new Grade 12 class, I observed that Dave typically spent thirty minutes to one hour a day, almost every day, teaching writing activities. At the beginning of a writing unit, Dave would spend a lot of time in the classroom attempting to motivate the students using wholegroup activities. After a couple of days, Dave would send twenty of the twenty-four students to the twenty-seat computer room to write rough drafts, and there they typically spent one or two days working on their rough drafts. After the rough drafts were completed, they would return to the classroom to discuss their essays. Usually, they could return to the computer room the following week to type in their changes. Dave stayed in his class to work with the four students who remained; another English teacher supervised the students in the computer room.

The computer room, with many defective computers and limited hard disk space, posed another challenge to Dave's instruction. The machines were prone to crashing and often students would lose all of the work of a class period. The machines were connected to two aging and slow dot matrix printers; students would often wait long periods of time for print-outs. As a result of these complications, students often took two-to-three days to write a two-page rough draft.

By the fourth or fifth day of writing instruction, most students had written and printed their rough drafts. Dave took these assignments home over the weekend and made comments on them. He returned the student assignments the following week and would spend a part of Monday's class reviewing the kinds of comments he had made. He hoped that when the students read his between-draft comments they would use them to revise their work. On the second day of the second week of writing, students would return to the computer room to make largely surface-level revisions. On average, most writing assignments took two weeks to complete. No materials were provided for two other topics required by the state of Ohio's *Model Competency-based Language Arts Program* (1996): visual literacy and oral communication.

When Dave consulted with other Grade 12 teachers as to how he might teach the course, a number of them recommended intensive vocabulary instruction, which, though not outlined as a principal form of instruction by the formal curriculum, he felt was an important part of his Grade 12 curriculum. Each day he used approximately thirty minutes of class time to review a set of twenty vocabulary words. At the end of the week, the students' knowledge of these words was tested, and new words were taught in the following week. As a result, approximately twenty to twenty-five percent of the total instructional time of 128 hours was used for the teaching of approximately 220 vocabulary words.

Although Dave had some control over his instructional choices, his instruction was clearly shaped both by institutional limitations and his own beliefs as shaped by the system. For example, Dave had been paid during the preceding summer to work with other teachers in revising the Grade 9 curriculum, evidence that there was at least a nod to collaborative planning; yet he received little help with the Grade 12 work. It is not surprising that Dave viewed his instruction as merely a set of procedural steps.

Constructing an Approach

The previous description accounts for Dave's use of ninety to 120 minutes per day with the class. During days when some time was available, Dave and I began to revise his traditional instructional approaches by including process drama. Occasionally, the alternative activities we designed took somewhat longer than thirty minutes; but because drama was used primarily to support reading, it was perceived as an integral part of literature instruction.

Process Drama

To give you a sense of the difference between the traditional theatrical approach and the more process-oriented approach, I will provide some background. Many educators have written extensively about "drama in education," or what increasingly in the United States is being called "process drama." Wagner (1998) offers this helpful description of drama in education:

> In drama in education (DIE), the starting point is usually an area of the curriculum that the students need to be introduced to. There is less emphasis on story and character development and more emphasis on problem solving or living through a particular moment in time. Through ritual, dramatic encounters, pantomime, *tableaux vivants* (still pictures made with the bodies of the participants), writing in role, and reflection, participants enter the mind of imagined characters and play out their responses to challenges and crises. Experienced teachers of DIE often initiate or move the drama along by assuming a role themselves and heighten the tension by challenging the participants to respond to dilemmas in authentic and believable ways. (7)

Drama in education has a different focus than traditional theatrical approaches.

O'Neill explains that drama does not depend on written scripts; rather, there is improvisation during which participants take different perspectives. Often, they change their views during the process. Scripts are generated through action and outcomes are not planned in advance but discovered in the process. In process drama, participants explore themes and ideas that are linked in an organic manner (see Figure 9–5).

Both creative drama and process drama are useful approaches because they support students in responding to lessons with what Wagner (1998, 8) calls an "authentic and spontaneous oral language." She notes that while a more traditional use of drama in classrooms has "engagement and authentic language" as a goal, process drama teachers have a different purpose. Wagner

---

Features of Process Drama
(*O'Neill 1995*)

- an ongoing event, rather than a finished object
- a dramatic elsewhere
- a process that is composed and rehearsed rather than improvised
- a series of episodes
- a gradual articulation of a complex dramatic world
- a group of participants who are an audience to their own acts
- a teacher or leader who can function both inside and outside the drama

FIGURE 9–5
Features of Process Drama

explains that for process drama teachers, "the goal goes beyond that to what has been learned from the experience—about history, human interactions, scientific discoveries, the role of persons in various professions, the texture of the lives of characters in literature—in short, the larger school curriculum."

Wagner offers weighty words and a wonderful vision of what process drama can be. Process drama, in the hands of a skilled teacher, can deliver on this promise; however, since Dave and I were only collaborating for a few months using a school curriculum that had a number of institutional constraints, we did not envision success at that level. Instead, we borrowed the concepts to implement what I called "process-oriented drama strategies." I coined this term to suggest the fledgling, experimental nature of the kinds of teaching we undertook.

Planning an Alternative to the Traditional

Figure 9–6 is a summary of the literary selections that were taught and the major writing tasks that were assigned to the students. Dave or I devised a drama activity to support each element of curricular contact, with the exception that during the last two weeks of the study, Dave wanted students to spend most of their time silently reading a novel.

Week	Curriculum Content: Vocabulary	Curriculum Content: Lit. selections	Curriculum Content: Writing assignments	Drama Activity	Leader of Drama Activity
	Summary of Drama Activities Used to Support Literary and Composition Teaching During the Study				
1	Vocabulary	Thurber *The Iliad*	Formal paper on ancient Greeks	Tableaus	Adrian
2	Vocabulary	*The Iliad* *The Aeneid*	Formal paper on ancient Greeks	Tableaus	Adrian
3	Vocabulary	*The Aeneid*	Complete formal paper Autobiography	Tableaus Hot-seating Small group discussion Ritual creation	Adrian
4	Vocabulary	*Beowulf*	Autobiography	Tableaus Writing-in-role Group discussion Ritual creation	Adrian
5	Vocabulary	*Beowulf*	Complete autobiography Begin legend	Hotseating	Adrian/Dave

FIGURE 9–6 *Summary of Drama Activities Used to Support Literary and Composition Teaching During the Study*

Our literary selections included classical literature, Old and Middle English, some poetry and short story selections, a Shakespearean play, and a novel. The novel *Things Fall Apart* by Chinua Achebe was selected because it was the only class set of novels that Dave was able to borrow from a teacher in the building. Since Dave was uncertain about the choice of this novel, he wanted to rely largely on silent in-class reading as the main form of instruction.

Dave also assigned an eclectic choice of writing tasks. Some writing assignments overlapped with the literary instruction; many others were independent of the literary selections. Dave used a number of activities to

Summary of Drama Activities Used to Support Literary and Composition Teaching During the Study					
Week	*Curriculum Content: Vocabulary*	*Curriculum Content: Lit. selections*	*Curriculum Content: Writing assignments*	*Drama Activity*	*Leader of Drama Activity*
6	Vocabulary	King Arthur's legends	Complete student legend Begin paper on "A journey"	Videotape of professional actors Writing-in-role	Dave
7	Vocabulary	Chaucer, *Canterbury Tales* (selections)	Journey papers ends Begin résumé	Teacher-in-role Mantle of expert Writing-in-role	Dave
8	Vocabulary	Poetry selections: *To an athlete dying young*	Complete résumé	Interviews Student-in-role Group discussion of interviews	Adrian/Dave
9	Vocabulary	*Macbeth*	Complete résumé Begin Process Analysis paper	Show videotape of pro. production create scenes Writing-in-role	Dave
10	Vocabulary	*Macbeth*	Complete process analysis	As above	Dave
11	Vocabulary	Novel: *Things Fall Apart*	No writing assignments Students keep notes on novel	No drama activities by teacher request	
12	Vocabulary	As above	As above	As above	
* Shading indicates these were weeks that were transcribed					

FIGURE 9–6 (cont'd.) *Summary of Drama Activities Used to Support Literary and Composition Teaching During the Study*

support students in their literature and writing lessons. Some of these activities included drama components. Briefly, the principle activities included the following techniques:

- *Tableaus*: students working in groups of three to five discuss and mold their bodies to form frozen pictures or scenes that depict what they have read or a moment from what they want to depict.
- *Hot-seating*: a student is placed in a role and responds to rapid-fire questions.
- *Group discussions and rituals*: students discuss events related to rituals and then depict them in a stylized and ceremonial way. In one case I discussed what occurs when a student meets someone they have not met in a long time. We then created a greeting ritual.
- *Writing-in-role*: students write a diary entry or similar writing responses as if they are in role as someone else.
- *Videotape of professional actors*: students view professional theatre on television.
- *Teacher-in-role*: the teacher takes on a role.
- *Mantle-of-the-expert*: students are endowed with the attributes of an expert and undertake activities as if they are experts.

LEARNING FROM THE EXPERIENCE IN COLLABORATIVE PLANNING

We learned much from our fledgling experiment in collaborative planning for alternative forms of instruction. We learned about the tensions, contextual factors, and powerful traditions that are very real forces in the progress of change efforts. In this section, I describe what Dave and I accomplished in the classroom. At the same time, I will reveal tensions and tension-causing factors such as the advice of peers, the powerful traditions associated with teaching English, the teacher's personal philosophy and background of experience, and conflicting views of appropriate student evaluation.

Tensions

Several tensions emerged as Dave and I engaged in our collaborative work.

These tensions were not necessarily damaging to Dave's and my collaboration; and they are helpful to think about today because they illustrate the complexity and difficulty of sustaining such collaborative effort in classrooms. Tension is useful: without it, rubber bands couldn't work. Dealing with tensions makes us realize that we are involved in a *process* rather than pinpointing right and wrong or success and failure.

Our planning sessions were a key element in understanding how we struggled with instructional strategies. This struggle represents an elaboration on the tension between Dave's insecurity in teaching a new course and my desire to explore process-oriented drama activities. In the case of *Beowulf*, a literary selection I knew fairly well but that Dave had not read since finishing college, I tried to explore alternatives in addition to having the students read the epic. I suggested to Dave that a critical motif in *Beowulf* is the recurrent threat to safety. I reasoned that "threat" was a motif the students might be interested in exploring. Our planning went something like this:

Dave: So what are you thinking about doing with threats?

Adrian: Well, . . . there are different kinds of threats in there. There's the threat of Grendel, but then there's also the threat from within and how they could support Beowulf. Could they possibly support Beowulf? That sort of thing.

Once Dave and I clarified and agreed on pursuing the motif of a threat, we proceeded with further planning. Dave was able to understand more precisely what I had in mind when we discussed the details:

Dave: So what do you think you're going to do?

Adrian: I had three or four things in mind. One was I was going to bring in a picture. . . . It's just a really barren landscape and get them to brainstorm about what kinds of threats might exist in that sort of place.

Dave: It's very desolate?

Adrian: Yeah. And another one was we could have a town meeting of people who live in this place. We'd imagine living in this place and we'd talk about what we're worried about.

Dave: So you're setting a scenario.

Adrian: Right.

Dave: O.K.

Adrian: And then we'll imagine—

Dave: Tell me more about this town meeting.

Adrian: I'll probably be sort of playing a role there and . . .

Dave: Such as?

Adrian: The roles that are usually best are sort of a bureaucrat—town clerk. . . .

Dave: O.K. Well—see I didn't know if you were going to be a town meeting moderator.

Adrian: Right. Moderator, right. A very bureaucratic function works best.

Dave: How are you going to organize them? Are you going to put them in a circle? . . .

Such discussions confirmed the idea, prominent in the literature, that a teacher's application of a new teaching approach is governed by already existing curricular knowledge and the meaning that the teacher derives from that knowledge. Dave and I needed to use the curriculum in a malleable way. In the example above, we began by talking about the plot, then threats, then heroes, and then how we could approach the material using a role-playing strategy so that the students could explore the issue of threats as if they themselves were being threatened. As we became more flexible in considering what we were going to do, Dave and I could also edge toward planning our lesson. Within a few weeks of beginning the study, we were able to explore possibilities beyond having the students summarize plot lines or the behaviors of the character. These patterns, emerging over the first few weeks of the study, indicated change in how these factors and tensions were changing over time in our planning.

Peer Influence

The traditionally held views of Dave's fellow teachers were another factor in shaping Dave's planning. Dave wanted to use his colleagues' suggestions, even though he also desired to pursue the alternative teaching strategies that were the purpose of our collaboration.

During the early part of the school year, Dave asked his colleagues how they taught the Grade 12 course. In most cases, teachers told Dave that they followed the chronological order of the text and that the writing assignments were used to evaluate the material learned in literature classes. As a result, Dave began the year by teaching *The Iliad* followed by the *Aeneid*. To complement his teaching of classical literature, he asked students to complete an assignment that required them to research and label mortals and gods depicted in the text.

Dave's colleagues also suggested that vocabulary should figure prominently in his course. They offered him copies of a weekly vocabulary skill-building exercise that had been published in the 1960s. The exercises featured twenty words per week and occasionally included some obscure choices. For Week 1, all of the words began with A, in the second week the words all began with the letter B, and so on. Here is the routine:

- Day 1: Use a dictionary to define the words.
- Day 2: Complete a fill-in-the-blank exercise using the appropriate word.
- Day 3: Write sentences using the featured word.
- Day 4: Take a test on the vocabulary words without reference to notes.

Following the suggestions of his colleagues, Dave used the prescribed handouts four days a week for thirty minutes per class. After the fourth week, Dave began to question the obscurity of some of the vocabulary words and abandoned the published vocabulary package in favor of using his own lists of vocabulary words. This kind of vocabulary instruction occupied one-quarter of each class four days a week.

One teacher suggested that Dave concentrate on having his students write essays to prepare them for the demands of college writing. Dave did not elaborate on what the teacher meant by college essays, and rejected the idea. He did, however, follow the school's guideline that every teacher undertake some activity that would support students in thinking about employment after graduation. To accomplish this, Dave required students to write résumés and an essay on career aspirations. These assignments were developed from his Grade 9 writing assignments, but he also revised them so that they would be age-level appropriate.

By the end of the course, in addition to reading classical literature, the students had read both *Beowulf* and *Macbeth*. Additionally, they had read a number of Twentieth century authors including Thurber and Achebe. Dave's evaluation of students included written tests on the classical literature. As a part of writing instruction, Dave had his students write a process analysis essay describing how to undertake a task, a compare–contrast essay, an auto-biographical essay, a career aspirations essay, and a personal résumé. Finally, Dave gave twelve vocabulary quizzes testing his students' ability to define 240 words. Dave did not communicate to the students exactly what portion of the final grade each piece of evaluation was worth, and he sometimes changed the value of tests and quizzes depending on student performances (sometimes with a view to weighing more heavily the tests where students performed better). In most cases though, the final grade was determined by weighing grades from the literature tests, the writing assignments, and the vocabulary quizzes.

Powerful Traditions

The traditions of the school and the English teachers at the school were powerful tensions in shaping how Dave worked with me when we planned lessons together. The traditions guided almost all of the writing assignments and the order of the literary selections that Dave taught. Consequently, there was little room for him to devise writing assignments or sequence readings in ways that could be more directly related to process-oriented drama activities. I originally thought Dave would have a high degree of flexibility when it came to thinking about writing assignments. In reality, because Dave sometimes expressed to me that he was "just staying afloat," he was loathe to ignore the advice of any of his colleagues who had previously taught the course. Indeed, he saw their advice as something that might assist him in his survival of the already arduous task of teaching the new course.

Personal Experiences and Philosophy

Another set of factors that influenced Dave's approach to our planning sessions was his personal philosophy of education and the instructional reper-toire that he had developed as a veteran teacher. During our planning sessions, Dave sometimes talked about his personal feelings behind what he wanted to do with students. He also responded to direct questions that I asked him regarding his philosophy. Because of his extensive experience teaching Grade 8 and 9 students, Dave reiterated many times that he thought that it was important for lessons to be activity based. Although Dave favored the use of activities in his teaching, he also felt that these activities should cover the plot of the literary selection in some way. Dave hoped that a discussion of plot would lead students to a larger understanding of themes or universal elements of a literary text, but their understandings proved to be extremely difficult for students. Often, Dave and I would end up talking to students about what the story was about rather than having a discussion of the author's artistic intentions. In the transcript from a planning session that follows, Dave illustrates that he wants his students to know about the war depicted in the *Iliad,* but he does not describe how we could get students to discuss the author's notion of war.

Adrian: What's your objective?

Dave: My objective is to, ah, cover content, and to get them thinking about some of the universal issues that will be part of their world. Now, it would make sense, that, you know, we started out with this *Iliad* so, I thought, we'll do something on war, because that seems to make sense. It's all about war.

Dave still wanted to have his students explore universal issues. I suggested that we plan a number of process-oriented drama activities that would give students an opportunity to think about themes. I attempted one of these activities in a class in which students discussed their feelings without reference to the plot of a literary work. When we were planning for a subsequent lesson, Dave questioned my approach:

Dave: I'm not sure what we accomplished today . . . whether it's just, ah, we had a nice talk today. I mean that's—is there anything beyond that? Do you want anything beyond that?

In another process-oriented drama activity, I explored cultural norms with students by leading students through a drama activity as if I were the narrator of the story and the students were the characters. During this process I asked them to concentrate on different kinds of rituals, such as what someone does when greeting another person. After the activity, I asked the students to evaluate their experiences. In a reflective journal he was writing, Dave questioned the academic value of exploring cultural norms with minimal reference to the plot of the story that we had just read:

Dave: With this activity I wondered about academic objectives—and I often wonder how important these objectives are. The exercise introduced the concept of cultural norms. . . . You are very good at setting scenes as the narrator of stills/slow motions. . . . Debriefing was interesting: "It's better than writing down things." . . . You know, again, . . . I thought they were terrifically interested, but I'm not sure beyond this fun we're having a good time.

Dave believed that learning should be measured by the students' ability to recollect the plots of stories. He was therefore uncertain as to how we could evaluate many of the process-oriented drama activities that I suggested. As an alternative to process-oriented drama, Dave suggested that we plan for the students to create products, such as student scripts and performances based on those scripts, that would demonstrate knowledge of what they had read.

Dave: How about trying to dramatize. . . . Teaching them how to write scripts? Too complicated?

I resisted Dave's desire to create products and suggested an activity that would emphasize the students' response to the literature being read:

Adrian: You know we could have them write a diary account of the death of Beowulf. . . .

Eventually we opted for my suggestion and Dave collected the student writing samples.

Innovator's Assumptions Versus Products As Evaluation

An additional factor that influenced our lesson planning was my assumption that both Dave and his students would embrace the alternatives to traditional evaluation that process-oriented drama approach offered. For example, when Dave and I planned classes together, he would ask me how we could get the students to create products in the form of performance. Specifically, he would consider units he was developing for teaching plays, storytelling, and résumé writing and ask what I could do to have students stage scenes, tell stories, and complete mock interviews. When I suggested that drama might be used with many different literary genres as a way of introducing a story, poem, play, or essay, Dave invariably insisted on discussing these product orientations.

Although some of the students' writing was interesting, Dave emphasized that students needed to demonstrate their knowledge of plots. He explained that his involvement in the Coalition of Essential Schools helped to persuade him of the need for students to demonstrate their understandings of literature. During one planning session he asked, "Are you familiar with the Coalition of Essential Schools? . . . One of the big things is exhibition. You know, that it's graduation by exhibition, and competency by exhibition, that type of thing."

IMPLICATIONS OF WHAT WE LEARNED

By the end of the study I realized that veteran teachers who are beginning to use an approach that is largely new are constrained by a number of factors. If teachers really want to move their teaching practices in alternative directions, a number of curricular supports from both the school and school district will be required. I have also come to understand that teachers need to develop fairly sophisticated knowledge about and skills for enabling students' understandings regarding the alternative pedagogy. Surely, for a Professional Development School active in a number of initiatives, more could have been done to support Dave in his lesson preparation and teaching. It is alarming that the virtually nonexistent support offered by the school and the district have been touted as being on the forefront of professional development. Just as Dave was limited by the institutional support he received, he was also shaped by the culture of the school in which he worked. The way he viewed the use of drama as a set of procedures was congruent with previous expectations. It is therefore no surprise that the students covered material but did not typically engage with the literary selections.

Because there was more support for a traditional approach than the kinds of instructional change I advocated, it is not surprising that I acted as a change agent who disrupted routines, but not one who could fully implement change. Based on this analysis, I am left to conclude that the successful application of the process-oriented approach that I attempted to implement is governed to a large degree by a teacher's system of curricular knowledge and meaning. A collaborative professional development approach, by itself, was not in this case sufficient to challenge the traditional way of doing things. Both Dave and I wanted a new teaching strategy, but additional supports were needed in order for the participants to fully implement the strategies that they were attempting.

These supports might include planning time before the beginning of the course for the participants to familiarize themselves with the curriculum content and the range of lesson objectives associated with that content. An additional support might include the provision of additional curricular materials so that the participants could have greater flexibility in selecting literature that is both relevant to the students and useful for implementing a process-oriented approach.

I have also concluded that teacher change can be difficult to achieve, even when an extensive collegial relationship already exists. A number of tensions arose and can exist either within the context of the collegial relationship, or between the participants and the institutional context in which they conduct their work. I initially believed that the close collegial relationship between Dave and myself and the fairly extensive time that he and I had set aside for the planning, teaching, and reflecting as well as the school-embedded, student-centered nature of the reform that we proposed to undertake would all combine to foster considerable changes in our teaching. I still believe that these features are necessary elements to foster professional development; but I now also believe that there must be a match between the teaching strategy and the teaching philosophy, the amount of experience with the proposed teaching strategy, and the content knowledge of the teacher.

Dave and I were challenged by factors such as time and materials. Collaborative professional development is more complex than calls to customize in-service development suggest. Although Dave and I thought we were initially "trying out some drama methods," in fact we were struggling with conflicting teaching repertoire, curricular meaning, and our ability to use appropriate activities in teaching students.

This study has implications related to both professional development and teachers in general English education in particular. Certainly, this study illustrates the complexity of professional development initiatives. Hundert (1996) has suggested that "three conditions of the teacher's work environment seem to impede the institutionalization of collaborative initiatives for site-based staff development: isolation, time constraints, and traditional role definition" (211). Although my work with Dave seemed to adequately deal with overcoming classroom teacher isolation, time constraints and Dave's interpretation of his role as one who should maintain the scholastic traditions of the English program were impediments not initially considered when I began the study. These impediments have even greater significance since this study took place in a school that was committed to professional development through a number of initiatives. Thus, it must be concluded that a school's and teacher's involvement in professional development does not by itself overcome barriers to change. Reform at the school district and school levels must connect to classroom practices if real change is to be realized in the way that students are taught.

It is important to note that this study was conducted within the context of a classroom, embedded as it was in all the buzz and confusion of school life. As such, this kind of field-based research is a valuable tool for viewing professional development initiatives. I found that the claims currently articulated by those interested in professional development—that reform needs to be longer-term, embedded in a school, related to students, and collegial rather than private—were very helpful for investigating this case. The need for protracted reforms undertaken in school-embedded, teacher- and student-centered contexts certainly suggests that those who undertake professional development through the one-shot, hour-long, in-service session need to give some thought as to how their work will be implemented on the ground.

My research here also illustrates a number of factors that complicate professional development initiatives conducted within the context of a Professional Development School (PDS). The analysis of these factors and the development of plans to address them is crucial if university-school partnerships are to function in an ongoing and sustained way. It is important for researchers not only to document exemplary cases that are judged to be successful by the participants, but also to focus on cases that have difficulty in surmounting challenges. Perhaps through the study of such challenges, educators might be able to surmount them. Clearly, the implication is that problems are our "friend" (Fullan 1993) and researchers must study the problem so we can reap the benefits of problem resolution.

Although I attempted to conduct a collaborative investigation with my cooperating teacher, this tale is not a co-authored story. If teachers and teacher-educators are to collaborate together on a methodological level, it is important for teachers to join researchers as collaborative storytellers who relate the narrative of their professional development journey when they report their research. Dave and I took a small step towards true collaboration, but it is incumbent on the teacher-educators to support the teachers in being equal partners and participants by telling the tale of collaborative professional development.

Our experience illustrates that teachers rely on established routines even when they are learning a new teaching strategy and that the development of new routines is a time-consuming process. These findings challenge the current school practices of a time-pressured world where increasing demands are placed on teachers. Clearly, time management and a long-term view of assigning teacher duties should to be considered if school districts are to support collaborative professional development.

Finally, this study suggests that process-oriented drama strategies are demanding for English teachers. Perhaps the strategies are demanding because the activities are so complex and powerful. They offer a reservoir of potential for those who are interested in developing their teaching repertoire. The power of drama strategies lies not in the activities, but in the interaction between the activities, the students' life experiences, and the teacher's ability to frame the drama and to lead students through the drama. The complexity of this interaction between drama as a teaching medium, student response, and a teacher's skill suggests that drama offers a rich, but demanding way for professional developers to explore the development of teachers' repertoires.

CONCLUSION

This study is not meant to characterize the teaching that Dave typically provides to all of his students. While I attempted to gather a rich picture of the way Dave and I worked with students regarding process-oriented drama approaches, it is certainly not a complete picture of all of Dave's teaching practices. All of the events have been filtered through my interpretive lenses, and since I have been doing the describing, I have controlled the tale.

Teacher ownership dramatically changes the way teacher education research can be represented. In the future, teams of teachers and researchers will need to study what happens when they mutually construct research questions, when they overlap teaching and researching responsibilities, and when they consider multiple ways of representing data.

For the past several years, some Americans have expressed concern regarding the quality of public schools. Regardless of the messenger, the quality of initial and ongoing teacher preparation, and the quality of the teachers themselves, are always at the center of such concern. It is therefore essential that teachers and teacher-researchers work together to address teacher preparation generally, and professional development specifically.

Although collaborative professional development conducted in classroom contexts can be demanding because of the myriad of factors that challenge the participants, it can also be a powerful vehicle to explore changing teaching practices. Visionary and collaborative reform is difficult to sustain and the participants must be cautious, but rewards in the way of solutions to old problems and the discovery of interesting new problems await collaborative professional development participants.

10 | LESSONS FROM A SUCCESSFUL REFORM INITIATIVE

Emily M. Rodgers

With every new report on the American educational system, citizens and educators sense a prevailing urgency to reform. National reports such as *What Matters Most: Teaching for America's Future* (National Commission on Teaching and America's Future 1996) underscore the impetus for change. According to this report, graduate rates and achievement levels have changed little, causing the authors to note that "There has been no previous time in history when the success, indeed the survival of actions and people has been tied so tightly to their ability to learn" (3). This assertion is consistent with the findings of a previous report that indicated reading achievement among children in the United States is at an unacceptably low level (*National Education Goals Report* 1995). More recently, federal initiatives have called for sweeping changes in literacy education and in the way schools operate. It isn't that achievement has plummeted; the call is for higher levels of literacy that are needed now and in the future.

Reform is needed, but reform usually fails, given all that we know about the tendency for educational reform efforts to come and go with little lasting change (Fullan 1993; Wilson and Daviss 1994). The prognosis for change seems bleak; failure is predictable (Sarason 1990). According to Fullan (1991) the complexity and intractability of problems in education make it difficult for real reform to occur.

Wilson and Daviss argue that a paradigm shift is needed so that the education system itself can be examined. For example, before real reform can occur, we need a thorough re-examination of traditional models of teacher preparation, the use of research to inform practice, and the ways problems are addressed. Fullan (1993) notes that as long as the focus remains on changing things that do not really matter, "fundamental, instructional reform" will not occur (46). Without a shift, educators are doomed to enact one idea after another with little hope that the new program will be sustainable for more than a few years.

Wilson and Daviss (1994) describe Reading Recovery as at least one program that has achieved a paradigm shift. According to these writers, Reading Recovery represents a good example of systemic reform and a rich context within which to observe the change process. In the next section I

This research was supported by a grant from the research fund of the Reading Recovery Council of North America.

will describe the design of Reading Recovery and justify using it as a context to study educational reform.

READING RECOVERY: AN EXAMPLE OF A SUCCESSFUL EDUCATIONAL REFORM INITIATIVE

Reading Recovery is a short-term literacy intervention strategy designed for first graders who are identified as being at risk of failing to learn to read and write. Evidence that Reading Recovery is an example of a successful reform effort comes from two features of the program: its dissemination and the success of the students served.

Dissemination of Reading Recovery

Reading Recovery has been replicated numerous times since it was first implemented in the United States about sixteen years ago. As of 1999, Reading Recovery has been implemented in 11,262 schools in 3,505 districts. Also 19,085 educators, including teachers and university faculty members, have taken the year-long training, and 701,475 students have been served (National Data Evaluation Center 2000). These data document the rapid dissemination of the program in a climate where, according to Walmsley and Allington (1995), the "process of change inevitably will be slow and . . . vigorously challenged" (26).

Progress of Students

As Reading Recovery expanded, the students served each year continued to make gains in reading. For example, 77,882 of all students served in 1999 ($n = 122,935$) made sufficient gains in reading achievement to reach the average band of their classmates on measures of reading and writing ability. This rate has remained fairly constant over the last sixteen years of the program's implementation (National Data Evaluation Center 2000).

The success of the program can also be measured in terms of

- accelerated progress that students make in literacy (Walmsley and Allington 1995; Dyer 1992; Hovest and Day 1997; Shanahan and Barr 1995)
- the maintenance of student gains over time (Jaggar 1997; Wang and Johnstone 1997)
- the reduction in the numbers of students referred to special education or learning disabilities services (Lyons 1994; Lyons, Pinnell, and DeFord 1993)

The widespread dissemination of Reading Recovery across the United States in tandem with consistent gains in reading achievement over sixteen years provide evidence that Reading Recovery is an example of a successful reform effort in education, making it a valid context to learn more about what it takes to bring about change to the system.

DESIGN VERSUS TINKERING

I agree with Wilson and Daviss (1994), who theorize that educational reform efforts fail because efforts are piecemeal; reformers do not consider redesigning the whole system. As a consequence, changes come and go and innovations are regarded as "fads" lasting only as long as the present school or school district administration. Fullan (1993) describes this cycle as "waves of change, episodic projects, fragmentation of effort and grinding overload" (42).

The concepts of design and redesign are important ones. In the field of education, we seem to spend more time on inventing, or "tinkering," instead of improving design. In other fields, however, careful attention is given to design (Lyons and Pinnell 2001). Engineers, for example, work on the design and redesign of innovations, whether it is the way the lead in a pencil is adhered to its case or how bridges can be made to span greater and greater distances (Petroski 2001). For these reasons, it seems that it might be helpful to examine the design of a successful educational innovation in order to better understand what it may take to bring about real change in education.

Methodology

I used a qualitative cross-case study approach to examine the design features of Reading Recovery as one example of an educational reform effort that has been successfully implemented. According to Patton (1990) the purpose of the case study approach is to gather comprehensive, systematic and in-depth information about each case (384). This approach can be particularly useful when the study aims to understand some special situation in great depth (54). In this study, there were multiple cases of school districts that had implemented Reading Recovery with great success.

Participants

In order to examine the design features of Reading Recovery, I identified high-performing school districts according to data collected by the National Data Evaluation Center (NDEC). The NDEC is a research center at The Ohio State University. Data on every child served by Reading Recovery are sent to NDEC at entry to and exit from lessons and at the end of the year. Reading Recovery teachers collect the information on each student they teach and these data document important aspects of the program's implementation, including the number of children served at the site, the number of Reading Recovery teachers, and the percentage of children reaching average band levels of their classmates on various literacy measures.

With the cooperation of NDEC, I selected districts where Reading Recovery had been successfully implemented. The following criteria were used:

- Reading Recovery had been implemented for at least three years and each Reading Recovery teacher taught at least eight students by the end of the school year. (Reading Recovery teachers work individually with four students at a time and the maximum length of a program is twenty weeks; therefore, it seemed reasonable to expect that a teacher could teach eight students in a school year.)

- Of *all* the children served by Reading Recovery in the site, at least sixty percent reached the average band of their classmates on measures of Text Reading Level, Writing Vocabulary, and Hearing and Recording Sounds in Words. (These are measures from Clay's *An Observation Survey of Early Literacy Achievement*, 1993.) Performing within average range enabled these originally low-achieving children to profit from participating in classroom instruction. Moreover, qualitative judgments and scores confirmed that children had acquired the body of strategies and skills needed to read independently.

Using these criteria, thirty-one high-performing school districts were identified in the country where Reading Recovery was implemented with excellence. For this study, I selected just three of the sites, and I was granted permission to conduct interviews and have access to their Reading Recovery research reports.

Two school districts are located in midwestern states and the third in a southeastern state. All three school districts are relatively small, having no more than eight elementary schools in the largest district. One is located in a suburban area near a large midwestern city and the other two are located in rural areas.

Data Collection

Glesne and Peshkin (1992) recommend the use of "multiple data collection methods" (24) and note that participant observation, interviewing, and document analyses are the data-gathering techniques most often used. For this study, on the continuum from observer to participant, I took the role of observer. I visited each selected district for several days in order to conduct interviews and gather documents for analyses, but I did not participate in the settings in any other way. I conducted audiotaped in-depth structured interviews, semi-structured focus group interviews, and unstructured individual interviews. In all, I interviewed twenty-eight teachers, ten principals, eight school board personnel, and four former or present superintendents. At each site I also interviewed three teacher-leaders (the specialists who train Reading Recovery teachers; a fuller description of this role is provided in the Findings section). Finally, I collected and analyzed annual research-based site reports and any other documents produced at the school district that related to implementation. See Figure 10–1 for a summary.

Data Analyses

According to Marshall and Rossman (1995) three broad phases are involved in data analyses: data reduction, data display, and conclusion drawing. I applied these three phases of analyses on two levels: *within* cases and *across* cases.

The audiotaped interviews were completely transcribed and then mailed to each participant for a "member check." They were asked to correct inaccuracies in the transcriptions, strike out any passages that they did not wish to be cited, and to add any additional comments for clarification or informational purposes as they saw fit.

These data were reduced through a process of generating codes or categories of data from the notes. I started with the factors which Askew et al. (1998) identified as necessary for sound implementation of Reading Recovery (see Figure 10–2). Based on a long history of implementation at a large variety of sites across North America, Askew and her colleagues determined that district and school leaders' active involvement in Reading Recovery was an important element in success. Broad ownership for the program and its goals, particularly the focus on reducing the number of below grade-level students, was seen as very important. Finally, successful implementers paid close attention to the data on student outcomes. Other codes emerged through the process of data reduction.

Once the codes were generated within cases, I looked across the cases for similar codes by stacking the cases in one matrix (an analysis strategy suggested by Miles and Huberman 1984). This display simplified the task of looking at the categories across the cases in a systematic way. My goal at the within- and cross-case level of analyses was to generate theories about the design of the Reading Recovery program specifically, and in general, what it takes to reform educational practices.

FINDINGS

Reading Recovery has become an integral part of the educational landscape in all three high-performing sites. Individuals involved with Reading Recovery, whether they were teachers, district-level personnel, or principals, described Reading Recovery as being a part of their "way of thinking." For example, one district coordinator said, "I haven't heard anyone say anything about not funding Reading Recovery since we've been established. Reading Recovery is a given. It's a part of us." A principal with another district voiced a similar point of view when he said, "[Reading Recovery] is known in the

FIGURE 10–1
Interviews

Interviews	
Reading Recovery Teachers	23
Classroom Teachers	5
School Administrators	10
District Office Administrators	12
Teacher-Leaders	3

community as well. All the new [elementary] buildings [have it]—it's part of the culture from the day you open the doors."

How has Reading Recovery come to be regarded as a vital, integral part of the culture of these school systems and not simply a passing fad? In the remainder of this section, I will present findings that describe three phases of implementation that each site experienced, including the last phase that all three sites are currently going through. I will also describe two kinds of factors that are present in the last phase: those that sustain the implementation of Reading Recovery and those that threaten it. Finally, I will describe the design features of Reading Recovery that emerged as a result of my analysis of the implementation phases.

Three Phases of Implementation: Inquiring, Inspecting, and Maintaining

Stakeholders in these sites went through an initial phase of *inquiring* about Reading Recovery before committing to it. This initial period was immediately followed by a time of closely *inspecting* the outcomes of implementing the initiative. Finally, in the current phase, each site is presently working on *maintaining* Reading Recovery. In this phase, the sites are dealing with factors that threaten the implementation and cultivating those that sustain it. The three phases are outlined in Figure 10–3.

Inquiring

Before Reading Recovery was adopted in each district, stakeholders first gathered information about it. This period lasted from one to three years. They observed Reading Recovery lessons in nearby districts—in one case, by transporting reading specialists, classroom teachers, and principals by van, five at a time, for several weeks. Viewing these lessons seemed to be an important way, and a common way, of learning more about Reading Recovery firsthand. One teacher said, "Once I observed the lesson I wondered where Reading Recovery had been all my life. It just made sense." Similarly, a district supervisor said, "Just going to the school and seeing what she was doing, she sold it."

Factors Recommended for Sound Implementation of Reading Recovery

- Ownership of the program
- Watching for full implementation
- Involvement of district administration
- Involvement of school administration
- Attention to data on student programs
- Shared focus (teachers and administrators) on reducing number of students below grade level

Source: Askew, B., Fountas, I., Lyons, C., Pinnell, G., and Schmitt, M. (1998).

FIGURE 10–2
Factors Recommended for Sound Implementation of Reading Recovery

Stakeholders also learned more about Reading Recovery from published articles and reports. These reports, which documented the progress of students, seemed to be important in convincing people, particularly school district personnel, that Reading Recovery was the program they wanted to improve the reading ability of their young at-risk students. The information in the published reports was also used in presentations to school board members to make a case for adopting Reading Recovery.

Inspecting

Once Reading Recovery was adopted, the results were carefully inspected and documented, especially in the first year. In each case, entry and exit data were collected for each student and the results made available in a research report. (This research plan is a requirement for all school districts that implement Reading Recovery.) In all three cases, additional research has been carried out, often in the form of follow-up studies that tracked the progress of students who had received Reading Recovery or studies that compared the progress of all children at one particular grade level over time. Student progress was also reported anecdotally. At every site, it seemed as though someone could describe a child who had made incredible progress, beyond what would have been expected without Reading Recovery. These concrete results spurred on the effort to more fully implement Reading Recovery in the sites.

Maintaining

Each of the three sites has now implemented Reading Recovery for at least three years and is now maintaining the program as an integral part of their system. In one particular district, the phrase "it's a [Reading Recovery] state

FIGURE 10–3
Three Phases of Program Implementation

Three Phases of Program Implementation		
Phase	*Actions*	*Time Period*
Inquiring	Gathering information Observing lessons and teacher training classes Examining research	1–3 years
Inspecting	Evaluating student outcomes Publishing research reports Gathering additional data (follow-up study) Gathering anecdotal notes	3 years
Maintaining	Continuing to monitor student achievement Making it an integral part of the system	Ongoing

of mind" was echoed a number of times by teachers, principals, and district-level personnel.

In the maintaining phase, there are at least two kinds of factors that affect the fidelity of the implementation of Reading Recovery:

- those that sustain the quality and stability of the implementation through the key role of the teacher-leader, taking notice of student achievement gains, and a shared focus on continual improvement in teaching;
- those that threaten the quality and stability of the implementation through a drop-off in results or changes in district philosophy and funding patterns.

Sustaining Factors

It became evident to me as I looked across the transcripts of my interviews that several features of the program were key to its maintenance in the district.

Teacher-Leader As Point Person

Interview data revealed that the single most important factor in each district was the presence of a point person who is at the center of the design of Reading Recovery at the level of the site. (A Reading Recovery site may or may not be made up of more than one school district.) This person, called a teacher-leader, is responsible for

- training new Reading Recovery teachers
- providing ongoing professional development to already trained teachers
- gathering and organizing the data collected each year on each child served by Reading Recovery
- submitting the data to NDEC for analysis
- writing an annual research report based on that analysis. The teacher-leader, who also teaches two to four students him/herself, serves as a consultant to Reading Recovery teachers working with children who are not making fast progress. The teacher-leaders that I interviewed in these three sites were also involved in teaching literacy courses and/or gathering data for additional research that they were conducting on Reading Recovery students

Each teacher-leader, described in each district as enthusiastic and tireless, was credited with his/her site's success. These people were well respected for their knowledge and their ability to work with others. They were also noted for their tough standards and high expectations of the teachers with whom they worked. These individuals were carefully selected for their role and, in one case, aggressively recruited from the classroom for the position. We could call the teacher-leader the point person.

The presence of this point person is the single most important sustaining factor to maintaining Reading Recovery, because all of the other sustaining factors are connected to and dependent upon the teacher-leader in some way. These other sustaining factors include the existence of locally collected data documenting the progress of the students and a shared focus on the teaching of children.

Collecting Data to Document Student Progress

At each site I was told that an important reason for keeping Reading Recovery was the continuing progress of the students served. This progress was documented in the annual site research report. The graphs and tables in the report were used in different ways to make the students' progress evident to different audiences. At one site, a few important results were written in lay terms and disseminated as part of an informational brochure about Reading Recovery. These brochures were left in public places, including for example, a doctor's office, in order to make the community more knowledgeable about Reading Recovery. One Reading Recovery teacher at that site explained the rationale behind this:

> I think that when a program stays only within educational circles we have a tendency for people to speculate. When people are asked, if they don't know if it's good or bad, they automatically think it's not good, whereas, we put [the information about Reading Recovery] out in places.

With the leadership of their teacher-leader, the teachers in that district focused in particular on making school board members knowledgeable about student progress in Reading Recovery. These teachers adopted a school board member for the year, thereby becoming responsible for keeping that member up-to-date about a particular student's progress. They planned to do this by sending videotapes of that child's lessons to the board member, throughout the year.

This view was repeated during a different interview by an assistant superintendent in the same district; he talked about the importance of keeping board members informed about Reading Recovery because of the many competing voices for funding. A principal agreed with his statement, saying,

> If you haven't done what [the assistant superintendent] was saying about educating [the board members], giving them concrete data—not just explaining the program but something they can look at to see the benefit . . . they want to see that it is resulting in increased achievement—if you don't take the time to communicate with the staff at your schools, they may not support the program out of a lack of understanding.

It is interesting that the same view—a lack of knowledge about Reading Recovery might lead stakeholders to withhold their support—was expressed separately by a teacher, principal, and assistant superintendent in the same district.

Shared Focus on Teaching

Finally, a third sustaining factor is a shared focus on teaching. Teachers, school board personnel, and principals across the sites shared this focus. Principals were flexible with their schedules to ensure little interference with the daily teaching of Reading Recovery students. If, for example, it was projected that school would be closing in the afternoon due to weather, one principal altered schedules so that the Reading Recovery teacher could teach all of her students in the morning. In most cases, it was rare to ask Reading Recovery teachers to act as substitutes, although they were willing to do so, if needed. The principals did not view Reading Recovery teachers as available subs who could readily give up their teaching time; if circumstances required their services, the teacher who had taught the most number of lessons that day would provide the substitute service.

Teachers frequently commented that they were always working on improving their own teaching. They were particularly pleased when they had an opportunity to share a teaching space with another Reading Recovery teacher because of the opportunity for dialogue with other teachers. They could talk about their teaching and their students' progress. One teacher said,

> I've even had one of my partners jump up in the middle of a lesson and come over to me and say, "Ahhh!" I think there is so much power to have the chance to share at that exact moment when you're ready to learn, and the child is ready to learn, and you have someone there who can give you that support.

Another teacher at a different site seemed to share the same focus on improving teaching when she said, "We are always searching to become better."

Teachers also highly value more formalized opportunities to work collaboratively with their colleagues. These opportunities come in the form of continuing contact sessions in which trained teachers meet about six times a year with the teacher-leader. Usually during these sessions, two of the teachers teach behind a one-way mirror while the rest of the group observes and comments on the lessons from the other side. Teachers also conduct cluster visits to one another, especially to problemsolve about a particular area of teaching or a child who may not be making fast progress. In this setting, a small group of teachers visit another teacher who teaches a student. The rest of the group observes and talks afterwards about how the child is learning and ways the teacher might shift the teaching to better suit what the child needs to learn how to do.

Threatening Factors

All interview participants were asked what they thought might cause the district to drop the program. All stakeholders, across roles, cited three factors that might threaten the implementation of Reading Recovery.

Lack of Results

Another idea emerging from the data was that if results ceased to be positive, district personnel, teachers, and principals would look for another initiative to take the place of Reading Recovery. Some teachers qualified this observation by saying that a lack of results could happen only if the teaching were no longer strong—another reference back to their emphasis on teaching.

Change in Philosophy

Interviews also identified a change in the agenda or philosophy of school board members or school district personnel as threatening factors. For example, a new superintendent could bring with him/her a different programmatic emphasis, choosing to divert funds to secondary schools or math programs. Change in administration was related to the first factor, lack of results, which could either cause stakeholders to abandon the initiative and look for something to replace it or to put forward other agendas with less opposition.

Lack of Funding

Each district has funded Reading Recovery in different ways: federal Title I monies (largely based on the school's number of free and reduced lunches), a state grant that supplements existing district funds, or district funds alone. In the cases where district board money was used, a decrease in results would be especially threatening because school board members, who hold the purse strings, might be likely to decide not to fund Reading Recovery, no matter what the district administrators recommended.

These three factors that threaten the implementation of Reading Recovery at these sites are interrelated because they depend on the first factor: student results. Without positive results from Reading Recovery, other decisions would follow and lead to the demise of the program. See Figure 10–4.

FIGURE 10–4
Factors Affecting Success in the Maintenance Phase

Factors Affecting Success in the Maintenance Phase	
Sustaining Factors	• Teacher-Leader Role
	• Student Success
	• Shared Focus
Threatening Factors	• Poor Results
	• Change in District Philosophy
	• Changes in Funding

DESIGN FEATURES OF READING RECOVERY

I noted distinct similarities in the implementation of Reading Recovery at these three successful sites. The stakeholders seemed to go through phases of inquiring, inspecting, and maintaining. Interviewees perceived the same threats to continued existence, including decline in results. While teacher-leaders had not experienced this decline, they were continually on guard.

This analysis of the implementation process across sites revealed key design features of Reading Recovery at these sites: rigorous evaluation, the teacher-leader's role, and professional development.

Research and Accountability

A key design feature of Reading Recovery is the ongoing evaluation of student progress.

To implement Reading Recovery, site administrators must agree to gather data in response to six research questions that describe the progress of Reading Recovery students. Data are systematically recorded and submitted to a central evaluation center, the National Data Evaluation Center, for analysis. Results are provided as print-outs to the districts, and the teacher-leader writes a technical report. Having a research plan to collect data on the progress of each student and to report local results is an integral component of each phase of implementing Reading Recovery at these three sites. People in varied positions frequently mentioned the evaluation process as being key to their decision to try Reading Recovery and key to their resolve to continue with it. In addition, the results are shared widely for various purposes with other stakeholders, including parents and school board members, creating broader ownership and pride and commitment internally.

Teacher-Leader

A second important design feature is the creation of a new role in a school district, that of a teacher-leader. The other important features of Reading Recovery—the training of teachers, advocacy for the program, research, and everything related to the fidelity of the intervention at the site—seem to depend on the teacher-leader.

Professional Development

A third key design feature of Reading Recovery is the element of ongoing professional development for teachers, either with the teacher-leader or with other teachers, both in preplanned sessions or on the spur of the moment. The teachers have a mind-set that they are continually learning and working on their teaching because there is always more to learn. They seem to value the opportunities to dialogue with and learn from their colleagues.

LEARNING ABOUT EDUCATIONAL REFORM FROM THE EXAMPLE OF READING RECOVERY

In systems where an educational innovation is being considered, it is vitally necessary for teachers to be involved first in recognizing the educational problems that have to be tackled and then in identifying reforms that might meet those needs (Datnow and Castellano 2001) because teacher "buy-in" is more likely to be achieved in this way. It is interesting that in all three of the sites in this study, teachers were involved in just that way. Teachers were the ones to initially bring Reading Recovery to the attention of school district personnel at two of the sites. They were involved in observing Reading Recovery lessons at other sites during the inquiry phase of the implementation, either by seeking out these experiences themselves or through arrangements made by school district personnel. When an innovation comes to a system in this way, as opposed to coming from the outside, support for the innovation is stronger and there is a better guarantee that the fidelity of the implementation will be maintained (Datnow and Castellano 2001).

When reform is imposed from the outside, Datnow and Castellano note a greater mismatch between what the system needs and what the innovation has to offer. In these three sites, not only was there a match between *what* the stakeholders felt they needed and what Reading Recovery had to offer, but also there was agreement *across* the stakeholders. When searching for an innovation, the teachers, principals, and school district personnel shared a common belief: the most pressing problem facing the district was improving the reading ability of young at-risk students. They also believed that by placing the bulk of their resources in early intervention for literacy, the whole district would eventually benefit. One former district supervisor, who was key to implementing Reading Recovery in his district, described this view as "the only decent philosophy" that one could have. In another district, a principal expressed the same belief when he said, "it's worth the money to invest in younger children." The teachers who were the first to be trained in these sites also identified the same need as facing their district before Reading Recovery was implemented.

Identifying and adopting an innovation that matches agreed-upon needs in a district is a good start but in no way guarantees that the innovation will last. The innovation must survive the pressures brought to bear upon it by forces such as changing personnel in the district or new ideas about teaching that may have popular appeal but be unsubstantiated by theory or research. Clay (1994) notes that the teacher-leader is a key component in the design because of his/her role in maintaining the fidelity of Reading Recovery in the face of these pressures. Citing Goodlad, Clay calls the teacher-leader the "agent of redirection" because of her/his pivotal role in redirecting learning across the system. Every part of the system has to change, including the child learning, the teacher learning, the system learning, and the community learning. Clay (1994) says that teacher-leaders are redirecting systems because they "teach children, train teachers, educate the local educators, negotiate the implementation of the program, act as advocates for whatever cannot be compromised in the interests of effective results, and talk to the public and media, correcting misconceptions" (127). The teacher-leader, therefore, is responsible for orchestrating fundamental changes in the system, the kind of reform where things that really matter are changed, which as Fullan (1993) has noted is so critical for reform to occur.

The role of the teacher-leader in redirecting the system does not diminish or take on less importance the longer Reading Recovery has been implemented. In fact, the role probably takes on greater significance because of a tendency for good designs to be "pared down," as Petroski (2001) describes it. Although Petroski is writing about design from an engineering perspective, there are lessons to be learned for the educational field. Petroski notes that the more successful a design is, the more likely it is to be replicated. Original designs, however, even though they are highly regarded, are also likely to be diluted because of influences such as "aesthetics, economics, and yes, ethics or their absence" (15). Petroski says that paring down of designs can take the form of

- upscaling without a proportional increase in strength
- streamlining or doing away with things deemed superfluous
- cheating (leaving out or substituting for something inferior)

"The cumulative effect of such paring down of strength is a product that can more readily fail. If the trend continues indefinitely, failure is sure to occur" (16). Teacher-leaders play a pivotal role in ensuring that the design is not pared away by stakeholders who do not understand the significance of the design features of Reading Recovery or by stakeholders who understand the design but are driven by other influences.

Here is a tension that must be managed sensitively. On the one hand, there is a need to guard against the paring down of good designs. On the other hand, there is a need to adapt a design to new situations so that it will not fail. Petroski provides the example of the collapse of the Tacoma Narrows Bridge as an example of the need to redesign in order to prevent failure. In this example, engineers, using the same, well-respected design of suspension bridges in common use, failed to take into account the effect of the wind in this new context. As a result, this traditionally successful design failed, and the bridge collapsed. Similarly in education, a successful design for an innovation in one setting cannot guarantee success in another setting with unanticipated differences.

On a national scale, changes were made to the design of Reading Recovery to take into account differences in the educational context between the United States and New Zealand, where it originated (Clay 1994). On local levels, in the sites involved in this study, small but significant changes were also engineered to adjust the innovation to fit the new setting. For example, Reading Recovery teachers usually teach four to five children individually for a half-day. During the remaining half-day they take a variety of roles depending on local decisions. In one site, the teachers, who all have graduate degrees, work a half-day as Reading Recovery teachers and the other half-day as literacy specialists to other classroom teachers. In another site, they work as Reading Recovery teachers for fifty percent of their job and Title I teachers for the other fifty percent. In the third site, they work solely as Reading Recovery teachers, teaching up to seven or eight students a day. Administrators and teachers at each site were struggling with their arrangements, but all were seeking to make the reform fit into their existing system.

In summary, Reading Recovery became a vital, integral part of these educational settings, perhaps because it has a design, and also because the design includes provision for a teacher-leader—someone at the site who is a focal point in maintaining the fidelity of the innovation against the continuous tendency to pare down its design.

The findings of this case study suggest that it is possible for an innovation to be successful and long-lasting in education, despite the strong tendency of innovations to fail and become just a passing fad. Lessons from Reading Recovery demonstrate the importance of having a well-articulated design that is informed by continuous data collection on the progress of the students served. It also needs to be maintained in the district by someone like a teacher-leader who, in effect, redirects the entire system.

Further study of successful examples of other educational reform initiatives may be useful to cross-check the features identified by this study and to determine other key features.

11 | MAKING DECISIONS AS PROFESSIONAL DEVELOPERS

Gay Su Pinnell
Emily M. Rodgers

Each of the chapters in this book represents a journey into teachers' learning. While the findings of the studies reported here have affirmed our respect for teachers, including their success and their commitment to student learning, we also hear some repeating themes that give us pause to think. Is professional development really the "answer" we claim it is? Or is it—at present—a blunt instrument that must be refined if it is to fulfill its promise? Perhaps there is no one answer. Maybe we need to think about different forms of professional development to be used for different purposes.

Let's examine some of the recurring themes that echo through the research and descriptions of practice reported here. Our colleagues have implied and directly said that professional development for literacy education:

- Is hard to do.
- Takes a large amount of time and effort.
- Will be expensive.
- Requires a high level of capacity within schools and districts.
- Will not get results right away.
- Is hard to measure.
- Is vulnerable to a myriad of "outside" forces that work against change.
- May have results that can be dissolved overnight by federal, state, or district changes.
- May encounter resistance.
- Must be implemented over and over again for different approaches.

In spite of these themes, our colleagues also imply that professional development *can* make a lasting difference and they generally support a constructivist view of learning. That is, the goal of all professional development is teachers' acquisition of the ability to:

- Make better decisions "on the run" while teaching.

- Vary their instruction to meet the needs of students.
- Go beyond a "materials" approach to tailoring instruction in ways that increase individuals' learning.
- Engage in powerful learning conversations with students within whatever instructional framework is used.
- Recognize their students' strengths in terms of both individual abilities and background and culture as they plan instruction.
- Learn from their teaching in a way that constantly increases their effectiveness over time.

The school is a social environment—a culture—within which new ideas and approaches must be assimilated. Teachers within a school or district may have very strong (although implicitly held) beliefs about "what works." New ideas that represent radical change may require deep changes in the culturally held belief systems. We asked ourselves, "Why is change so difficult?" And, again examining the chapters in this book, we found some possible reasons:

- As teachers, we tend to see only the results in front of us at the moment. Whatever approach we take, most children are learning and we do not have the perspective of knowing how these same children would fare in other contexts. Thus, we seem successful, and if some children are not learning, there are always explanations—home problems, learning disabilities, delayed development, and so on. Inside the elementary school, it is sometimes hard to see reasons for change.
- When we take on new approaches, we often do not see results right away. In fact, because we feel awkward with the new techniques, we sometimes see negative results. Fear starts to set in and we feel insecure. We are not supported by evidence that we can see or know how to see.
- Because of the discrepancy between state mandates or testing programs that measure our work in ways that are so different from practice, we feel torn between what we are told is sound practice and the tasks we see our students required to perform on a test. It is hard to see testing and instruction as different, and testing becomes instruction, whatever the new approaches we are asked to try.
- Finally, teachers often feel powerless within the larger system. Administrators constantly change (or change their minds). The new approach comes to be treated as "the flavor of the month." New criticism, new mandates, and new solutions constantly arise. Teachers feel at the mercy of administrative whims that move first in one direction and then in another. They may have small decision-making power within classrooms but no power where it counts. In fact, sometimes the only power they have is to resist change by passive participation and no action.

The experts who have written this book tell us that schools are social systems that must be developed into learning cultures where teachers are active considerers and decision makers in the construction of curriculum. We agree with that idealized view, but we are also rooted in the practicalities of making reform work within less-than-ideal situations.

In our work we have found some tenets of successful reform through professional development (see Figure 11–1).

To take on new practice successfully, teachers need efficient ways to take on the new practice right away in terms of routines, procedures, and logistics. Much as we would like to present philosophies and theories and engage teachers in a long series of discussions to discover implications for practice, we do not have that luxury and teachers do not have and can not expend the extra time needed to do so. In other words, we can not expect teachers to reconstruct every practice to assure greater literacy achievement. Implementing an extreme "constructivist" approach would leave a whole generation of children behind. While teachers would probably be excited by new ideas, they may become discouraged and flounder. Moreover, the experimentally and tentatively applied new approaches will be vulnerable to criticism and will probably disappear before they have a chance to become rooted and refined.

We have also learned that the chance of success is greater if, rather than leaving them to search for materials, teachers are provided with the basics. It also helps if they are arranged in a logical order so that it is easy for teachers to use them. These materials may be organized to greater and lesser degrees; for example, teachers may be given a sequence of books or stories to work through, or they may have books organized into "levels" so that they have a clear idea of how to use them with children.

Teachers also need help over the rough spots. It is pretty clear that you can not engage in a deep, analytical discussion of learning after observing a lesson in which the teacher has spent an entire hour of reading instruction struggling with four children reading a text that is too hard. Effectiveness and efficiency, not to mention caring for children, take precedence. Here are some common rough spots that need immediate intervention:

- There are twenty-one other children in the classroom who need instruction.
- The instruction that is being provided is ineffective.
- The teacher is becoming highly frustrated and will not continue to use the approach much longer.

Tenets of Taking on New Practice

- Efficient ways to take on routines and procedures.
- Materials to support the process.
- Specific guidance over the rough spots.
- A feeling of competence from the beginning.
- Early, easy-to-see successful impact on students.

FIGURE 11–1
Tenets of Taking on New
Practice

- Children are not learning reading but probably are learning that reading is tedious, uninteresting, and hard.

In such situations, coaching should take the form of immediately improving text selection, prescribing the amount of time for working with a group, streamlining instruction, and injecting a note of enjoyment into the entire process. The teacher needs direction and help, and a "questioning" technique may not work so well as some gentle, direct suggestions.

Immediate, competent execution of the particular technique or approach is a more important factor in long-term teacher development than we may have previously thought. There is an inherent dilemma in the situation. We know from research that change takes time and success doesn't emerge right away. Some researchers have even described an "implementation dip." That means that implementing a new program may so disrupt instruction in areas like pace, timing, and smoothness of instruction, that learning will also be interrupted or decrease for a very short time followed by a spurt in achievement. That's all very well, but living through that dip is a scary thing for teachers, students, and parents.

Teachers are accustomed to feeling competent; by necessity, they have developed routines so that they can give less attention to management. Usually, the more practiced and smooth they are, the better they feel about their work. Taking on a new approach disrupts everything; suddenly, you may actually feel incompetent. You fumble with materials; your timing is off. You may lose some attention from students. All of those factors make it hard to continue the learning. Providing more structure and support as teachers take on a new approach may help in avoiding such problems and increase teachers' confidence from the beginning.

Finally, evidence of student success is critical to the staying power of an innovative technique or school reform project. If we are working with agriculture or mechanical processes, we may wait patiently for the designated period of time—a season, a year—to draw conclusions about success. The human beings who work in schools tend to lack that patience because they are engaged in work that is critical for the children in front of them. In fact, that is one reason why it is so difficult to get teachers to participate in field-based research projects with control groups. No one wants to be in the "control" group (which is expected not to succeed) for an entire year. Teachers want to see success.

Innovations that have built-in processes for looking at evidence of success will have greater sticking power, provided that they really are working with students. We take the position that most effective approaches have some strong frameworks that, implemented with the routines in place, do bring about increased student learning. Over time, we would expect teachers to refine their work for maximum effectiveness with a variety of students, but the basic framework must be sound even for the beginner. If we can help teachers take on new approaches efficiently (without unduly floundering in the routines) and assure that they see early success, the motivation will be there to continue.

LEARNING FROM THE IMPLEMENTATION OF COMPLEX APPROACHES

Our work in professional development has been influenced by extensive experience in helping teachers learn about and implement two complex instructional procedures. We'll briefly explain how professional development works to support teachers in these two contexts. In Figure 11–2, these professional development approaches are outlined for each of the five ways to support teachers we described in Figure 11–1.

Reading Recovery

Reading Recovery is not *an* approach to teaching literacy. It is a dynamic combination of approaches that teachers use in varying ways to meet the needs of struggling readers. The decision-making process is quite complex, but teachers plunge into their application of the program right away during the training year. They are given the lesson framework, for example, and asked to try it out within a thirty-minute period of time. The framework consists of:

1. Familiar rereading of texts.
2. Second reading of a text while the teacher records and assesses reading behavior for accuracy and use of strategies.
3. "Making and breaking," which is working with magnetic letters in order to learn about letters, sounds, and how words work.
4. Composing and writing a message or story, with extensive work on a "practice" page to hear sounds and learn to spell words.
5. Reading, cutting up, and reconstructing the message or story to give greater attention to visual details.
6. Being introduced to and reading a new text.

Teacher-leaders provide clear demonstrations of every component of the framework and help teachers practice the instructional moves they need. They also provide a set of books that are leveled in terms of difficulty so that text selection will be easier. They are even provided with specific written guidelines and suggestions for language to use. Teachers meet in weekly sessions to see example after example of lessons. While there are explanations and explicit rationales, the emphasis in the beginning is on becoming skilled in the process. Each week, teachers use a systematic way of recording and analyzing children's behaviors so that they can plot progress. Keep in mind that Reading Recovery teachers are working one-on-one with young children who are having difficulty learning to read and write.

	Reading Recovery	Classroom Practice—Guided Reading
Taking on New Practice		
Efficient ways to take on routines and procedures.	Teachers are provided with a structured lesson framework and specific directions for each component.	Teachers are provided with a structured lesson framework and specific directions for each component.
	Clear language is suggested to help children attend to aspects of reading.	Examples are demonstrated through videotape.
Materials to support the process.	Teachers receive a set of books that are leveled in terms of difficulty and specific guidance in assessing children's reading levels.	Teachers use a gradient of text as a guide to book selection. The have a "beginning" collection of texts that they are expected to get to know well so that they can use them effectively with students.
	Teachers receive writing materials and magnetic letters with instructions as to when and how to use them.	They receive magnetic letters and white boards, with directions for use.
Specific guidance over the rough spots.	Teachers are observed and observe others with specific attention to procedures.	Literacy coaches demonstrate lessons in classrooms so that teachers can see the procedures with their own students.
	They are shown how to refer to a reference that provides detailed and specific directions.	They provide coaching and feedback to help teachers refine use of the lesson framework, materials, and time.
A feeling of competence from the beginning.	Within a few days, teachers find that they can follow the steps of the lesson.	Teachers find the steps of introducing, reading, discussing, and teaching about the text to be a structured way of implementing the technique.
	Although they know they are not yet expert, they are using the language and working with the techniques with enough sophistication that they can show their teaching to others.	With support in text selection and grouping, they can begin to refine routines in terms of time and pacing.
Early, easy-to-see success.	Teachers measure children's reading and writing progress every day, using specific recording forms. They look at evidence of learning with the help of a teacher-leader, and they also discuss progress in learning (with evidence) in class.	Teachers regularly sample children's reading, taking notes of accuracy to determine competent reading of the text level. They also note evidence of comprehension and fluency. These data are discussed with the literacy coach in the process of learning to determine the appropriate level of text to introduce next.

FIGURE 11–2 *Taking on New Practice*

Reading Recovery training places maximum emphasis on learning by doing; teachers provide lessons behind a one-way glass screen so that they can learn from each other. Rather than waiting until they become expert, these novice teachers get started right away in showing their teaching to their peers. No one is expected to be perfect; but, sometimes to their amazement, they find themselves using the language of lessons and demonstrating the process within a week or so of beginning their training.

Guided Reading

Guided reading is a complex approach that is new to most teachers. Guided reading is a *classroom* instructional technique designed to help all children move forward in the development of a reading process. The teacher works with small groups of students.

Using a structured framework for lessons, teachers group children who are similar in the development of a reading process and then select texts that will be within their control but offer opportunities to learn. Teachers first introduce texts; then students read the text individually with the teacher sampling their reading and interacting briefly to prompt for strategies. After reading, the teacher guides students to discuss the meaning of the text and then demonstrates and invites students to engage in using the processing strategies that are involved in comprehending the text. Finally, the teacher might extend understanding through writing exercises or work with isolated words to promote flexible word solving.

Professional development in guided reading involves explicit demonstrations of lessons and written descriptions of each component of the lesson framework. In the ideal arrangement, teachers are provided assistance in grouping children, as well as a gradient of text difficulty to guide selection. They also receive magnetic letters and other materials along with instructions on how to use them. Literacy coaches typically work alongside teachers; they may take turns providing lessons to a particular group and recording and discussing progress. Teachers are given specific ways of determining whether children are successfully processing (solving words and comprehending) texts, and their progress is plotted along a chart reflecting the gradient.

The structure and support of guided reading makes it possible for teachers to get started on lessons right away. Once management issues are settled for the rest of the children in the class, coaches help teachers work with small groups using lesson components. Teachers have the opportunity to hear and feel their own implementation of the components of guided reading.

VARYING PROFESSIONAL DEVELOPMENT SUPPORT

The two situations described previously may seem to be "top-down" in nature. After all, we are telling teachers much about the instructional techniques rather than letting them discover the techniques for themselves. We have a strong belief that teachers should not be forced to use a particular practice, but we are asking them to put some pretty specific ideas into place. The idea is to say something like this, "Trust me for a while and try this out. Here's how to do it."

These days we are asking for profound changes in classroom practice, and we are seeking teachers who will become lifelong learners who develop their theories and their practice over time. The promise of professional development is that it may be built into the daily work of teachers just as it is in other technical fields, for example, health professions. That means there is time and we need to take a long view. We conclude this book by conceptualizing teacher development not as "prescribed" or "constructivist," two opposing views that often clash in school reform movement, but as a continuum of choices that may be employed at different times for different purposes. In Figure 11–3, we present a continuum of choices that we have given labels to and will describe in the following sections.

Dimensions of Professional Development Support

The choices are placed along a continuum from high-to-low professional development support. In this case, "high support" means a high level of direction along several dimensions, which are detailed in Figure 11–4 and listed here. Each of these dimensions represents a decision to be made by the provider of professional development. For purposes of description, we have identified categories along the continuum from high-to-low support,

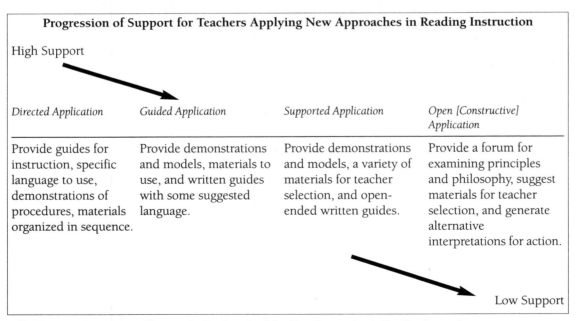

Progression of Support for Teachers Applying New Approaches in Reading Instruction			
High Support			
Directed Application	*Guided Application*	*Supported Application*	*Open [Constructive] Application*
Provide guides for instruction, specific language to use, demonstrations of procedures, materials organized in sequence.	Provide demonstrations and models, materials to use, and written guides with some suggested language.	Provide demonstrations and models, a variety of materials for teacher selection, and open-ended written guides.	Provide a forum for examining principles and philosophy, suggest materials for teacher selection, and generate alternative interpretations for action.
			Low Support

FIGURE 11–3 *Progression of Support for Teachers Applying New Approaches in Reading Instruction*

although staff developers would vary their work continuously in many different ways. We'll describe each category along the first four dimensions, which are briefly defined in the following sections. Self-analysis, a critical component of all categories, will be discussed later as the vehicle for moving from one category to another.

- *Materials* may be provided to support the implementation of a new approach, or teachers may be left to find and select their own materials. The degree of choice and freedom in materials use can be placed on a continuum from highly directed to open. At first glance, it may seem desirable to leave the choice of materials entirely in teachers' hands, but think about the labor involved and the complexity of these decisions. It may be overwhelming and involve long hours of labor to select materials for an instructional procedure you don't really know yet; mistakes may undermine early success. Deciding just how much to provide, as well as how much direction to give, is an important decision that is unique to each situation.

- *Demonstrations and directions* for procedures may be quite specific or very open in nature. Given an outline, general idea, or theoretical framework, teachers may be left to work out their own versions and applications. As a result, there will be creativity and there may be some degree of ownership; but wide variation will also be evident. At the other end of the continuum of support, the staff developer provides precise directions, even specifying the order of application and specific language to try out during lessons.

- At the low end of professional development support, *technical assistance* may take the form of being a sounding board for teachers as they try out new techniques and work out their own procedures. Staff developers may question and guide discussion, bringing issues to the forefront, and helping teachers engage in self-reflection. At the high end of support, the staff developer will walk through procedures with teachers, sometimes demonstrating and sometimes giving very specific suggestions to refine the "mechanics" of the approach. Teachers usually implement the approach with great consistency from the beginning but will vary their use of it as they learn to tailor it to individual students.

- *Data feedback* is defined as the essential and accepted evidence of student success that is needed for an approach to take root. At the low end of support, teachers will be left to their own impressions and individual ways to determine whether children are learning. These may vary from person to person, but will be strengthened as teachers work together to compare notes in collegial groups. High support would involve specific, systematic assessment procedures that are regularly examined, openly shared across groups of teachers, and used specifically to guide further instruction.

- *Self-analysis* is the mechanism for moving teachers from needing high support to an open or constructivist level. In a highly supportive

situation, self-analysis is heavily guided. The staff developer brings the practitioner's attention to specific details observed in his/her own behavior and that of children. Materials are brought out for examination and evaluation. Once routines are established and timing and pace are working, the analysis does not stop but concentrates on evidence of learning and teacher-student interactions, both those that "work" and those that do not. Through participating in self-analysis, teachers take on the role for themselves; working in collegial groups supports the process.

Open (Constructivist) Application

A constructivist approach is popular in the literature; we will begin there. The ultimate goal of professional development is to support teachers as decision makers; only then can we assure the expert teaching that will reach and provide for every child. Materials and scripts can go only so far. Excellent teachers know how to tailor instruction to meet children where they are and quickly intervene to help them understand the concepts and behaviors that will take them further. A well-designed approach will have the structure and directions that put sound practice into place. However, being effective with the approaches means "filling in the blanks" of those moment-to-moment interactions that make the difference for children who have difficulty learning or for those who need extra attention and excitement to become engaged.

Dimensions of Professional Development Support	
Dimensions	*Teachers' Needs*
Materials	• The basic materials to support the implementation of a new approach. • Lower-to-higher levels of organization to support the use of materials.
Demonstrations and Directions that Specify Procedures	• Clear demonstrations of the particular technique or approach. • Step-by-step descriptions of procedures. • Suggested language or beginning "scripts" to try out the approach.
Technical Assistance	• In-class demonstration to tease out the details of the procedures and untangle confusions. • Feedback on implementation of the procedures, including the use of materials, timing, and language.
Data Feedback	• Collection of evidence of students' learning as part of the process. • Guidance in looking at evidence of students' learning.
Self-Analysis	• Support in analyzing the new approach and its effects so that implementation becomes deeper. • Self-analysis to vary and adjust the technique or approach for maximum effectiveness with the particular students taught.

FIGURE 11–4 *Dimensions of Professional Development Support*

Materials

In an open application, teachers would have wide access to materials and would select them for their appropriateness for the approach and for the specific children they teach. Teachers would continually analyze materials to determine their effectiveness and appeal to children.

Demonstrations and Directions

In a constructivist approach, the focus is on underlying theory and the principles of learning. Teachers may employ a variety of procedures that they design themselves and/or adapt from seeing many different examples. They may encounter opposing views or procedures that conflict with each other as they examine the thinking of many different individuals, but their exposure helps them in building their *own* theories. They do not take on an approach with a "name." Instead, taking care to be consistent with a coherent theory, they construct the curriculum for themselves with their students in mind. Often, they seek and give advice, but the decisions are theirs.

Technical Assistance

Teachers use staff developers and other colleagues as a sounding board to help them reflect on and analyze their practice.

Data Feedback

In a constructivist approach, teachers have a strong sense of what counts as evidence of learning. They observe students in great detail, noting changes in behavior that provide evidence that their instructional approaches are resulting in learning. They may develop some of their own instruments and test them through use. Colleagues may work together to create standards and assessment systems that have a school-wide impact.

Supported Application

If a constructivist approach is considered ideal, then we need to back up and think about how to get there. It is obvious that the previous descriptions were of highly polished, reflective, and expert professionals who have read widely and developed tentative theories. For novices, it is pretty difficult to conceptualize and act on theory, even with the support of a staff developer. A higher level of support will be needed even for teachers who have gained some experience. *Supported application* of a new technique or approach means a light approach, but one that provides very specific suggestions. Still, the precise way a new technique is implemented is the individual teacher's decision and variation is expected.

Materials

Teachers are provided with some materials and asked to make decisions about using them in their instruction. They may explore and use other materials of their own choosing, often sharing them with their colleagues. As they work on their classroom innovations, teachers are expected to constantly evaluate materials and organize them for better use.

Demonstrations and Directions

Teachers receive overall frameworks with some specific directions for implementing techniques. They also see varied demonstrations, learning from several different experts. They are encouraged to adapt the techniques to suit their own styles and their views of the students they teach.

Technical Assistance

Teachers receive the ongoing support of visits from a staff developer or literacy coach who makes suggestions and engages in dialogue about classroom processes. The coach and teacher become problem solvers together in adapting and adjusting techniques.

Data Feedback

Staff developers suggest specific assessment procedures and discuss them with teachers. Teachers select ways of documenting students' behaviors and analyzing them, and they share their assessments with colleagues.

Guided Application

Guided application provides stronger support for teachers who are taking on challenging new techniques. In this category, teachers are asked to apply the technique as designed.

Materials

Teachers are provided with a set of materials and some specific directions for their use. Usually, materials are organized logically to make it easier for teachers to incorporate them into their instruction.

Demonstrations and Directions

The staff developer is explicit and specific in providing suggestions and models for instruction. Teachers are asked to try them out using specific directions and to reflect on their teaching afterwards. There is plenty of room for discussion and variation as teachers become more familiar with the approach.

Technical Assistance

Teachers are provided with coaching to help them implement techniques as designed and they engage in self-analytical discussion to refine their use and understanding.

Directed Application

When would you need an approach even more directive than guided application? We need to keep in mind that novice teachers or teachers who are taking on a very challenging new learning may be overwhelmed by the sheer number of concepts they have to keep in mind. They may need the relief of high support and direction while working to understand something new. They may need to puzzle out a new approach and its philosophical underpinnings while they see themselves actually doing it. In this case, a very strong support system, also called *directed application*, may be necessary. The staff developer provides materials, instructions that are roughly appropriate for the grade level or group of children, and asks the teacher to take on the technique exactly as directed.

Materials

In a directed application, teachers are provided with the specified materials they will need and told to use them in particular ways, including sequence. For example, teachers who are very new to guided reading may simply be given a set of books arranged along a gradient of difficulty and asked to use the books in sequence for a group of children. As the teachers use the materials, they learn more about them and about children's responses.

Demonstrations and Directions

Precise directions and even "scripts" are provided to help the teacher "jump start" instruction in a smooth, efficient way. For example, when implementing a word study program, teachers may be give some specific lessons, with scripted language, and asked to try them out with children. The idea is for teachers simply to enter the instructional situation trusting the staff developer enough to use the directions as a step-by-step guide.

Technical Assistance

First, staff developer helps to smooth out the rough spots by providing feedback on application, timing, and use of materials; but then, the staff developer helps the teacher understand the process through discussion.

Data Feedback

Integral to the instructional process is a set of assessment procedures that teachers are taught to use. There is regular examination of a specific set of assessment data collected on a required schedule. These data affirm the success of the approach but also help the staff developer know how to direct the teacher to adjust the technique if necessary.

REFLECTION AND SELF-ANALYSIS—THINKING OUR WAY FORWARD

Many of us have been involved in round after round of professional development along the whole range of categories. We have gradually developed concepts and skills that allow us to take on new techniques while at the same time evaluating and reflecting. We forget that we ourselves may have learned some of our repertoire through following some step-by-step directions. In Figure 11–5, we have outlined some advantages and disadvantages of each category along the continuum.

Directed application, for example, is helpful to novice teachers in that they do not have to consider every detail of instruction. Materials are provided and they follow explicit directions. Teachers see themselves using the approach with some competency right away. In general, approaches are followed with more fidelity from the beginning and staff developers and teachers can determine whether the approach is working.

On the other hand, these highly directed approaches have a long history of not working because they reduce teaching to a mechanical process and teachers soon become tired of following scripts and structured directions. Staff developers and curriculum people are required to come up with organizational systems and materials that work, but teachers may take little responsibility. The real problem is that these mechanical approaches are expected to endure year after year without teachers bringing their own thinking to the process; that simply doesn't make for job satisfaction or quality performance for most people, especially those who are concerned about the learning of children they serve every day. In any mechanically applied approach, teachers will see children falling through the cracks and want to do something about it.

Making Decisions As a Staff Developer

As a staff developer, the level of the continuum you select may depend on several factors:

- The experience level of teachers with whom you are working.
- The degree to which teachers are already familiar with the approach in question.
- The seriousness of the need for change.
- The speed at which change is needed.
- The complexity of the approach to be implemented.

Some classroom techniques are easy to take on in terms of routine, but do not lend themselves to scripted or structured approaches and also require a great deal of reflection and practice to make effective. An example might be reading aloud to children. While it's easy to get started, having powerful conversations with children that lead to increased comprehension strategies is quite difficult and requires a strong grasp of text analysis and theory of learning.

You might elect to use supported application in that you suggest books that are appropriate for the age level but give teachers wide leeway in selection. You might involve them over time in deep discussion and analysis of read-aloud sessions so that they learn to look for evidence of comprehension on the part of students and also think about the kinds of conversations that will be helpful. Constructive application would be a natural outgrowth of teachers' studying the read-aloud process. Only for novice teachers would

Advantages and Disadvantages of Approaches to Professional Development

Category of Support	Advantages	Disadvantages
Directed Application	• Helpful to novice teachers. • Provides time to understand complex techniques. • Provides for competent-looking performance right away. • Improves the structure and timing of instruction right away. • Takes less teacher time. • Works for consistency in the application of the approach from the beginning.	• Requires a larger amount of written guides and materials. • Requires much organization on the part of staff developers. • May lead teachers to implement approaches simplistically without adjusting them to the needs of children. • May reduce teaching to a mechanical process if self-reflection is not involved. • Produces data that can be examined to determine how the approach works.
Guided Application	• Provides the support teachers need to get started quickly. • Leaves room for reflection and adjustment. • Saves teachers time in gathering materials and designing instruction. • Involves teachers in looking at their results.	• Makes getting started slightly more complex for teachers. • Depends heavily on having a supportive and collegial group for the teacher to rely on. • May encounter some variation in the consistency with which the approach is implemented.
Supported Application	• Makes teachers feel supported as they take on new and challenging techniques. • Provides a forum for reflection on their work. • Leaves room for creativity and variation to suit individual teacher styles. • May engage teachers deeply in assessing the effect of an approach.	• Requires more teacher time and effort in planning and organizing materials. • Assumes that teachers bring knowledge and experience to the process. • Promotes wide variation in the application of the approach. • May provide inconclusive data to determine whether the approach works.
Open Application	• Promotes ownership of change. • Develops teachers as thinkers and individuals. • Communicates the primary importance of teacher decision making. • Leads to decision making based on theory.	• May result in wide variation in implementation or no implementation at all of the selected approach. • May mean that some teachers flounder and become discouraged. • Produces no conclusive results since teachers' implementations are idiosyncratic.

FIGURE 11–5 *Advantages and Disadvantages of Approaches to Professional Development*

you need directed application or guided application. In other words, beginners might actually need to learn how to have children sit, how to hold the book, modulate the voice, and so on.

Each component of guided reading, described previously, requires a high level of understanding and skill on the part of the teacher. Learning to implement this approach takes time and support. For most teachers, you might select directed or guided application as a way to begin learning. For example, text selection is complex; and it is hard to learn to use the lesson structure effectively if you can not select appropriate texts. You might provide teachers with a limited set of texts organized on a continuum of difficulty and tell them to get to know the texts very well. After assessing and grouping the children (another guided activity), teachers would begin on a level and select from a limited number of books those they would use for a group.

For very inexperienced teachers, you might even place books in a particular sequence and ask them to use these texts as a way of learning how children respond to guided reading. The texts would go up in difficulty. If they are easy, children would read through them quickly. If they are hard, you could have some "branch-out" texts so that they would stay at roughly the same place for a while. You might say that this approach is similar to telling teachers to use a basal reader, and you would be right; the difference is that teachers would be expected to observe children, practice their introductions and conversations, and learn from the process. They are working toward careful selection of texts with the students in mind. The highly supported beginning removes the variables to which teachers have to give attention and creates a strong likelihood of success. They have the opportunity to "get the feel of it" before taking full responsibility for all aspects.

The Role of Self-Analysis and Self-Reflection

Without analysis and reflection, professional development along the full range of the continuum will eventually have more disadvantages than advantages. Self-reflection is the vehicle that makes the experience have lasting effects. Teachers will realize the true potential of any instructional approach if they implement it well but they will also continue to learn about it and about children as they *respond* to the teaching. If they are truly to become expert in helping every child, they will also need to use the instruction they are engaged in as a way of learning more about teaching.

Whatever decision you make as a staff developer, you will want to build into your program design continuous opportunities for teachers to engage in self-analysis and self-reflection. The chapters in this book emphasize these dynamic processes, and they are essential every step of the way. Even when teachers are following a fairly directed sequence of actions, they can still ask themselves questions such as:

- Were children engaged?
- How did they respond to my questions or directions?

- How could I have brought [individual student] more into the group?
- What is it about this text that I have helped students understand?
- What did students learn today that was new?
- How did students change in their behavior (even slightly)?
- How have my students changed over time?

Talking with the coach and with colleagues about questions like these will help teachers to shift their focus from "right and wrong" ways of "doing" instructional procedures to discovering *how* children are responding and *what* they are learning. In fact, some highly supported work may actually free teachers sooner to focus on their students. Some ways to engage teachers in self-analysis and self-reflection follow (also see Figure 11–6):

- A primary way to promote analysis and reflection is through your regular classroom visits as a coach. Even though you may be offering very specific suggestions, you can still call to the teacher's attention important children's behaviors that provide evidence of learning; and you can invite the teacher to reflect and talk about what she/he was thinking at various points in the lesson.
- Sharing their problems and observations of students with others who are implementing the same approach will help teachers to become more analytical as they talk about their work.
- Observing more experienced teachers who are farther along in implementing the approach will provide contrast. Teachers will become more analytic as they make comparisons, discovering how their lessons are similar to and different from more experienced teachers.
- Observing and being observed by peers who are just learning the techniques will also heighten observational powers. When you know you are being observed, you may be more aware of your interactions with

---

Self-Analysis and Self-Reflection: Thinking Our Way Forward

- Inviting the observation of the literacy coach and discussing the lesson afterwards.
- Inviting peers to problem-solve problems related to lessons.
- Observing more experienced teachers using the technique; comparing one's own lessons.
- Observing and discussing with others who are just learning the same technique.
- Tape-recording lessons and listening for the language of introductions or teacher-child interactions.
- Reading and reflecting on lessons as examples.
- Videotaping lessons and observing them with the literacy coach.
- Selecting specific goals for refinement and assessing their impact.
- Becoming a part of a learning community that actively promotes ongoing learning.

FIGURE 11–6
Self-Analysis and Self-Reflection: Thinking Our Way Forward

students and their performance; at the same time, your peers can feed back to you what you may not have noticed because you are so focused on managing the teaching. Observing others frees you from that management and allows for more analysis. The idea is not for teachers to imitate each other, but to assist each other in reflection.

- Listening to audiotape recordings of lessons rivets teachers' attention on the language of the lesson. They can examine their book introductions for clarity, conciseness, and connection with children's backgrounds and interests. They can listen to their interactions with children to reflect on how they supported (or interfered with) understanding.
- Through the professional development process, teachers will participate in reading about children's learning and about the particular instructional approaches they are working to implement. This reading should prompt them to think of examples from their own experience.
- Watching and analyzing videotapes of lessons provides still another experience to promote analysis and reflection. Here, teachers can observe the interplay between their instructional moves and children's responses. They can notice behavior that they might have missed.
- Working with the coach, teachers can identify actions that they want to take to improve their teaching.

The analytic/reflective cycle described in *Systems for Change* (Lyons and Pinnell 2001) is presented almost as if it is a final "stage" of learning; but we believe that it begins even when teachers are taking on new approaches in a somewhat mechanical way.

LEARNING: A CONSTANT PROCESS

As we reflect on the studies reported in this volume, we realize that learning is a continual process. Even as adults, we are learning through every action we take. We are the sum total of our experiences; that is true personally as well as professionally. Young teachers are formed by their initial work; in providing professional development for them, we are creating the framework of the profession for the next decades. We want to structure these experiences carefully so that young teachers have the level of support they need to grow into self-analysis and strong decision making. We want to assure early success but push for continued analysis so that they develop effective systems for improving teaching while in the process of doing it. Careful judgement on the part of professional developers, and a commitment to establishing analysis and reflection from the beginning, is a critical component of educational improvement and should not be overlooked.

REFERENCES

Allington, R. L. 1994. "The Schools We Have. The Schools We Need." *The Reading Teacher* 48: 14–29.

American Federation of Teachers. 1999. *Teaching Reading Is Rocket Science: What Expert Teachers of Reading Should Know and Be Able to Do* (June, Item No. 372). Washington, DC: American Federation of Teachers.

Anders, P. L. & K. S. Evens. 1994. "Relationship Between Teachers' Beliefs and Their Instructional Practice in Reading." In *Beliefs About Text and Instruction with Text,* edited by R. Garner & P. Alexander, 137–54. Hillsdale, NJ: Lawrence Erlbaum.

Anders, P. L., J. V. Hoffman, & G. G. Duffy. 2000. "Teaching Teachers to Teach Reading: Paradigm Shifts, Persistent Problems, and Challenges." In *Handbook of Reading Research: Volume III,* edited by M. Kamil, P. B. Mosenthal, P. D. Pearson, & R. Barr, 719–42. Mahwah, NJ: Lawrence Earlbaum.

Anderson, N. A. 1991. "Improving Reading Inservice." *Kansas Journal of Reading* 7 (1): 37–39. Department of Education's Strategic Plan, 2002–2008, (2002, March), *http://www.ed.gov/pubs/stratplan2002-07/stratplan2002-07.pdf*

Askew, B. J., I. C. Fountas, C. A. Lyons, G. S. Pinnell, & M. C. Schmitt. 1998. *Reading Recovery Review: Understandings, Outcomes, and Implications.* Columbus, OH: Reading Recovery Council of North America.

Atwell, N. 1991. *Side By Side: Essays on Teaching to Learn.* Portsmouth, NH: Heinemann.

Au, K. 1997. "Changing Views of Literacy Instruction and Teacher Development." *Teacher Education and Special Education* 20 (1): 74–82.

Baker, S. & S. Smith. 1999. "Starting Off on the Right Foot: The Influence of Four Principles of Professional Development in Improving Literacy Instruction in Two Kindergarten Classrooms." *Learning Disabilities Research and Practice* 14 (4): 239–53.

Ben-Peretz, M. 2001. "The Impossible Role of Teacher Educators in a Changing World." *Journal of Teacher Education* 52 (1): 48–56.

Bos, C. S. & P. L. Anders. 1994. "The Study of Student Change." In *Teacher Change and the Staff Development Process: A Case in Reading Instruction,* edited by V. Richardson, 181–98. New York: Teachers College Press.

Botel, M., P. M. Ripley, & L. A. Barnes. 1993. "A Case Study of an Implementation of the 'New Literacy' Paradigm." *Journal of Research in Reading* 16: 112–27.

Boyd, P. C., M. Boll, L. Brawner, S. K. Villaume. 1998. "Becoming Reflective Professionals: An Exploration of Preservice Teacher's Struggles as They Translate Language and Literacy Theory into Practice." *Action in Teacher Education* 19 (4): 61–75.

Broaddus, K. & J. W. Bloodgood. 1999. "'We're Supposed to Already Know How to Teach Reading': Teacher Change to Support Struggling Readers." *Reading Research Quarterly* 34 (4): 426–51.

Bruner, J. S. 1978. "The Role of Dialogue in Language Acquisition." In *The Child's Concept of Language,* edited by A. Sinclair. New York: Springer-Verlag.

Bussell, J. F. 2001. "Teacher Leadership: A Key Factor in Reading Recovery's Success." *Literacy Teaching and Learning: An International Journal of Early Reading and Writing* 5: 53–83.

Butler, A. & J. Turbill. 1984. *Towards a Reading-Writing Classroom.* Portsmouth, NH: Heinemann.

Calhoun, E. F. 1994. *How to Use Action Research in the Self-Renewing School.* Alexandria, VA: Association for Supervision and Curriculum Development.

Cashdan, A. 1976. "Who Teaches the Child to Read?" In *New Horizons in Reading,* edited by J. Merritt, 80–85. Newark, DE: International Reading Association.

Check, J. W. 1997. "Teacher Research As Powerful Professional Development." *The Harvard Education Letter* 13: 6–8.

Clay, M. M. 1989. "Involving Teachers in Classroom Research." In *Teachers and Research: Language Learning in the Classroom,* edited by G. S. Pinnell & M. M. Matlin, 29–46. Newark, DE: International Reading Association.

————. 1991. *Becoming Literate: The Construction of Inner Control.* Auckland, NZ: Heinemann.

————. 1993. *An Observation Survey of Early Literacy Achievement.* Portsmouth, NH: Heinemann.

————. 1994. "Reading Recovery: The Wider Implications of an Educational Innovation." *Literacy, Teaching and Learning* 1 (1): 121–41.

————. 2001. *Change over Time in Literacy Learning.* Auckland, NZ: Heinemann.

Clay, M. M. & C. Cazden. 1990. "A Vygoyskian Interpretation of Reading Recovery." In *Vygotsky and Education,* edited by L. Moll. New York: Cambridge University Press.

Cochran-Smith, M. & S. L. Lytle. 1990. "Research on Teaching and Teacher Research: The Issues That Divide." *Educational Researcher* 19 (2): 2–10.

————. 1993. *Inside/Outside: Teacher Research and Knowledge.* New York: Teachers College Press.

Combs, M. 1994. "Implementing a Holistic Reading Series in First Grade: Experiences with a Conversation Group." *Reading Horizons* 34 (3): 196–207.

Corcoran, T. B. 1995 (June). *Helping Teachers Teach Well: Transforming Professional Development* [On-line]. Available: *http://www.ed.gov/pubs/ CPRE/t61/*

Costa, A. L. & R. J. Garmston. 1994. *Cognitive Coaching.* Norwood, MA: Christopher-Gordon.

Cronbach, L. J. 1975. "Beyond the Two Disciplines of Scientific Inquiry." *American Psychologist* 30: 116–27.

Cunningham, P. M. & J. W. Cunningham. 1992. "Making Words: Enhancing the Invented Spelling-Decoding Connection." *The Reading Teacher* 46: 106–15.

Daniels, H. 1994. *Literature Circles: Voice and Choice in the Student-Centered Classroom.* York, ME: Stenhouse.

Darling-Hammond, L. 1996a. "The Right to Learn and the Advancement of Teaching: Research, Policy, and Practice for Democratic Education." *Educational Researcher* 25: 5–17.

————. 1996b. "What Matters Most: A Competent Teacher for Every Child." *Phi Delta Kappan* 78: 193–200.

————. 2000. "Teacher Quality and Student Achievement: A Review of State Policy Evidence." *Education Policy Analysis Archives* [On-line], 8, 1. Available: *http://epaa.asu.edu/epaa/v8n1/*

Darling-Hammond, L. & M. W. McLaughlin. 1995. "Policies That Support Professional Development in an Era of Reform." *Phi Delta Kappan* 76: 597–604.

Datnow, A. & M. Castellano. 2001. "Teachers' Responses to Success for All: How Beliefs, Experiences, and Adaptations Shape Implementation." *American Educational Research Journal* 37 (3): 775–99.

Dewey, J. 1933. *How We Think: A Restatement of the Relations of Reflective Thinking to the Educative Process* (2nd rev. ed.). Lexington, MA: D. C. Heath.

Downhower, S., M. P. Melvin, & P. Sizemore. 1990. "Improving Writing Instruction Through Teacher Action Research." *Journal of Staff Development* 11: 22–27.

Duffy, G. G., L. R. Roehler, & J. Putnam. 1987. "Putting the Teacher in Control: Basal Reading Textbooks and Instructional Decision Making." *Elementary School Journal* 87: 357–66.

Dyer, P. 1992. "Reading Recovery: A Cost-Effectiveness and Educational-Outcomes Analysis." *ERS Spectrum* 10 (1): 10–19.

Eby, J. W. 1997. *Reflective Planning, Teaching, and Education for the Elementary School.* New Jersey: Prentice-Hall.

Eeds, M. & D. Wells. 1989. "Grand Conversations: An Exploration of Meaning Construction in Literature Study Groups." *Research in the Teaching of English* 23 (10): 4–29.

El-Dinary, P. B. & T. Schuder. 1993. "Seven Teachers' Acceptance of Transactional Strategies Instruction During Their First Year Using It." *Elementary School Journal* 94 (2): 207–19.

Erickson, F. 1986. "Qualitative Methods in Research on Teaching." In *Handbook of Research on Teaching* (3rd ed.), edited by M. C. Wittrock, 119–61. New York: Macmillan.

Ferguson, R. F. 1991. "Racial Patterns in How School and Teacher Quality Affect Achievement and Earnings." *Challenge* 2: 1–35.

Finch, C. 1999. "Using Professional Development to Meet Teachers' Changing Needs: What We Have Learned." *Centerpoint* 2 (1): 1–14.

Flood, J., D. Lapp, W. Ranck-Buhr, & J. Moore. 1995. "What Happens When Teachers Get Together to Talk About Books? Gaining a Multicultural Perspective from Literature." *Reading Teacher* 48: 720–23.

Fountas, I. C. & G. S. Pinnell. 1996. *Guided Reading: Good First Teaching for All Children.* Portsmouth, NH: Heinemann.

———. 1999a. *Matching Books to Readers: Using Leveled Books in Guided Reading, K–3.* Portsmouth, NH: Heinemann.

———. 1999b. "What Does Good First Teaching Mean?" In *Stirring the Waters: The Influence of Marie Clay,* edited by J. S. Gaffney & B. J. Askew, 165–85. Portsmouth, NH: Heinemann.

Fullan, M. G. 1993. *Change Forces: Probing the Depth of Educational Reform.* New York: Falmer Press.

———. 2001. *The New Meaning of Educational Change (Third Edition).* New York: Teachers College Press.

Fullerton, S. K. & M. P. Quinn. 1996–1997. "Establishing the Learning Context: Connecting Learning Through Grouping and Structure." *Greater Washington Reading Council Journal* 21: 27–31.

Glaser, B. G. & A. L. Strauss. 1967. *The Discovery of Grounded Theory.* Chicago: Aldine.

Glesne, C. & A. Peshkin. 1992. *Becoming Qualitative Researchers: An Introduction.* White Plains, NY: Longman.

Goatley, V., K. Highfield, J. Bentley, L. S. Pardo, J. Folkert, P. Scherer, T. E. Raphael & K. Grattan. 1994. "Empowering Teachers to Be Researchers: A Collaborative Approach." *Teacher Research: The Journal of Classroom Inquiry* 1 (2): 128–44.

Goswami, D., & P. R. Stillman, eds. 1987. *Reclaiming the Classroom: Teacher Research As an Agency for Change.* Portsmouth, NH: Boynton/Cook.

Gray-Schlegel, M. A. & J. B. Matanzo. 1993. "Action Research: Classroom Teachers' Perceptions of Its Impact on the Teaching of Reading." In *Inquiries in Literacy Learning and Instruction,* edited by T. B. Rasinski & N. P. Padak, 135–42. Pittsburgh, KS: College Reading Association.

Guskey, T. R. 1997. "Research Needs to Link Professional Development and Student Learning." *Journal of Staff Development* 18 (2): 36–40.

————. 2000. *Evaluating Professional Development*. Thousand Oaks: Corwin Press, Inc.

Guskey, T. R. & D. Sparks. 1996. "Exploring the Relationship Between Staff Development and Improvements in Student Learning." *Journal of Staff Development* 17 (4): 34–38.

Hargreaves, A. 1994. *Changing Teachers, Changing Times: Teachers' Work and Culture in the Postmodern Age*. New York: Teachers College Press.

Hargreaves, A. & M. Fullan. 1998. *What's Worth Fighting for Out There*. New York: Teachers College Press.

Herman, R. & S. Stringfield. 1997. *Ten Promising Programs for Educating All Children: Evidence of Impact*. Arlington, VA: Educational Research Service.

Hoffman, J. 1996. "Teacher and School Effects in Learning to Read." In *Handbook of Reading Research: Volume II*, edited by R. Barr, M. Kamil, P. B. Mosenthal, & P. D. Pearson, 911–50. Mahwah, NJ: Lawrence Erlbaum.

Hoffman, J. & P. D. Pearson. 2000. "Reading Teacher Education in the Next Millennium: What Your Grandmother's Teacher Didn't Know That Your Granddaughter's Teacher Should." *Reading Research Quarterly* 35: 28–44.

Hollingsworth, S. 1994. *Teacher Research and Urban Literacy Education: Lessons and Conversations in a Feminist Key*. New York: Teachers College Press.

The Holmes Group. 1986. *Tomorrow's Teachers: A Report of The Holmes Group*. East Lansing, MI: The Holmes Group.

Hovest, C. & J. Day. 1997 (February). "Sustaining Gains: Ohio's Reading Recovery Students in Fourth Grade." Paper presented at the 12th Annual Reading Recovery Conference and National Institute, Columbus, Ohio.

Hubbard, R. & B. Power. 1993. *The Art of Classroom Inquiry: A Handbook for Teacher Researchers*. Portsmouth, NH: Heinemann.

Hundert, D. 1996. "Collaborating on Drama and the Curriculum: A Site-Based, Peer-Mediated, Teacher In-Service Project." *Research in Drama Education* 1 (2): 201–14.

Jadallah, E. 1996. "Reflective Theory and Practice: A Constructivist Process for Curriculum and Instructional Decisions." *Action in Teacher Education* 18 (2): 73–85.

Jaggar, A. 1997 (March). "Do Reading Recovery Children Sustain Their Gains?" Paper presented at the annual meeting of the American Educational Research Association, Chicago.

Jennings, J. H., J. A. Hieshima, D. L. Pearce, S. Shapiro, & A. K. Ambardar. 1994. "A Staff Development Project to Improve Literacy Instruction in an Urban School." *Illinois Reading Council Journal* 22: 44–59.

Johnson, B. 1993. *Teacher-As-Researcher*. ERIC Digest 92–7. Washington, DC: ERIC Clearinghouse on Teacher Education. ED355205

Joyce, B. & B. Showers. 1980. "Improving Inservice Training: The Messages of Research." *Educational Leadership* 37 (5): 379–85.

————. 1988. *Student Achievement Through Staff Development: Fundamentals of School Renewal* (2nd ed.). White Plains, NY: Longman.

————. 1995. *Student Achievement Through Staff Development: Fundamentals of School Renewal* (2nd ed.). White Plains, NY: Longman.

Juel, C. 1988. "Learning to Read and Write: A Longitudinal Study of Fifty-four Children from First Through Fourth Grade." *Journal of Educational Psychology* 80: 437–47.

Kieffer, R. D. & M. A. Faust. 1994. "Portfolio Process and Teacher Change: Elementary, Middle, and Secondary Teachers Reflect on Their Initial Experiences with Portfolio Evaluation." In *Multidimensional Aspects of Literacy Research, Theory, and Practice,* edited by C. K. Kinzer & D. J. Leu, 82–88. Chicago: National Reading Conference.

Killion, J. 1998. "Scaling the Elusive Summit." *Journal of Staff Development* 19 (4): 12–16.

Klingner, J. L. & S. Vaughn. 1996. "Reciprocal Teaching of Reading Comprehension Strategies for Students with Learning Disabilities Who Use English as a Second Language." *Elementary School Journal* 96 (3): 275–93.

LaBoskey, V. K. 1997. "Teaching to Teach with a Purpose and Passion: Pedagogy for Reflective Practice." In *Teaching About Teaching: Purpose, Passion and Pedagogy in Teacher Education,* edited by J. Loughran & T. Russell, 150–63. Washington, D.C.: The Falmer Press.

Lampert, M. & C. M. Clark. 1990. "Expert Knowledge and Expert Thinking in Teaching: A Response to Floden and Klinzing." *Educational Researcher* 19 (5): 21–23, 42.

Lewis, A. C. 1997. "A Conversation with Linda Darling-Hammond." The *Harvard Education Letter* 13: 4–5.

Lieberman, A. E. 1995a. "Practices That Support Teacher Development: Transforming Conceptions of Professional Learning." *Phi Delta Kappan* 76: 591–96.

———. 1995b. *The Work of Reconstructing Schools: Building from the Ground Up.* New York: Teachers College Press.

Lieberman, A. & L. Miller. 1984. *Teachers, Their World and Their Work.* Arlington, VA: Association for Supervision and Curriculum Development.

———. 1999. *Teachers Transforming Their World and Their Work.* New York: Teachers College Press.

Lindfors, J. 1999. *Children's Inquiry: Using Language to Make Sense of the World.* New York: Teachers College Press.

Little, J. W. 1987. *Staff Development in California. Public and Personal Investments, Program Patterns, and Policy Choices. California Postsecondary Education Commission Report.* ERIC accession number 300342.

———. 1996. OERI Working paper on "Excellence in Professional Development and Professional Community."

Lyons, C. 1994. "Reading Recovery and Learning Disabilities: Issues, Challenges and Implications." *Literacy, Teaching and Learning* 1 (1): 110–19.

Lyons, C. A. & G. S. Pinnell. 1999. "Teacher Development: The Best Investment in Literacy Education." In *Stirring the Waters: The Influence of Marie Clay*, edited by J. S. Gaffney & B. Askew, 302–31. Portsmouth, NH: Heinemann.

———. 2001. *Systems for Change in Literacy Education.* Portsmouth, NH: Heinemann.

Lyons, C. A., G. S. Pinnell, & D. DeFord. 1993. *Partners in Learning: Teachers and Children in Reading Recovery.* New York: Teachers College Press.

Maeroff, G. I. 1993. *Team Building for School Change: Equipping Teachers for New Roles.* New York: Teachers College Press.

Malouf, D. B. & E. P. Schiller. 1995. "Practice and Research in Special Education." *Exceptional Children* 61 (5): 414–24.

Marshall, C. M. & C. B. Rossman. 1995. *Designing Qualitative Research.* Thousand Oaks, CA: Sage.

Mathison, S. 1988. "Why Triangulate?" *Educational Researcher* 17 (2): 13–17.

McCarrier, A. M., G. S. Pinnell, & I. C. Fountas. 2000. *Interactive Writing: How Language and Literacy Come Together, K–2.* Portsmouth, NH: Heinemann.

McKay, J. A. 1992. "Professional Development Through Action Research." *Journal of Staff Development* 13: 18–21.

Miles, M. B. & A. M. Huberman. 1984. *Qualitative Data Analysis: A Sourcebook of New Methods.* Beverly Hills, CA: Sage.

Milz, V. E. 1989. "Comments from a Teacher Researcher." In *Teachers and Research: Language Learning in the Classroom,* edited by G. S. Pinnell & M. M. Matlin, 25–28. Newark, DE: International Reading Association.

Mohr, M. M. & M. S. Maclean. 1987. *Working Together: A Guide for Teacher-Researchers.* Urbana, IL: National Council of Teachers of English.

Moore, M. 1991. "Reflective Teaching and Learning Through the Use of Learning Logs." *Journal of Reading Education* 17: 35–49.

National Board for Professional Teaching Standards (NBPTS). 1993. *What Should Teachers Know and Be Able to Do?* Detroit, MI.

The National Commission on Teaching and America's Future. 1996. *What Matters Most: Teaching for America's Future.* New York: NCTAF.

National Data Evaluation Center. 2000. *Reading Recovery and Descubriendo La Lectura National Report, 1998–99.* Columbus, OH: The Ohio State University.

National Education Goals Report: Building a Nation of Learners. 1995. Washington, DC: U.S. Government Printing Office.

National Reading Panel. 2000. *Teaching Children to Read: An Evidence-Based Assessment of the Scientific Research Literature on Reading and its Implications for Reading Instruction* [On-line]. Available: *http://www.nichd.nih.gov/ publications/nrp/smallbook.pdf*

National Staff Development Council. 1995. *Standards for Staff Development: Elementary School Edition.* Oxford, OH: National Staff Development Council.

Newmann, F. M., G. Lopez, & A. S. Bryk. 1998. *The Quality of Intellectual Work in Chicago Schools: A Baseline Report.* Chicago, IL: Consortium on Chicago School Research.

O'Flahavan, J. F. 1994/95. "Teacher Role Options in Peer Discussions About Literature." *The Reading Teacher* 48 (4): 354–56.

O'Neill, C. 1995. *Drama Worlds: A Framework for Process Drama.* Portsmouth, NH: Heinemann.

Ohio Department of Education. 1996. *Model Competency-Based Language Arts Program.* Columbus, OH: Department of Education, State of Ohio.

Olson, L. 2001 (January). *Quality Counts 2001: A Better Balance: Standards, Tests, and Tools to Succeed.* [On-line]. Available: *http://www.edweek.org/ew/ew_printstory. cfm?slug=16qc.h20*

Pappas, C. C., B. Z. Kiefer, & L. S. Levstik. 1990. *An Integrated Language Perspective in the Elementary School.* White Plains, NY: Longman.

Patterson, L., C. M. Santa, K. G. Short, & K. Smith. 1993. *Teachers Are Researchers: Reflection and Action.* Newark, DE: International Reading Association.

Patton, M. Q. 1990. *Qualitative Evaluation and Research Methods.* (2nd ed.). Newbury Park, CA: Sage.

Petroski, H. 2001 (Winter). "Success and Failure in Engineering." *National Forum* 10–17.

Piaget, J. 1955. *The Language and Thought of the Child.* Cleveland, OH: World.

Pinnell, G. S. 1997. "An Inquiry-Based Model for Educating Teachers of Literacy." In *Research in Reading Recovery,* edited by S. L. Swartz & A. F. Klein, 6–17. Portsmouth, NH: Heinemann.

Pinnell, G. S. & I. C. Fountas. 1998. *Word Matters: Teaching Phonics and Spelling in the Reading/Writing Classroom.* Portsmouth, NH: Heinemann.

Pinnell, G. S. & D. Kerbow. 2000. "Acquiring Conceptual Understandings and Knowledge." Paper presented at 2000 NRC 50th Annual Conference, Scottsdale, AZ.

Pinnell, G. S. & C. A. Lyons. 1999. "Literacy Coordinator as Instructional Leader: The Development of Technical Knowledge and Skill." Paper presented at the American Educational Research Conference. Toronto, Canada.

Porter, A. C., M. S. Garrett, L. Desimone, K. S. Yoon, & B. F. Birman. 2000. *Does Professional Development Change Teaching Practice? Results from a Three-Year Study* (Report No. 2000-04). Washington, DC: U. S. Department of Education.

Potts, A., S. Moore, S. Frye, M. Kile, C. Wojerta, & D. Criswell. 2000. "Evolving Partnerships: A Framework for Creating Cultures of Teacher Learning." In *National Reading Conference Yearbook,* edited by T. Shanahan & F. V. Rodriguez-Brown 49: 165–77. Chicago: National Reading Conference.

Raphael, T. E. & S. I. McMahon. 1994. "Book Club: An Alternative Framework for Reading Instruction." *The Reading Teacher* 48: 102–16.

Rentel, V. M. & G. S. Pinnell. 1989 (December). *Staking That Claim: The Content of Pedagogical Reasoning.* Presented at the Annual Meeting of the National Reading Conference, Austin, TX.

Report of the National Reading Panel, Teaching Children to Read. 2000 (December). Washington, DC: U.S. Department of Health and Human Services.

Richardson, V. 1994. *Teacher Change and the Staff Development Process: A Case of Reading Instruction.* New York: Teachers College Press.

Richardson, V. & P. C. Anders. 1994. "The Study of Teacher Change." In *Teacher Change and the Staff Development Process: A Case in Reading Instruction,* edited by V. Richardson. New York: Teachers College Press.

Robb, L. 2000. *Redefining Staff Development: A Collaborative Model for Teachers and Administrators.* Portsmouth, NH: Heinemann.

Roskos, K., V. J. Risko, & C. Vukelich. 1998. "Conversations: Head, Heart, and the Practice of Literacy Pedagogy." *Reading Research Quarterly* 33: 228–39.

Rylant, C. 1996. *Henry and Mudge: The First Book of Their Adventures.* New York: Aladdin Paperbacks.

Sarason, S. 1990. *The Predictable Failure of Educational Reform.* San Francisco: Jossey-Bass
———. 1995. *School Change: The Personal Development of a Point of View.* New York: Teachers College Press.

Scharer, P., J. Williams, & G. Pinnell. 2001. *Literacy Collaborative* 2001 *Research Report.*

Senge, P. 1990. *The Fifth Dimension: The Art and Practice of the Learning Organization.* New York: Doubleday.

Shanahan, T. & R. Barr. 1995. "Reading Recovery: An Independent Evaluation of the Effects of an Early Instructional Intervention for At-Risk Learners." *Reading Research Quarterly* 30 (4): 958–96.

Shanker, A. 1996. "Quality Assurance: What Must Be Done to Strengthen the Teaching Profession." *Phi Delta Kappan* 78: 220–24.

Sherin, M. G. 2000. "Viewing Teaching on Videotape." *Educational Leadership* 57: 6–38.

Short, K. G. & G. P. Kauffman. 1992. "Hearing Students' Voices: The Role of Reflection in Learning." *Teachers Networking: The Whole Language Newsletter* 11 (3): 1–6.

Sizer, T. R. 1992. *Horace's School: Redesigning the American High School.* New York: Houghton Mifflin.

Snow, C. E., M. S. Burns, & P. Griffin, eds. 1998. *Preventing Reading Difficulties in Young Children.* Washington, DC: National Academy Press.

Sparks, D. 1997. "A New Vision for Staff Development." *Principal* 77, 20–22.

Sykes, G. 1996. "Reform as Professional Development." *Phi Delta Kappan* 77 (7): 464–67.

Teale, W. H. 1986. "Home Background and Young Children's Literacy Development." In *Emergent Literacy: Writing and Reading,* edited by W. H. Teale & E. Sulzby, 173–206. Norwood, NJ: Ablex.

Teitel, L. 2001. "An Assessment Framework for Professional Development Schools Going Beyond the Leap of Faith." *Journal of Teacher Education* 52 (1): 57–69.

Tierney, R., D. Tucker, M. Gallagher, A. Crismore, & P. D. Pearson. 1988. "The Metcalf Project: A Teacher-Researcher Collaboration." In *Changing School Reading Programs,* edited by S. J. Samuels & P. D. Pearson, 207–26. Newark, DE: International Reading Association.

U.S. Department of Education. 2001. *The Nation's Report Card: Fourth-Grade Reading 2000.* Washington, DC: Office of Educational Research and Improvement and the National Center for Education Statistics.

University of Georgia & University of Maryland. 1991. *National Reading Research Center: A Proposal from the University of Georgia and the University of Maryland.* Athens, GA & College Park, MD: University of Georgia and University of Maryland.

Vygotsky, L. S. 1978. *Mind in Society: The Development of Higher Psychological Processes.* (M. Cole, V. John-Steiner, S. Scribner, & E. Souberman, Eds. and Trans.). Cambridge, MA: Harvard University Press.

Wagner, B. J. 1998. *Educational Drama and Language Arts: What Research Shows.* Portsmouth, NH: Heinemann.

Walmsley, S. & R. Allington. 1995. "Redefining and Reforming Instructional Support Programs for At-Risk Students." In *No Quick Fix: Rethinking Literacy Programs in America's Elementary Schools,* edited by R. L. Allington & S. A. Walmsley. New York: Teachers College Press.

Wang, Y. L. & W. Johnstone. 1997 (March 24–28). "Evaluation of Reading Recovery Program." Paper presented at the Annual Meeting of the American Educational Research Association, Chicago, IL.

Wasley, P. A., R. L. Hampel, & R. W. Clark. 1997. *Kids and School Reform.* San Francisco: Jossey-Bass.

Wilson, K. & B. Daviss. 1994. *Redesigning Education.* New York: Henry Holt.

Wold, L. S. 2000. "An Examination of Teachers' 'Learning to Act' on Reflection." Paper presented at 2000 NRC 50th Annual Conference, Scottsdale, AZ.

Wright, B. D. 1977. "Solving Problems with the Rasch Model." *Journal of Educational Measurement* 14: 97–116.

Wright, B. D. & N. Masters. 1983. *Rating Scale Analysis (Rasch Measurement series).* Pluribus Press.

Yost, D. S., S. M. Sentner, & A. Forlenza-Bailey. 2000. "An Examination of the Construct of Critical Reflection for Teacher Education Programming in the 21st Century." *Journal of Teacher Education* 51 (1): 39–49.

Zeichner, K. 1980. "Myths and Realities: Field-based Experiences in Preservice Teacher Education." *Journal of Teacher Education* 31 (6): 45–55.

Zimpher, N. L. & K. R. Howey. 1992. *Policy & Practice Toward the Improvement of Teacher Education: An Analysis of Issues from Recruitment to Continuing Professional Development with Recommendations.* Oak Brook, IL: North Central Regional Educational Laboratory.

READINGS CITED BY CLASSROOM LITERACY FACILITATORS

Bedrova, E. & D. J. Leong. 1996. *Tools of the Mind: The Vygotskian Approach to Early Childhood Education.* Columbus, OH: Merrill/Prentice Hall.

Clay, M. M. 1998. *By Different Paths to Common Outcomes.* Portsmouth, NH: Heinemann.

Dandy, E. B. 1991. *Black Communications: Breaking Down the Barriers.* Chicago: African American Images.

DeStefano, J. S. 1978. *Language the Learner and the School.* New York: John Wiley & Sons.

Dorn, L. J., C. French, & T. Jones. 1998. *Apprenticeship in Literacy: Transitions Across Reading and Writing.* York, ME: Stenhouse.

McNaughton, S. 1999. Developmental Diversity and Beginning Literacy Instruction at School. In *Stirring the Waters: The Influence of Marie Clay,* edited by J. S. Gaffney & B. J. Askew, 3–25. Portsmouth, NH: Heinemann.

Pinnell, G. S. & I. C. Fountas. 1998. *Word Matters: Teaching Phonics and Spelling in the Reading/Writing Classroom.* Portsmouth, NH: Heinemann.

Wood, D. 1988. *How Children Think and Learn.* Oxford: Basil Blackwell.

CONTRIBUTORS

Suzette Ahwee is a Senior Research Associate at the University of Miami. She obtained her master's degree in the area of Emotional Handicaps and Learning Disabilities and is currently a doctoral student in Special Education at the University of Miami. She now serves as project coordinator for a federally funded research grant focusing on the implementation and sustainability of effective research-based practices.

Nancy Anderson is an Assistant Professor in the Department of Reading at Texas Woman's University. Experiences as a classroom teacher, language arts specialist, teacher-educator, and Reading Recovery university trainer fuel her commitment to providing meaningful professional development opportunities for teachers. Her research and publications center on the coaching aspect of professional development and helping leaders learn how to effectively support teacher learning.

Billie J. Askew is Professor Emerita in the Department of Reading at Texas Woman's University. She has worked in the field of literacy as a classroom teacher, reading specialist, administrator, and teacher-educator. Professional interests include early literacy and the prevention of literacy difficulties. Her commitment to comprehensive literacy efforts in schools has been influenced by her work in Reading Recovery and in classroom literacy projects.

Michele Mits Cash is a Research Assistant at the University of Miami. She earned a Ph.D. in Reading from the University of Miami. She is currently conducting research on the implementation and sustainability of effective research-based practices for students with disabilities in general education classrooms. Her research interests include secondary reading and professional development.

Diane DeFord is the John E. Swearingen Chair of Literacy Education at the University of South Carolina, where she teaches courses in reading and writing methodology and assessment in literacy. Dr. DeFord has published numerous articles and chapters in books, and is the author of a new assessment program for pre-kindergarten through eighth grade.

Teddi Fulenwider has worked in the field of early literacy for twenty years as a classroom teacher and teacher-educator. She is currently the Early Literacy Facilitator for the Mesquite, Texas public schools. For the past three years she has participated in the Verizon Early Literacy Project at Texas Woman's University. She works with teachers in classrooms, supporting their efforts in the field of early literacy.

Susan King Fullerton is a trainer of Reading Recovery teacher-leaders and an Assistant Professor in the School of Teaching and Learning at The Ohio

State University, where she teaches graduate courses in Reading Recovery and literacy education. She is a recipient of several teacher research grants and continues to support teacher research through her work with teachers and through committee work with the International Reading Association.

Marie Tejero Hughes is an Assistant Professor at the University of Illinois at Chicago in Special Education. She received her doctorate from the University of Miami in the areas of Reading and Learning Disabilities. Her current research projects focus on reading instruction for students with disabilities in general education classrooms, professional development, and family involvement.

Janette Klingner is an Associate Professor at the University of Colorado at Boulder in Bilingual Special Education. She earned a Ph.D. in Reading and Learning Disabilities from the University of Miami. Research *foci* include outcomes for students with learning disabilities in inclusive classrooms, professional development in research-based practices, and the disproportionate representation of culturally and linguistically diverse students in special education.

Robyn Kordick is a Classroom Literacy Facilitator for Little Elm ISD. She has worked in the field of literacy as a primary classroom teacher and a Reading Recovery teacher. Professional interests include early literacy and staff development in the area of literacy.

Carol A. Lyons is Professor Emeritus at The Ohio State University. She is the author of a forthcoming book, *The Making of Mind: The Making of a Reader and Writer*, and coauthor of *Systems for Change in Literacy Education: A Guide to Professional Development*, which informed the chapter for this book.

Gay Su Pinnell is a professor in the School of Teaching and Learning of the College of Education at The Ohio State University. She has received the Charles Dana Award for Pioneering Achievement in Health and Education as well as the Albert Harris Award of the International Reading Association. She is a member of the Reading Hall of Fame. She is currently working on comprehensive approaches to improving literacy education.

Mary Quinn began teaching in Fairfax County, Virginia and has twelve years of classroom and resource experience. An active teacher-researcher, she has cowritten several grants and made numerous local, state, and national presentations based on her studies. Quinn is currently the Elementary Reading Specialist and Primary Reading and Language Arts Curriculum Leader in Upper St. Clair, Pennsylvania.

Adrian Rodgers taught secondary English and Drama for eight years in Labrador, Canada. His interest areas include professional development, English & drama education, and qualitative research. He is currently an Assistant Professor of Teacher Education at The University of Dayton.

Emily M. Rodgers taught for ten years in Newfoundland prior to joining the faculty of The Ohio State University as an Assistant Professor in the College of Education. Her research focuses on the professional development of teachers and the nature of effective scaffolding of literacy learning. She received the National Reading Conference Outstanding Student Research Award in 1999.

Yvonne G. Rodríguez is an Assistant Professor at Texas Woman's University in the Department of Reading. Her teaching experiences encompass special education, bilingual education, and reading. With her bilingual background, Dr. Rodríguez has been instrumental in reconstructing Reading Recovery for the Spanish-speaking child, known as Descubriendo la Lectura. Dr. Rodríguez's research interests involve assessment of bilingual students, Spanish literacy acquisition, oral language, and working with the adult learner.

Sarah Scheuermann is a Classroom Literacy Facilitator for Arlington, Texas public schools in collaboration with Texas Woman's University. She teaches a graduate level Foundations of Literacy course and provides classroom support for participating teachers. She is an Adjunct Instructor for Texas Woman's University and provides staff development for Arlington Schools. Her experience includes classroom and Reading Recovery teaching.

Pat Vollenweider is a Classroom Literacy Facilitator in the Arlington, Texas public schools. She teaches the Foundations of Literacy graduate course to kindergarten through second-grade teachers in Arlington through Texas Woman's University. As a Classroom Literacy Facilitator, she also supports teachers by demonstrating, observing, and discussing their classroom practices and literacy understandings. She supports the school district by conducting literacy presentations at the campus and district level. Pat taught in the primary grades for twenty-one years and was a Reading Recovery teacher for five years.

Linda Wold is an Assistant Professor at Purdue University Calumet, teaching preservice and practicing teachers to be reflective literacy educators. Her areas of research and publication are self-study in teacher assessment, teacher reflection and action, children's literature, and language learning routines. She enjoys writing poetry and is actively involved in professional readers' groups to extend literacy borders.